Both glucose and oxygen pass from the blood into the cells by **diffusion**. Diffusion is the movement of molecules from an area where they are densely packed together (a high concentration) to an area where they are spread out (a low concentration).

Cells in the body are supplied with glucose and oxygen by tiny blood vessels called **capillaries**. They have very thin walls just one cell thick, so that substances can diffuse through them easily. A working cell will be respiring and using up glucose and oxygen. This means that there will be a low concentration of these substances inside the cell, and a high concentration of them in the blood capillaries next to the cell. The oxygen and glucose will be able to diffuse into the cell.

Carbon dioxide is made by respiration in the cell. This means there is a high concentration of it inside the cell and a low concentration outside the cell. The carbon dioxide will diffuse out of the cell into the capillaries.

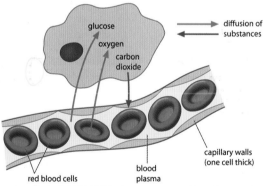

glucose

oxygen

carbon dioxide

diffusion of substances

capillary walls (one cell thick)

blood plasma

red blood cells

**C** A respiring cell gets its oxygen and glucose, and loses carbon dioxide, by diffusion.

**Glossary words**
You will need to know the meaning of some key words. These are shown in **bold**. The glossary at the back of each topic gives you a list of all the key words and what they mean.

**A**

**P**

4 What is diffusion?

5 Explain why oxygen diffuses into respiring cells.

6 Why does carbon dioxide diffuse out of respiring cells?

**H** When you exercise, your muscles need extra energy to contract. This energy comes from respiration, so the rate of respiration needs to increase. You take in more oxygen and remove the extra carbon dioxide by increasing your breathing rate.

At the same time, your heart beats more quickly to take the oxygen away from your lungs to your body cells more rapidly. This maintains a large concentration difference between the gases in your lungs and in your capillaries. Gas exchange occurs more quickly – more oxygen diffuses from your lungs into your blood and more carbon dioxide diffuses from your blood into your lungs.

**P**

7 Why does respiration need to increase in your muscles when you exercise?

8 Why does your breathing rate need to increase during exercise?

**Questions**
There are lots of questions on the page to help you think about the main points in each double-page section.

Summary Exercise

Higher Questions

# How to use your ActiveBook

The ActiveBook is an electronic copy of the book, which you can use on a compatible computer. The CD-ROM will only play while the disc is in the computer. The ActiveBook has these features:

## Glossary
Click this tab to see all of the key words and what they mean. Click 'play' to listen to someone read them out to help you pronounce them.

## DigiList
Click on this tab to see menus which list all the electronic files on the ActiveBook.

## ActiveBook tab
Click this tab at the top of the screen to access the electronic version of the book.

## Key words
Click on any of the words in **bold** to see a box with the word and what it means. Click 'play' to listen to someone read it out for you to help you pronounce it.

## Interactive view
Click this button to see all the bits on the page that link to electronic files, like documents and spreadsheets. You have access to all of the features that are useful for you to use at home on your own. If you don't want to see these links you can return to **Book view**.

---

 ActiveBook    DigiList     Glossary

**P2.9**

## 2. Acceleration

*By the end of these two pages you should be able to:*
- explain what acceleration is and how it is calculated
- describe how to use a velocity–time graph to find the acceleration of an object.

**A** The acceleration in a dragster …

**B** … is much greater than any normal car.

Very few things that are moving stay at a constant velocity. They are always speeding up or slowing down. This change in velocity is called **acceleration**. Acceleration is a vector, like velocity, so it can be positive (speeding up) or negative (slowing down). Remember that vectors have direction as well as size. This means that acceleration also refers to changing direction, not just changing speed.

To work out the acceleration of something, you need to know:
- the velocity it started at (in metres per second) – this is written as $u$
- the velocity it ends up at (in metres per second) – this is written as $v$
- the time it took to change velocity (in seconds) – this is written as $t$.

The equation is:

$$\text{acceleration (m/s}^2) = \frac{\text{change in velocity (m/s)}}{\text{time (s)}}$$

This can also be written as: $a = (v - u)/t$

For example, a cheetah can start from rest and reach 26 m/s in 2 seconds. How can you find its acceleration?

Answer: $a = (v - u)/t$
$= (26 \text{ m/s} - 0 \text{ m/s})/2 \text{ s}$
$= +13 \text{ m/s}^2.$

1 What units is acceleration measured in?
2 What do the symbols $u$ and $v$ represent?
3 Write down the equation used to calculate acceleration in words and in symbols.

**C** Acceleration of +4 m/s² means that every second the velocity goes up by 4 m/s.

| Time (s) | Velocity (m/s) |
|----------|----------------|
| 0 | 0 |
| 1 | 4 |
| 2 | 8 |
| 3 | 12 |
| 4 | 16 |

204

Turn off  Go Interactive   Page

advancing learning, changing lives

advancing learning, changing lives

## GCSE Additional Science
## Students' Book

# Edexcel
# 360Science

Edexcel's own course for the new specification

**Phil Bradfield**

**James de Winter**

**Andrew Harmsworth**

**Cliff Porter**

**Nigel Saunders**

**Richard Shewry**

**Martin Stirrup**

**Charles Tracy**

This book also includes

Active Book

A PEARSON COMPANY

# How to use this book

The book is divided into 12 topics. Each topic has a one-page introduction and is then divided into ten double page sections. At the end of each topic there is a set of questions that will help you practise for your exams and a glossary of key words for the unit.

As well as the paper version of the book there is a CD-ROM called an ActiveBook. For more information on the ActiveBook please see the next two pages.

What to look for on the pages of this book:

**Learning outcomes**
These tell you what you should know after you have studied these two pages.

**Higher material**
If you are hoping to get a grade between A* and C you need to make sure that you understand the bits with this symbol **H** next to it (as well as everything else in the book). Even if you don't think you will get a grade above a C have a go and look at these bits – you might surprise yourself (and your teacher!).

**'Have You Ever Wondered?'**
These questions are there to help you think about the way science works in your life. Your teacher might ask you what you think.

---

B2.1

## 6. Aerobic respiration

**By the end of these two pages you should be able to:**

- recall that aerobic respiration provides energy for work
- explain how glucose and oxygen are supplied to respiring cells and how carbon dioxide is removed
- explain why respiration is increased in exercising muscles
- explain why gas exchange in the lungs is increased during exercise.

### Have you ever wondered?

What processes in cells keep you alive?

Your body needs **glucose** in order to release energy. Most of this comes from the digestion of carbohydrates. You also need oxygen. When you breathe in, oxygen enters the blood in the lungs and travels around the body in the bloodstream. The oxygen and glucose react in your body to produce carbon dioxide and water. The reaction gives out energy:

glucose + oxygen ➞ carbon dioxide + water (+ energy)

This process is called **respiration**. Because it uses oxygen, it is also known as **aerobic** respiration. The energy from aerobic respiration is needed to drive many processes in your body. Examples are muscle contraction, building proteins and sending messages through nerves.

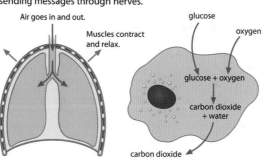

**A** Foods containing carbohydrates are needed for energy. The glucose from these foods is absorbed by the bloodstream and taken into the cells of the body.

Air goes in and out.

Muscles contract and relax.

glucose

oxygen

glucose + oxygen

carbon dioxide + water

carbon dioxide

Breathing is the way that air is forced in and out of the lungs.

Aerobic respiration is a reaction that happens in the cells.

**B** Breathing occurs in the lungs, but respiration is a chemical reaction that occurs in the cells.

**1** Explain the difference between breathing and respiration.

**2** What are the products of aerobic respiration?

**3** Give three uses of the energy from respiration.

20

Velocity–time graphs can also tell you about the acceleration of an object. If the line slopes upwards this means that the object's velocity is increasing (accelerating). The steeper the line, the greater the acceleration. If the line slopes downwards the object is slowing down. This is called **deceleration**.

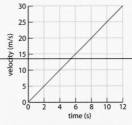

**D** Both C and D are accelerating but C is accelerating more than D.

> **Have you ever wondered?**
>
> Did you realise how much you know of the laws of physics if you skate, snowboard or play flight simulators?

You can calculate the acceleration of an object using a velocity–time graph. First, look at the velocity axis and read the starting velocity ($u$) and final velocity ($v$). Then find the time ($t$) between these two values. From this, calculate the **gradient** (or slope) of the line. This gradient is the acceleration.

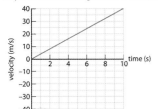

change in velocity = 40 m/s – 0 m/s = +40 m/s
time for change = 10 seconds
Acceleration = +30m/s/10s = +3m/s²

**E** The gradient of a velocity–time graph gives the acceleration.

When using velocity–time graphs to calculate acceleration:
• make sure that you read both the initial *and* final velocities from the graph
• remember that acceleration can be negative if the velocity decreases – you must include the minus sign.

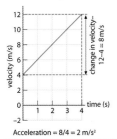

change in velocity – 12–4 = 8m/s

Acceleration = 8/4 = 2 m/s²

**F** The change in velocity here is 8 m/s (not 12 m/s).

change in velocity = –20m/s

Acceleration = 20/5 = – 4 m/s²

Acceleration doesn't always have to be positive.

**4** An object accelerates at +3 m/s². If it starts at 0 m/s what is its velocity after 5 seconds?

**5** If the line on a velocity–time graph slopes downwards, what does this tell you about the movement of the object?

**6** It is possible for a stationary dragster to accelerate at +50 m/s². What will its velocity be after 0.5 seconds?

**7** A sprinter travelling at 10 m/s takes 2 seconds to come to a stop. What is his deceleration?

**8** Calculate the acceleration of the object from the graph.

**9** The Space Shuttle can accelerate initially at almost +30 m/s². Write a page from a NASA guidebook that explains what this means and how velocity–time graphs can show the motion of any object.

Summary Exercise

Higher Questions

205

# Contents

# Inside living cells

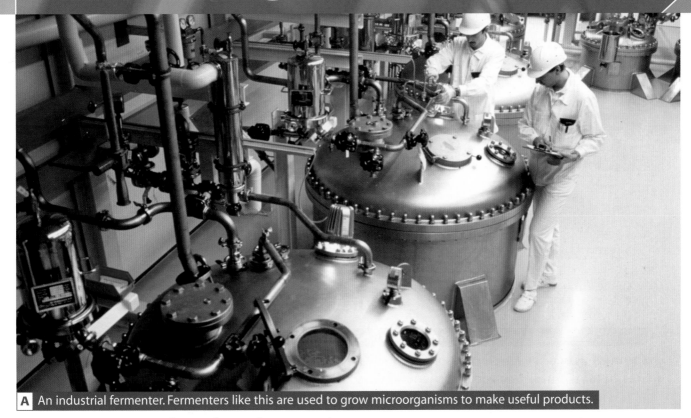

**A** An industrial fermenter. Fermenters like this are used to grow microorganisms to make useful products.

Microorganisms are tiny living things that cannot be seen without a microscope. They include bacteria, as well as single-celled fungi, called yeasts. Microorganisms can be grown on a large scale in metal tanks called fermenters. They are grown to produce chemicals that are useful to us.

One example of a useful chemical is the hormone insulin, which is needed to treat people with the disease diabetes. Bacteria do not normally make human insulin. Scientists have altered the genes of the bacteria so that they will make the hormone. To change the genes of bacteria so they can make useful products like insulin, scientists needed to know about the chemical that makes up genes – DNA.

**In this topic you will learn that:**

- the chemical reactions essential for life take place inside cells
- respiring cells need a supply of glucose and oxygen, producing carbon dioxide as a waste product
- genes are the template for protein synthesis inside cells
- the digestive, circulatory and respiratory systems provide cells with the basic materials they need to carry out their functions.

Insulin is a hormone that is produced by special cells in an organ called the pancreas.

- Write down three other types of cell found in the human body.

- Draw up a table with two columns. In one column make a list of any things you can think of that cells need to keep them alive, and in the second column make a list of any things you can think of that cells make.

# 1. DNA

> **By the end of these two pages you should be able to:**
> - describe the structure of a DNA molecule
> - explain that a DNA molecule controls how amino acids join together to form proteins in a cell.

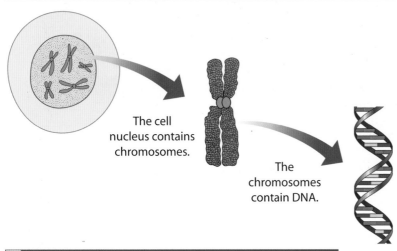

The cell nucleus contains chromosomes.

The chromosomes contain DNA.

**A** The nucleus of a cell contains the genetic material – DNA.

In the nucleus of a cell are chromosomes, which are made up of **genes**. In turn, genes are made of a chemical called **DNA**. DNA contains instructions for making the cell and telling it what to do. These instructions are called the **genetic code**. The DNA tells the cell to make particular **proteins**. A gene is a length of DNA that gives the instructions for making a certain protein.

Some proteins make up the framework that builds the cell. Other proteins are not part of the cell's structure, but have special jobs to do. For example the hormone **insulin** is a protein that controls the level of glucose in the blood. One important group of proteins is **enzymes**, which control all chemical reactions in cells.

## Have you ever wondered?

How does my body know which enzymes to produce?

A molecule of DNA is shaped like a twisted ladder. The sides of the ladder are made of a sugar called deoxyribose, and phosphate groups. These are linked together alternately:

– sugar – phosphate – sugar – phosphate – sugar –

The rungs of the ladder, which join the two sides – or **strands** – together, are made up of pairs of **bases**, called **adenine** (A), **thymine** (T), **cytosine** (C) and **guanine** (G). The bases are always paired in the same way: adenine pairs with thymine (A–T), and cytosine pairs with guanine (C–G).

1 What is the genetic code?

2 What does the DNA tell the cell to make?

3 What is a gene?

The twisted ladder is shaped like a double-coil. A coil is called a helix, so the DNA molecule is known as the **double helix**.

The DNA double helix

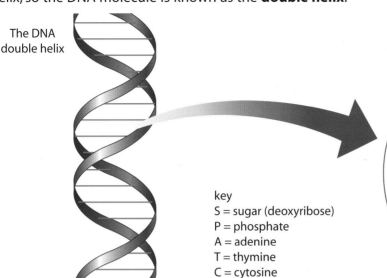

key
S = sugar (deoxyribose)
P = phosphate
A = adenine
T = thymine
C = cytosine
G = guanine

Pairs of bases form the 'rungs' of the ladder, sugars and phosphates form its sides.

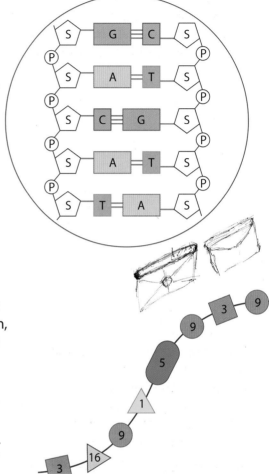

**B** The structure of part of a DNA molecule.

Proteins are made of long chains of tens to hundreds of **amino acids** joined up in a particular order. There are about 20 different amino acids. The order of amino acids is different for each protein, and it is this order that controls the structure and function of the protein. The DNA gives the order of the amino acids.

Only one side of the DNA ladder acts as a code for making proteins. This is called the **coding** strand. When the genetic code needs to be used in the cell, the DNA molecule unzips down the middle, exposing the bases along the coding strand. A sequence of three bases in the coding strand such as CTA or TTC, is called a **triplet**. The triplet decides where one amino acid is to be put into the protein. In other words, it 'codes for' an amino acid.

**C** Protein molecules are made of long chains of 20 different amino acids arranged in different orders.

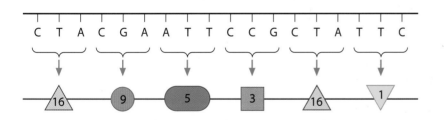

| C | T | A | C | G | A | A | T | T | C | C | G | C | T | A | T | T | C |

16     9     5     3     16     1

**D** The order of base triplets in the DNA coding strand produces the order of amino acids in the protein.

**Have you ever wondered?**

Why are plants and animals so different?

**Summary Exercise**

4 Explain how amino acids are arranged in a protein.

5 Part of the coding strand of DNA has the base sequence …AAGCGATTCAGG… How many amino acids would this code for?

6 Explain how DNA controls the order that amino acids are put together to form a protein.

**Higher Questions**

P

A

?

11

# 2. Fermentation

**By the end of these two pages you should be able to:**

- explain that microorganisms can be cultivated in fermenters to produce useful substances
- explain that DNA can be transferred into microorganisms.

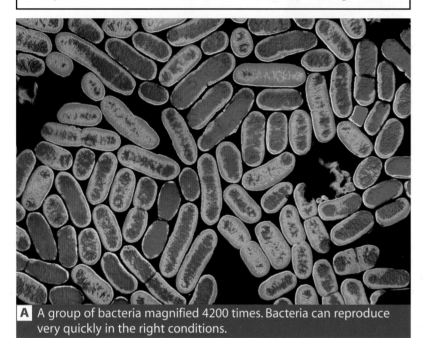

**A** A group of bacteria magnified 4200 times. Bacteria can reproduce very quickly in the right conditions.

A **microorganism** is a living thing that is so tiny it can only be seen through a microscope. Bacteria, yeasts and moulds are all examples of microorganisms. Scientists **cultivate**, or grow, microorganisms in a liquid that contains nutrients and a source of energy. This liquid is called the **culture medium**. The scientists must control the growth conditions carefully. If they do this, the microorganisms will reproduce very quickly. Some types of bacteria can divide into two every two hours. This means that after just two days, one bacterial cell could produce over 16 million cells. After three days, this number could increase to over 60 billion cells!

As they grow, the microorganisms use up the nutrients in the culture medium, and produce waste products and other substances. This process is called **fermentation**. One use of fermentation is making wine or beer using yeast. The yeast is given sugar. It uses the sugar as a nutrient, and also as a source of energy. The sugar is broken down to leave two waste products: carbon dioxide and alcohol (ethanol). When making wine or beer, the alcohol is the product that is wanted. However, fermentation by microorganisms can be used to produce many other useful products, not just alcohol. To do this, the microorganisms are cultivated in tanks called fermenters.

1 Explain the meaning of fermentation.

The nutrients and energy source that are added depend on the type of microorganism used. Some microorganisms use different sugars, such as sucrose or glucose. Other nutrients like amino acids may have to be added to the fermenter, so that the microorganism can use these as the building blocks for proteins. Some microorganisms will not grow unless certain minerals or vitamins are added too.

**B** An industrial fermenter can hold up to 200 000 dm³ of culture medium for growing bacteria or other microorganisms.

Microorganisms are grown in fermenters to make many different products. Fermentation of milk by bacteria is used to make yoghurt and cheese, and microorganisms are used to make other food products like vinegar and soy sauce. Microorganisms are also used to make a range of different enzymes needed in industrial processes, for example in the food industry and in biological detergents. Moulds and bacteria are grown to make antibiotics such as penicillin, which is used to cure infections. These are all examples of fermentation.

Bacteria and other microorganisms contain DNA. They use the same genetic code as humans and other organisms. Scientists can make the bacteria produce new products by changing their DNA. First they identify a protein that is needed as a medicine, such as insulin, which is needed to control diabetes. Next, they 'cut out' the section of the human DNA that is used for making insulin. They then put this piece of DNA into the bacteria. The bacteria now contain the gene for making insulin. If they are cultivated in a fermenter, this will grow massive numbers of bacteria, and produce lots of insulin. In the past, insulin had to be extracted from animal organs. Using fermentation is a much better method.

Some medicines and other useful products are now made in this way, such as enzymes and human growth hormone.

2 In wine making, what food source is given to the yeast as a source of energy?

3 Name three nutrients that might be added to a fermenter.

4 Name five useful products that are made from fermentation by microorganisms.

5 Describe the method scientists use to produce human proteins from bacteria.

6 Bacteria reproduce in a particular way. How does this make them good for producing products like human insulin?

**Summary Exercise**

**Higher Questions**

# 3. Using microorganisms

**By the end of these two pages you should be able to:**

- explain the advantages of using microorganisms for food production
- describe how a fermenter is used to cultivate microorganisms.

Industrial fermenters are used to make a wide range of products. As well as human insulin, a number of medicines are made, such as the antibiotic penicillin, which is a product of a mould called *Penicillium*. Many other species of microorganisms are grown in fermenters to produce foods and drinks.

People have been using microorganisms to make foods and drinks for thousands of years. Yeast is a single-celled fungus. It is used to make bread, wine and beer. Cheese and yoghurt can be made from milk using microorganisms called lactic acid bacteria. Blue cheeses are made using types of mould. The most widely used fermented food in the world is soy sauce, which is made in China, Japan and many other parts of Asia. Three microorganisms are used to produce soy sauce: a mould, a bacterium, and yeast.

Another food is actually made of microorganisms. Mycoprotein is a meat substitute that you have probably heard of as Quorn™. It is used to make a range of pies, burgers, ready meals and other foods. Mycoprotein consists of fine threads of a fungus.

**A** All of these foods are made by fermentation by microorganisms.

**1** List six foods or drinks made using microorganisms.

There are advantages in using microorganisms for food production. They reproduce at a very fast rate, so the food can be produced quickly and efficiently. Microorganisms are easy to keep and manipulate in a fermenter. They can also be grown in any country, in any climate. Some microorganisms can be fed on waste products from other industries, which saves resources. For example, the mould that makes Quorn™ can be grown using waste from flour making.

**B** Some foods made from Quorn™.

**2** It has been suggested that food made from microorganisms could be a solution to food shortage problems in some developing countries. Explain why this might be true.

**H** There are conditions in which each species of microorganism grows best. These are known as the optimum conditions for growth. They include a particular mixture of nutrients, an optimum temperature and an optimum pH. The conditions inside the fermenter can be carefully controlled so that the microorganisms will produce as much of the product as possible. This is called the maximum yield.

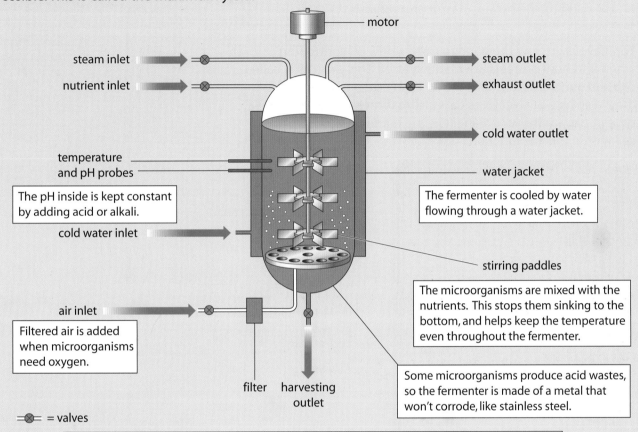

motor

steam inlet

nutrient inlet

steam outlet

exhaust outlet

cold water outlet

temperature and pH probes

water jacket

The pH inside is kept constant by adding acid or alkali.

The fermenter is cooled by water flowing through a water jacket.

cold water inlet

stirring paddles

air inlet

The microorganisms are mixed with the nutrients. This stops them sinking to the bottom, and helps keep the temperature even throughout the fermenter.

Filtered air is added when microorganisms need oxygen.

filter    harvesting outlet

Some microorganisms produce acid wastes, so the fermenter is made of a metal that won't corrode, like stainless steel.

= valves

The contents of the fermenter are monitored by special probes. These record the concentration of nutrients, temperature, pH, oxygen and carbon dioxide levels. The data is fed into a computer, which automatically controls the conditions in the fermenter.

**C** An industrial fermenter.

Before the fermenter is filled with fresh nutrients and culture, measures must be taken to avoid contamination by unwanted organisms. These measures are called **aseptic** precautions. The inside of the tank and all the pipes are cleaned and sterilised. This is usually done with very hot steam under high pressure. If these precautions are not taken, two problems might arise. Firstly, any bacteria or fungi that managed to get into the fermenter would contaminate the product with their cells or waste chemicals. Secondly, the contaminating microorganisms would compete with the organism in the culture, reducing the yield of product.

3 What are aseptic precautions? Explain why they are necessary.

4 Explain why the contents of the fermenter need to be stirred by the paddles.

5 Why do conditions such as temperature, pH, oxygen levels and nutrient concentrations need to be maintained in the fermenter?

Summary Exercise

Higher Questions

# 4. Making proteins

**By the end of these two pages you should be able to:**

- describe the organelles in the cell that are involved with making proteins
- describe the first stage of protein synthesis.

You have seen how the genetic code works by controlling when and how proteins are made in a cell. This process is called **protein synthesis**. Proteins are assembled from amino acids in the cytoplasm at structures called **ribosomes**. Ribosomes are a type of **organelle**. An organelle is the name for any part of a cell with a specific function.

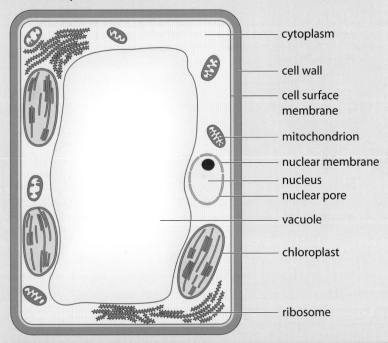

- cytoplasm
- cell wall
- cell surface membrane
- mitochondrion
- nuclear membrane
- nucleus
- nuclear pore
- vacuole
- chloroplast
- ribosome

**A** Organelles are the structures in a cell which carry out particular jobs.

To make proteins, two things must happen:

- the instructions from the code must be carried from the DNA in the nucleus to the ribosomes
- amino acids must be brought to the ribosomes to be built up into a protein.

Both of these stages are carried out by a chemical called **RNA** (ribonucleic acid). RNA has a similar structure to DNA, but the RNA molecule is a single strand. Like DNA, RNA has a sequence of bases on it, but the DNA base thymine (T) is replaced in RNA by a base called uracil (U).

One sort of RNA carries the code out to the ribosomes, this is called **messenger RNA**, or mRNA. A different sort brings the amino acids to the ribosomes and 'reads' the code for making a protein.

1 Name three cell organelles.

2 Describe two differences in the structure of DNA and RNA.

The process of copying the DNA code to form mRNA is called **transcription**. The DNA acts as a **template** for forming the mRNA (and eventually the protein). A template is a pattern, a bit like a stencil, that can be used over and over again to produce the same structure every time. The code in part of the DNA produces a similar code in an mRNA molecule. This molecule then leaves the nucleus to assemble a protein at the ribosome.

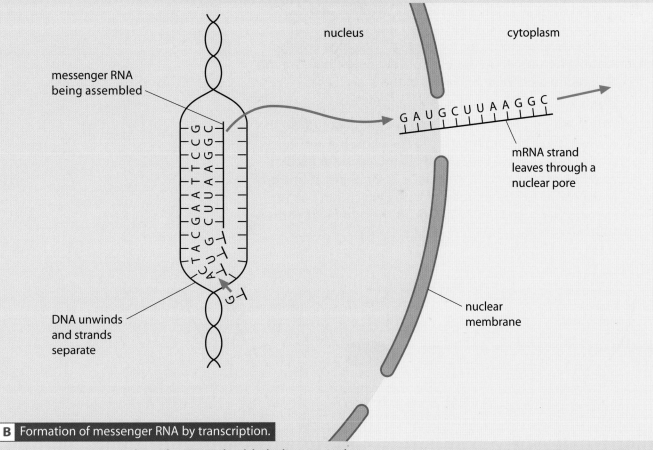

**B** Formation of messenger RNA by transcription.

Transcription starts when the DNA double helix unwinds, exposing the bases. An mRNA molecule then forms next to the DNA. Remember that in the DNA, the bases are paired: A pairs with T, and C pairs with G. The mRNA bases match up with the bases in the DNA in the same way. However, because there is no T in RNA, the A in the DNA pairs with U in the mRNA.

For example:
DNA sequence:                 A T C|C T G|G A C|G A T
mRNA sequence:           U A G|G A C|C U G|C U A

When the mRNA has been made, it breaks away from the DNA and leaves the nucleus through a nuclear pore. The DNA molecule then 'zips up' again. It can be used at a later time if more of the protein needs to be made.

3  Where does transcription occur?

4  What would be the order of mRNA bases corresponding to this sequence of bases on a DNA strand: ACCTAGCAG

5  Write a brief description of the process of transcription as a series of bullet points.

**Summary Exercise**

**Higher Questions**

**H** *By the end of these two pages you should be able to:*

- describe the second stage of protein synthesis.

The second stage of protein synthesis takes place at the ribosome. Here, the mRNA code is 'read' and a chain of amino acids is joined together to form a protein. This stage is called **translation**, because it translates the sequence of bases of the mRNA into the order of amino acids in the chain.

Once the strand of mRNA attaches to a ribosome, the code is 'read' by a second sort of RNA, called **transfer RNA** (tRNA). The job of tRNA is to carry amino acids to the ribosome and link up with the mRNA. There is a specific tRNA molecule for each of the 20 different amino acids that make up proteins. At one end of the tRNA is an exposed triplet of bases, which can pair up with a particular triplet on the mRNA. At the other end of the tRNA is a place where the amino acid attaches.

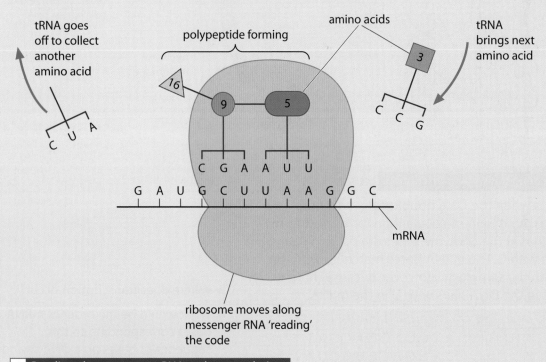

**A** Reading the messenger RNA code – translation.

The triplet of bases on the tRNA matches a triplet on the mRNA, following the base-pairing rules. The first amino acid is now held in a fixed place by the tRNA, ready to start a chain.

1 What is the job of tRNA?

2 A tRNA molecule has an exposed triplet of bases UAC. What will be the triplet of bases on the mRNA strand that will match with these bases?

Another tRNA molecule then brings along a second amino acid. This tRNA has a triplet of bases matching the next triplet on the mRNA. These bases again pair up with the bases on the mRNA. A chemical bond now forms between the first amino acid and the second one. A third tRNA now arrives, carrying another amino acid, and this tRNA links to the mRNA as before. The third amino acid is added to the growing chain.

Meanwhile, the first tRNA goes off to collect a new amino acid, leaving its first one behind in the chain. The tRNA molecules operate a sort of shuttle service, bringing amino acids to the ribosome and stringing them together according to the code on the mRNA. Eventually a long chain of tens or hundreds of amino acids is made. This is called a **polypeptide**.

**Insulin**

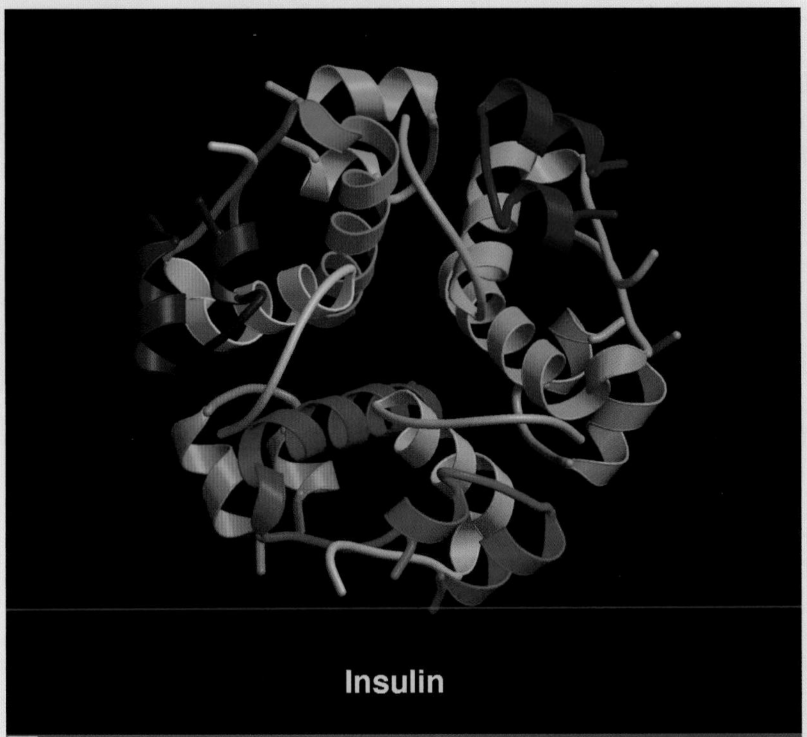

**B** A protein is made of one or more polypeptides folded into a certain shape.

A protein is not just a long chain of amino acids. The polypeptide has to be folded into a particular shape to form the protein's working structure. For example, in the hormone insulin the polypeptide chain is folded into a complicated shape like a ball of string. This is why it is called a globular protein.

**3** How many different tRNA molecules are there?

**4** What is a polypeptide?

**5** Explain the difference between a polypeptide and a protein.

**6** Write a list of the steps involved in translation, starting from when the mRNA leaves the nucleus. Make sure you put these steps into the correct order.

Summary Exercise

Higher Questions

# 6. Aerobic respiration

**P**

**H**

- recall that aerobic respiration provides energy for work
- explain how glucose and oxygen are supplied to respiring cells and how carbon dioxide is removed
- explain why respiration is increased in exercising muscles
- explain why gas exchange in the lungs is increased during exercise.

**?**

## Have you ever wondered?

What processes in cells keep you alive?

Your body needs **glucose** in order to release energy. Most of this comes from the digestion of carbohydrates. You also need oxygen. When you breathe in, oxygen enters the blood in the lungs and travels around the body in the bloodstream. The oxygen and glucose react in your body to produce carbon dioxide and water. The reaction gives out energy:

glucose + oxygen → carbon dioxide + water (+ energy)

This process is called **respiration**. Because it uses oxygen, it is also known as **aerobic** respiration. The energy from aerobic respiration is needed to drive many processes in your body. Examples are muscle contraction, building proteins and sending messages through nerves.

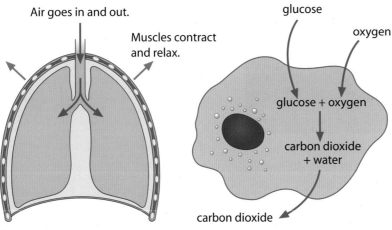

**A** Foods containing carbohydrates are needed for energy. The glucose from these foods is absorbed by the bloodstream and taken into the cells of the body.

Air goes in and out.

Muscles contract and relax.

glucose

oxygen

glucose + oxygen

carbon dioxide + water

carbon dioxide

Breathing is the way that air is forced in and out of the lungs.

Aerobic respiration is a reaction that happens in the cells.

**B** Breathing occurs in the lungs, but respiration is a chemical reaction that occurs in the cells.

**P**

1 Explain the difference between breathing and respiration.

2 What are the products of aerobic respiration?

3 Give three uses of the energy from respiration.

Both glucose and oxygen pass from the blood into the cells by **diffusion**. Diffusion is the movement of molecules from an area where they are densely packed together (a high concentration) to an area where they are spread out (a low concentration).

Cells in the body are supplied with glucose and oxygen by tiny blood vessels called **capillaries**. They have very thin walls just one cell thick, so that substances can diffuse through them easily. A working cell will be respiring and using up glucose and oxygen. This means that there will be a low concentration of these substances inside the cell, and a high concentration of them in the blood capillaries next to the cell. The oxygen and glucose will be able to diffuse into the cell.

Carbon dioxide is made by respiration in the cell. This means there is a high concentration of it inside the cell and a low concentration outside the cell. The carbon dioxide will diffuse out of the cell into the capillaries.

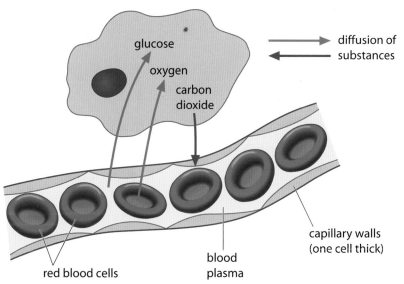

glucose

oxygen

carbon dioxide

diffusion of substances

capillary walls (one cell thick)

blood plasma

red blood cells

**C** A respiring cell gets its oxygen and glucose, and loses carbon dioxide, by diffusion.

4 What is diffusion?

5 Explain why oxygen diffuses into respiring cells.

6 Why does carbon dioxide diffuse out of respiring cells?

**H** When you exercise, your muscles need extra energy to contract. This energy comes from respiration, so the rate of respiration needs to increase. You take in more oxygen and remove the extra carbon dioxide by increasing your breathing rate.

At the same time, your heart beats more quickly to take the oxygen away from your lungs to your body cells more rapidly. This maintains a large concentration difference between the gases in your lungs and in your capillaries. Gas exchange occurs more quickly – more oxygen diffuses from your lungs into your blood and more carbon dioxide diffuses from your blood into your lungs.

7 Why does respiration need to increase in your muscles when you exercise?

8 Why does your breathing rate need to increase during exercise?

**Summary Exercise**

**Higher Questions**

P

**By the end of these two pages you should be able to:**

- explain why the heart rate and breathing rate increase with exercise
- interpret data on these measurements.

?

## Have you ever wondered?

Why does my heart beat faster when I exercise?

When you exercise, your muscles get energy from respiration. Glucose and oxygen must be supplied to your muscles, while the waste product carbon dioxide must be removed:

glucose + oxygen ⟶ carbon dioxide + water (+ energy)

If you exercise more vigorously, your muscle cells need more energy to do the extra work, so they need to respire faster. This means:

- more oxygen must be absorbed by your lungs
- more carbon dioxide must be removed by your lungs
- more glucose and oxygen must be delivered to your muscles by your blood
- more carbon dioxide must be removed from your muscles by your blood.

For these changes to happen, both your breathing system and your heart have to work harder. You breathe faster and more deeply. This increases the rate of gas exchange in your lungs: more oxygen is absorbed into your blood and more carbon dioxide is removed. Your heart rate also increases, pumping more blood to your muscles.

P

**1** State three changes that can take place to increase the amount of oxygen delivered to exercising muscles.

You can measure your breathing rate by counting the number of breaths you take in 30 seconds, then multiplying by two to give the number of breaths per minute. You can also measure your heart rate by counting your pulse over 30 seconds, and multiplying by two to give the number of beats per minute.

The table shows the results of an investigation using an exercise bike carried out by Kelly and Rutvi. They started by resting for 10 minutes. Then they cycled for 15 minutes at the same pace, and then rested for another 10 minutes. They measured their breathing rates and heart rates before, during and after the exercise. They started cycling at 0 minutes and stopped cycling at 15 minutes.

**A** You can use an exercise bike to find the effect of exercise on your heart rate and breathing rate.

| | Time (minutes) | Kelly's results | | Rutvi's results | |
|---|---|---|---|---|---|
| | | Breathing rate (breaths/minute) | Heart rate (beats/minute) | Breathing rate (breaths/minute) | Heart rate (beats/minute) |
| Cycling | 0 | 14 | 74 | 12 | 76 |
| | 5 | 19 | 122 | 16 | 99 |
| | 10 | 24 | 139 | 16 | 103 |
| | 15 | 27 | 145 | 16 | 103 |
| Resting | 20 | 13 | 90 | 12 | 75 |
| | 25 | 14 | 75 | 12 | 76 |

**B** Table showing the effect of exercise on breathing and heart rate.

You can see that the girls responded to exercise very differently. For example, Kelly's breathing rate increased from 14 to 27 breaths per minute in 15 minutes. This is an increase of 13 breaths per minute. Rutvi's breathing rate only increased from 12 to 16 breaths per minute in the same time.

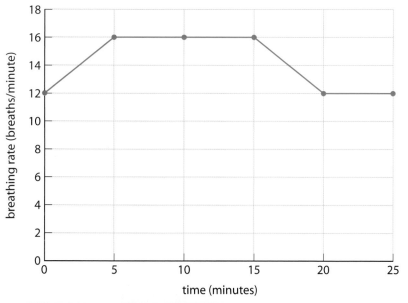

**C** This graph shows how Rutvi's breathing rate changed over the 25-minute period.

2 Suggest why the girls measured their breathing rate and heart rate before the exercise.

3 Explain the reasons for the changes in Kelly's breathing rate over the 25-minute period.

4 Why was it important that the two girls carried out the same amount of exercise?

5 At rest, Kelly's breathing rate and heart rate were different from Rutvi's.
   a What effect might this have on the results of the investigation?
   b Could this variable be controlled? Explain your answer.

6 Describe the shape of the curve in the graph of Rutvi's breathing rate.

7 The girls' heart rates also changed during exercise, but by different amounts. Which student showed the greatest increase in heart rate?

8 Plot a line graph of Kelly's heart rate against time.

9 Explain why the girls' heart and breathing rates both increased during exercise.

Summary Exercise

Higher Questions

**By the end of these two pages you should be able to:**

- explain why breathing and heart rate monitors, and digital thermometers, can provide more reliable data than traditional methods.

You can measure your breathing rate and heart rate by counting them using a timer. But these results can be unreliable. To measure your heart rate you need to find your pulse in your wrist. But the pulse is quite faint, and it is easy to miss a beat and make a mistake when you count it over 30 seconds. Another problem is that you have to stop the exercise to take a measurement.

Sports physiologists need to make measurements of the working of the human body. When they need to find out how exercise affects things like heart rate and breathing rate, they use machines called monitors. These are much more reliable than taking measurements by hand, as they give you a correct result every time. They are also more precise, as they can measure very small values. For example, a thermometer that measures to 0.01 °C is more precise than one that measures to 1 °C.

Monitoring equipment like this can cost thousands of pounds. A digital pulse monitor is much cheaper, costing less than £20. It detects the pulse in your skin by sensing the heat from the blood flowing through your wrist or thumb. You can even get pulse meters that clip onto an earlobe. Some pulse monitors can be used while you are exercising. Like the expensive equipment, you can feed the output from some kinds of pulse monitor into a computer, to give a permanent record.

1 Give two problems with taking your pulse by hand.

2 Explain what is meant by the term 'reliable'.

**A** A machine can continuously monitor heart rate and breathing rate. There is no need to stop the exercise to take a measurement. The data can be fed into a computer and used to plot graphs.

When you exercise, respiration also produces heat. Your body has methods to cool you down, like sweating, so that your temperature stays constant. But there may be a slight rise in your core body temperature. This is the temperature in the middle of your body, rather than on your skin. The average core temperature of a person at rest is about 37 °C. When you exercise, it might rise by a few tenths of a degree.

Physiologists sometimes want to measure these small changes in core temperature. They used to use an ordinary mercury thermometer to do this, which was placed under the tongue. These thermometers are not very precise, measuring the temperature to about 0.1 °C at best. Now digital thermometers are available. These give a readout in numbers, so you don't need to read from a scale. They are much more reliable, and can be as precise as 0.01 °C.

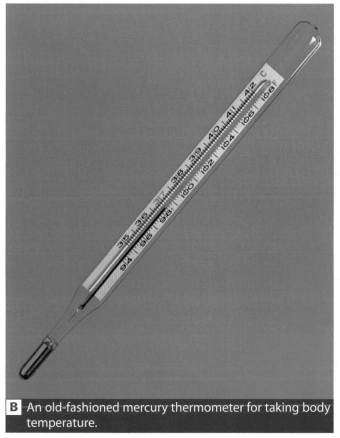

**B** An old-fashioned mercury thermometer for taking body temperature.

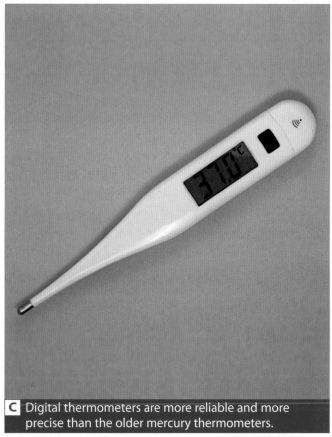

**C** Digital thermometers are more reliable and more precise than the older mercury thermometers.

A digital thermometer senses the temperature, and gives a reading when it is stable. This happens more quickly than with a mercury thermometer. You can also get expensive digital thermometers, or probes, that give a continuous output to a computer, like the heart rate monitors.

3 What is the average core body temperature?

4 By how much does the core body temperature change when you exercise?

5 How precise is a digital thermometer, compared with a mercury thermometer?

6 Explain why breathing and heart-rate monitors are more reliable than traditional methods.

**Summary Exercise**

**Higher Questions**

# 9. Anaerobic respiration and exercise

**By the end of these two pages you should be able to:**

P

- explain why, during vigorous exercise, muscle cells may not receive enough oxygen for their needs
- describe how anaerobic respiration releases energy by changing glucose into lactic acid

H

- explain why extra oxygen is needed to remove the lactic acid.

P

Aerobic respiration uses oxygen to change glucose into carbon dioxide and water, producing energy. If you carry out a low or moderate amount of exercise, you will be able to get all the energy you need from aerobic respiration. If you exercise vigorously, your blood will not be able to reach your muscle cells fast enough to deliver the oxygen they need for aerobic respiration. This would happen if you took part in a 'burst' activity, such as a sprint, or if you quickly lifted a heavy weight.

A burst event still needs energy, but the energy is not gained from aerobic respiration. Instead, energy comes from breaking down glucose into a chemical called **lactic acid**:

glucose $\longrightarrow$ lactic acid (+ some energy)

This is also a type of respiration, but because it does not use oxygen to react with the glucose, it is called **anaerobic** respiration.

**1** Which of the following sports are 'burst' events?
- throwing a javelin
- running a marathon
- putting the shot
- jogging

V

**A** 'Burst' events like sprinting use anaerobic respiration.

**B** If too much lactic acid builds up in the blood it causes cramp.

Why do I get cramp?

Anaerobic respiration produces enough energy to keep the overworked muscles going for a short time. But it has two disadvantages:

- anaerobic respiration produces much less energy than aerobic respiration
- when lactic acid builds up in the bloodstream, it causes muscle **cramp**.

100-metre runners get most of their energy from anaerobic respiration. Long-distance runners get most of theirs from aerobic respiration. Even a trained athlete cannot run a marathon at the speed of a sprinter! After a short distance, lactic acid would build up in the body, causing muscle cramp. Instead, long-distance runners have to pace themselves so that their muscles do not start to respire anaerobically. With practice, long-distance runners learn to keep something in reserve, so that they can sprint down the finishing straight.

**2** What does anaerobic mean?

**3** Explain why your muscles can only use anaerobic respiration for a short time.

**H** When a 'burst' event such as a sprint is over, the lactic acid in the blood has to be removed. Your body breaks it down into carbon dioxide and water, using aerobic respiration. Your body needs more oxygen to do this, so this is called the oxygen debt. After the race, your breathing gradually returns to normal, and the lactic acid in your blood is gradually broken down. The oxygen debt is repaid. The oxygen debt is the difference between how much oxygen you would need if you gained all the energy by aerobic respiration, and how much oxygen is actually available. This can be shown as a graph.

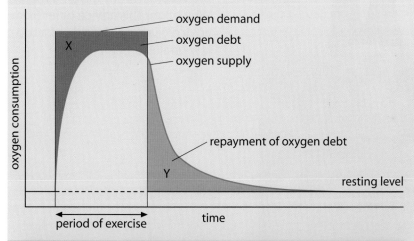

**C** Area X shows the extra oxygen needed for the period of exercise (the oxygen debt). Area Y is the oxygen repaid after the exercise. Area X = area Y.

**4** Explain why a sprinter develops an oxygen debt during a race.

**5** Explain what repaying the oxygen debt means.

Summary Exercise

Higher Questions

# 10. Which diet? How much exercise?

**By the end of these two pages you should be able to:**

- discuss why official advice on diet and exercise changes over time
- consider the scientific basis of fashionable diets.

Everyone knows that it is a good idea to eat a healthy diet and take regular exercise. But how do you know what a healthy diet is? Since the 1950s, people have been advised to avoid eating foods with high cholesterol, like butter and eggs. It was believed that the more cholesterol in your diet, the higher your risk of coronary heart disease. The Framingham Heart Study was one of the many studies carried out to investigate this idea. It was started in 1948 and is still running today.

The Framingham study did find a link between the cholesterol people ate and their risk of heart disease. But it also found that there are many other factors that can increase your risk of heart disease. These include smoking, weight, high blood pressure and diabetes as well as genetic factors. Many people now think that foods like butter and eggs are not so bad after all, as they contain proteins, vitamins and minerals. New findings can change the advice we are given on health and diets. But good research can take a long time to carry out.

**A** Butter used to be considered healthy. Now many people are turning to low-cholesterol foods.

1 The Framingham study has been going on for over 50 years. Why does this make it an important source of information?

2 Advice on diets and healthy living often comes from the government. Why might this advice differ from advice given on the side of a tub of low-cholesterol margarine?

**B** Exercise advice has also changed over the years. In the 1930s people thought that outdoor activities were the best way to keep fit. Since the 1980s, indoor exercise has been popular. These have included fads like spinning, trampolining and exercise balls.

Fashion and the media often suggest new diets to help you lose weight or stay healthy. Examples are the Atkins diet, the cabbage soup diet and 'food combining'. People following the Atkins diet have to cut down on carbohydrates, but they can eat high levels of protein and fat. Many types of fruit and vegetables are also forbidden at the start of the diet. But what is the evidence that this diet works?

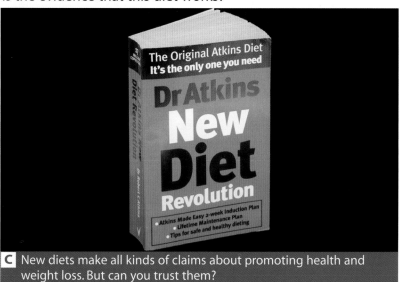

**C** New diets make all kinds of claims about promoting health and weight loss. But can you trust them?

| Diet followed | Average weight loss after 3 months (% of body mass) | Average weight loss after 6 months (% of body mass) | Average weight loss after 12 months (% of body mass) |
|---|---|---|---|
| Low calorie | 2.7 | 3.2 | 2.5 |
| Low carbohydrate | 6.8 | 7.0 | 4.4 |

**D** This table shows the results from a study done on 63 obese people. Source: *New England Journal of Medicine* Volume 348, 22 May 2003, Number 21.

This study found that lots of people had trouble sticking to the diets and many dropped out. Although the people who continued with the low-carbohydrate diet did lose weight, there may be negative side effects. Avoiding fruits and vegetables can increase the risk of some forms of cancer. Eating a lot of protein is linked to a higher risk of cancer of the colon, and the diet puts a lot of strain on the kidneys and the liver. It may also stop people absorbing calcium properly, which can lead to brittle bones. People often feel very tired when they start the diet, and they may suffer from bad breath.

Advice on healthy living can vary, but there is no argument that people need regular exercise and a varied diet containing plenty of fresh fruits and vegetables. It is important to consider the evidence behind a claim and the people who are making it, and not to be too influenced by popular opinion.

3 Look at the results table. Explain what the results show.

4 Do you think that the diet is worth doing? Explain your reasons.

5 What sort of information would you need to know if you were making up your mind about a new diet?

6 Why does official advice about diet and exercise change over time?

**Summary Exercise**

**Higher Questions**

## Multiple choice questions

**1** In a DNA molecule
  A cytosine pairs with guanine.
  B thymine pairs with cytosine.
  C guanine pairs with adenine.
  D adenine pairs with cytosine.

**2** Fermentation means
  A changing the genes of microorganisms.
  B growing microorganisms in a culture medium.
  C keeping microorganisms in aseptic conditions.
  D using microorganisms to break down nutrients into useful products.

**3** Mycoprotein (Quorn™) is made from
  A bread.
  B mould.
  C bacteria.
  D beef burgers.

**4** Oxygen enters a cell by a process called
  A respiration.
  B breathing.
  C fermentation.
  D diffusion.

**5** Aerobic respiration
  A makes lactic acid.
  B produces glucose.
  C needs oxygen.
  D uses carbon dioxide.

**6** Human body temperature
  A stays constant at 73 °C.
  B can be measured with a digital thermometer.
  C varies a lot with exercise.
  D cannot be measured with a mercury thermometer.

**7** A sport that is most likely to use anaerobic respiration is
  A shot put.
  B jogging.
  C marathon running.
  D long-distance swimming.

**8** Anaerobic respiration
  A produces carbon dioxide, water and a lot of energy.
  B produces lactic acid and a little energy.
  C uses glucose and oxygen and produces a little energy.
  D uses glucose and produces carbon dioxide and a little energy.

**9** Your muscle cells may not receive enough oxygen for their energy requirements
  A when you walk slowly.
  B if you take deep breaths.
  C if your heart beats faster.
  D if you carry out vigorous exercise.

**10** During exercise
  A less carbon dioxide is removed by the lungs.
  B more glucose is removed from the muscle cells.
  C more oxygen enters the muscle cells.
  D less glucose is needed by the lungs.

**H 11** The oxygen debt is
  A built up before a race to save energy.
  B used up in oxidising glucose.
  C greatest in a long-distance race.
  D paid off after a race to remove lactic acid.

**12** In the genetic code
  A one base is the code for a gene.
  B two bases are the code for a protein.
  C three bases are the code for an amino acid.
  D four bases are the code for an enzyme.

**13** The molecule that carries amino acids to the ribosomes is called
  A DNA.
  B polypeptide.
  C protein.
  D RNA.

**14** The order of molecules in protein synthesis is
  A DNA → RNA → polypeptide
  B RNA → polypeptide → DNA
  C polypeptide → RNA → DNA
  D RNA → DNA → polypeptide

**15** In the second stage of protein synthesis
  A triplets of DNA bases are used to produce RNA.
  B amino acids are brought to the ribosome by DNA.
  C RNA and amino acids are linked to ribosomes.
  D amino acids are linked to produce ribosomes.

## Short-answer questions

Jake and Anthony are doing a project on the effects of exercise on the body. Jake has been exercising on a running machine which records his heart rate. Anthony has recorded Jake's breathing rate. Their results are shown in the table.

| Measurement | At rest | Walking | Running |
|---|---|---|---|
| Heart rate (beats per minute) | 73 | 95 | 165 |
| Breathing rate (breaths per minute) | 16 | 20 | 32 |

**A** Measurements of Jake's heart rate and breathing rate with different amounts of exercise.

1 Anthony thinks that Jake's heart beats faster when he is exercising so that more blood will go to his muscles, carrying oxygen.
   a The blood also supplies a substance that is a source of energy for the muscles. What is the name of this substance?
   b Name the gas which is carried away from the muscles by the blood.

2 Oxygen is needed by the muscle cells for aerobic respiration.
   a Explain the purpose of aerobic respiration.
   b What gas is needed for aerobic respiration, and what gas does it produce?

3 Anthony has noticed that Jake's breathing rate has also changed.
   a Describe the difference in Jake's breathing rate with the different levels of exercise.
   b Explain why Jake's breathing rate changes like this.
   c Explain how diffusion is important in the lungs.

4 Jake tried sprinting on the running machine. He had to stop after a while, because he felt an ache in his legs. Anthony said this was muscle cramp.
   a Name the chemical that built up to cause muscle cramp.
   b What type of respiration produced this chemical?
   c Explain why Jake did not get muscle cramp when he was walking.

**H** 5 Jake knows that oxygen passes from the blood capillaries to the muscle cells by diffusion. He is confused about this process.
   a Explain how diffusion of molecules like oxygen happens.
   b How is the structure of a capillary adapted to increase the rate of diffusion?
   c Explain how breathing maintains a diffusion gradient for oxygen in the lungs.

# 12. Glossary

D

*adenine  A base found in DNA and RNA.

*aerobic  A process using oxygen. Aerobic respiration is respiration that needs oxygen.

*amino acid  One of about 20 different small molecules that link together in long chains to form proteins. Often called the building blocks of proteins.

*anaerobic  A process that does not use oxygen. Anaerobic respiration is respiration that does not need oxygen.

*aseptic  Conditions that are free from contamination by unwanted microorganisms. Aseptic precautions are taken to avoid contamination by unwanted microorganisms in a fermenter.

*bases  Chemical groups making up part of the DNA and RNA molecules. The order of bases in the DNA forms the genetic code.

*capillary  Very small blood vessel with walls one cell thick. The site of exchange of materials between the blood and cells.

*coding  The strand of DNA that carries the genetic code.

*cramp  Muscle pain caused by build-up of lactic acid when a muscle is overworked.

*cultivated  The growth of organisms, such as plants and microorganisms, in controlled conditions.

culture medium  A liquid in which microorganisms are grown.

*cytosine  A base found in DNA and RNA.

*diffusion  The movement of molecules from a region where they are at a high concentration to a region where they are at a low concentration.

*DNA  The chemical that makes up genes (deoxyribonucleic acid).

*double helix  The shape of the DNA molecule, like a twisted ladder.

enzymes  Proteins in cells that control chemical reactions. They are biological catalysts.

*fermentation  Using microorganisms to break down nutrients into useful products.

genes  Sequences of DNA inside chromosomes that control the characteristics of an organism.

genetic code  The instructions carried by the DNA for making a cell and telling it what to do.

*glucose  A simple sugar that is broken down in cells to release energy. It is also produced during photosynthesis.

*guanine  A base found in DNA and RNA.

*insulin  A protein hormone that controls the level of blood glucose.

*lactic acid  The waste product of anaerobic respiration in muscle cells.

messenger RNA  A type of RNA that carries the genetic code out from the nucleus to the cytoplasm during protein synthesis.

*microorganism  A very small organism that can only be seen through a microscope. Bacteria, fungi and viruses are examples of microorganisms.

*organelle  A part of a cell with a specific function, such as the nucleus.

*polypeptide  A long chain of amino acids. A protein is made of one or more polypeptides folded into a particular shape.

*protein  A chemical made of chains of amino acids. Proteins form part of the cell's framework (structural proteins) or carry out a particular job (functional proteins).

protein synthesis  The way proteins are made in a cell.

*respiration  The chemical reaction occuring in all living cells. Glucose is broken down into carbon dioxide and water to release energy.

*ribosome  A tiny organelle in the cytoplasm of a cell where proteins are made.

*RNA  A chemical similar to DNA that is involved in protein synthesis.

*strand  One side of the DNA double helix. The two strands are joined by pairs of bases.

template  A pattern, like a stencil, which can be used over and over again. The DNA coding strand acts as a template for forming mRNA.

*thymine  A base found in DNA.

transcription  The first stage of protein synthesis, where the genetic code in the DNA is converted into a similar code in the mRNA.

transfer RNA  A type of RNA that carries amino acids to the ribosome to be built up into a protein.

translation  The second stage of protein synthesis, where the genetic code in the mRNA is converted into the sequence of amino acids in a protein.

*triplet  A group of three bases in DNA that codes for the placing of an amino acid in a protein during protein synthesis.

*glossary words from the specification

# Divide and develop

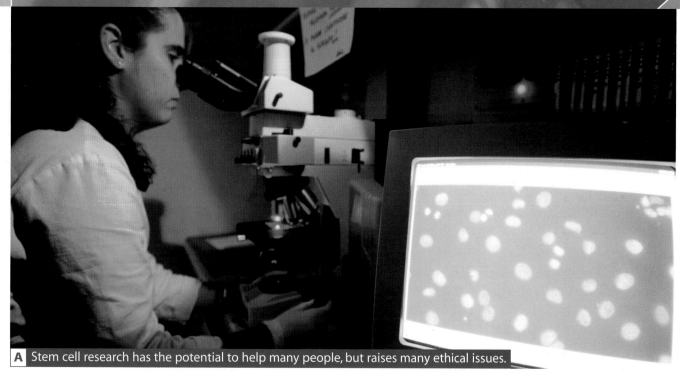

**A** Stem cell research has the potential to help many people, but raises many ethical issues.

All animals and plants are made from cells. Some organisms, like bacteria, are single-celled. A human body is built from thousands of millions of cells. Plants are also built from cells. Plant and animal cells have some differences but many similarities. Most cells can only divide to make more cells of the same kind. Some cells are very special as they can become any type of cell. They are called stem cells.

To understand why cells are so important, you will need to know more about their structure and what they do. You will need to know how cells divide and develop to form organisms. Knowing this can help you to understand more about techniques like cloning and gene therapy, and to think about the ethical issues surrounding them.

### In this topic you will learn that:

- organisms grow by cell division, elongation and differentiation of cells
- plants and animals are different and this results in different patterns of growth and development
- there is a variety of environmental factors that will influence the growth and distribution of plants
- human intervention can manipulate the outcome of reproduction.

Look at the following statements and sort them into the following categories:

I agree, I disagree, I need to find out more.

- A human being develops from just one cell.
- Plant and animal cells divide and develop using the same process.
- Dolly the sheep was a clone.
- A foetus can be legally aborted up until the 24th week of pregnancy.
- Gene therapy can cure genetic illnesses.

# 1. Cell division

All living organisms are made from cells. Organisms grow because these cells multiply. **Growth** is a permanent increase in the size of an organism. New cells are made by **cell division**. Body cells, which make up things like hair, teeth, skin and muscle, are made by a kind of cell division called **mitosis**. Mitosis produces cells for growth, repair or the replacement of older cells.

Most plants keep on growing all their lives. They grow from the tips of roots and shoots. Animals stop growing when they reach a certain size.

Most body cells have a **nucleus** containing **chromosomes**. The chromosomes carry the **genes** that control the characteristics of the organism. Before a cell can divide it must make a copy of all its chromosomes. When the cell splits, each new cell will contain identical chromosomes, carrying identical genes. The new cells are called daughter cells.

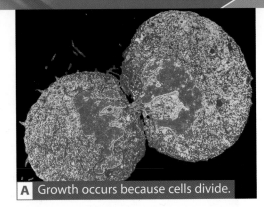

**A** Growth occurs because cells divide.

1 How do plants and animals grow?

2 What sort of cells are produced by mitosis?

3 Why is mitosis an important part of growth?

4 Explain how mitosis produces cells that are genetically identical.

5 Draw a series of diagrams to show how a body cell divides to make a new cell.

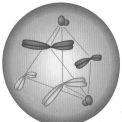

Each chromosome makes an identical copy of itself.

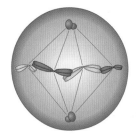

The chromosomes line up across the centre of the cell.

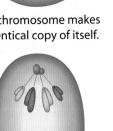

One complete set of chromosomes moves to each end of the cell.

The cell starts to divide in two and split apart. Each new cell is a daughter cell. The daughter cells contain identical chromosomes in their nuclei and carry identical genes to the parent cell.

**B** Mitosis is the division of a cell to produce two identical new cells.

**H** Another type of cell division is called **meiosis**. Meiosis produces sex cells such as **sperm**, **ova** and pollen grains. These are called **gametes**.

During human fertilisation, a sperm and an **ovum** come together eventually to form an embryo. Each of these cells must contain only half the number of chromosomes of a normal body cell, otherwise the **embryo** would have twice as many chromosomes as it should have. The process of meiosis halves the number of chromosomes when gametes are formed. This means that when fertilisation occurs the embryo has the right number of chromosomes. An embryo is a **diploid** cell, which means it contains a full set of 46 chromosomes. Half the chromosomes come from the mother, the other half from the father.

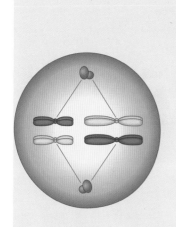 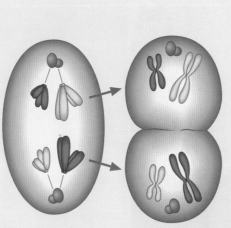 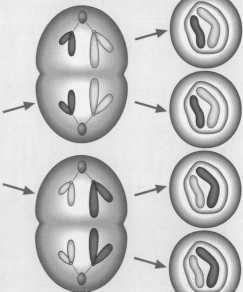

Each chromosome makes an identical copy of itself. The two copies stay in contact with each other.
The chromosomes line up in pairs. Each pair codes for the same characteristics.

The cell divides in two. One chromosome from each pair goes into each new cell. (This means there are no pairs of chromosomes in the new cells.)

The new cells divide again. Each chromosome splits in two. Each half goes into a new cell. This makes four haploid cells. These develop into gametes.

**C** Meiosis is the division of a cell to produce four haploid cells. These can then develop into gametes.

Mitosis and meiosis are both types of cell division that start with a diploid cell. But there are a number of important differences. The process of mitosis produces two identical cells with identical genes. These cells are also diploid. The process of meiosis produces four cells that do not have identical genes. These cells are **haploid**, which means they only contain 23 chromosomes. This process helps to provide genetic variation in offspring.

6 What sorts of cells are produced by meiosis?

7 Why is it important that gametes have half the number of chromosomes of normal body cells?

8 Draw up a list of the differences between mitosis and meiosis.

**Summary Exercise**

**Higher Questions**

# 2. What is growth?

**By the end of these two pages you should be able to:**

- explain what is meant by growth
- explain that growth occurs because of cell division, elongation and differentiation
- describe how growth can be measured.

P

V

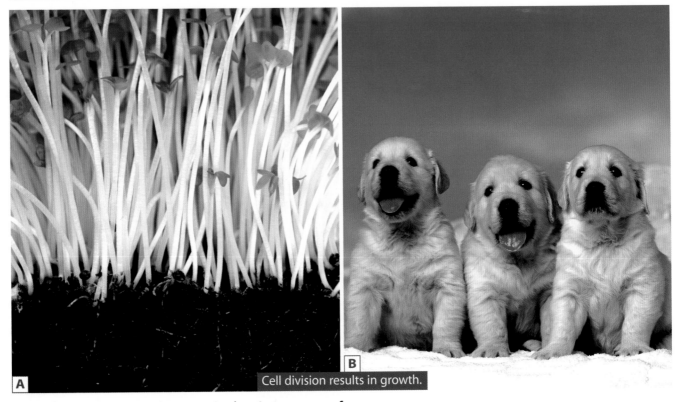

A

B

Cell division results in growth.

Growth is a permanent increase in the size or mass of an organism. All growth results from the production of new cells by mitosis. The bigger the organism the more cells it contains.

There are different ways of measuring growth in plants and other organisms. One is simply to weigh the organism. Body cells contain a large amount of water, so much of this weight will be water. This measure is called the **wet weight**. But the amount of water can vary, so this can give inaccurate results. A more accurate method is to dry the body out in an oven first. This is called the **dry weight**. This method kills the organism, so it is often used to compare growth in plants.

Another way to measure growth in plants is to look at size and length. Plants can be measured from the shoot tip to ground level to give their height. Measuring across the widest part of the plant is called its spread. Height and spread are used by garden centres and plant catalogues so customers know how big a plant will grow.

Most cells are made for specific purposes. When cells divide they may undergo **differentiation**. The new cells develop special characteristics to allow them to do their job. For example, red blood cells differentiate from special cells in bone marrow.

Similar cells may be grouped to form a **tissue**, such as heart muscle. Different tissues together may make an **organ**, such as the heart. Organs together make up a system, such as the circulatory system. A system may contain many types of differentiated cells.

## Have you ever wondered?

Why don't I keep growing forever?

C | You do not need to mow the lawn during winter.

Plants have a special way of growing. When new cells are formed around root and stem tips, their cell walls are still soft. The cells absorb water into their vacuoles and get longer. This process is called **elongation**. As the cells get longer the roots or shoots also get longer. The cell wall then hardens and the cell keeps its new shape.

There are several factors that can affect the way plants grow. In winter, plants grow more slowly. Lower temperatures mean slower rates of reaction inside cells, because enzymes work more slowly. Less light and shorter days means less photosynthesis, so plants grow more slowly, or stop growing altogether. Plants also need nutrients like nitrates. If they don't have enough of these minerals, they may stop growing.

1 What is meant by growth?

2 What causes growth?

3 Why are cells differentiated?

4 What is the difference between a tissue and an organ?

5 Explain how plant roots and shoots grow.

6 Why do plants need minerals like nitrates?

7 Why can insufficient light stop plants from growing?

8 Explain how cell division results in growth.

Summary Exercise

Higher Questions

# 3. Measuring growth

**By the end of these two pages you should be able to:**

- explain how size changes during human growth
- describe cell division and differentiation in human growth
- recall that a species will have a size range.

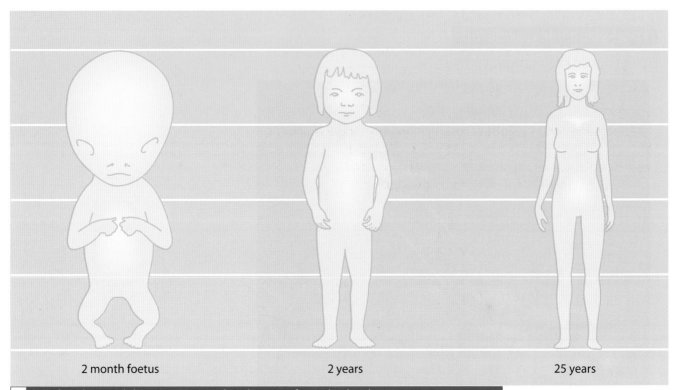

| 2 month foetus | 2 years | 25 years |

**A** Your head is much bigger compared to the rest of your body when you are very young.

All humans start life as a fertilised cell, called a **zygote**. The cell starts dividing and becomes a cluster of cells. At this stage all the cells are the same. As cell division increases cells become specialised, for example to make nerve cells or muscle cells. The zygote is now an embryo. As the embryo develops further, it becomes a **foetus**. The process of growth from fertilisation to birth takes about 40 weeks. In this time, the foetus grows rapidly. It increases its mass around 3000 times in the final 30 weeks.

After birth, growth continues at an even rate until puberty, when there is a growth spurt. During the growth spurt, the body grows rapidly. Parts of the body grow at different rates, and boys and girls develop differently. Girls usually start their growth spurt earlier. They also finish earlier, at about 18. Boys may continue growing for another two years.

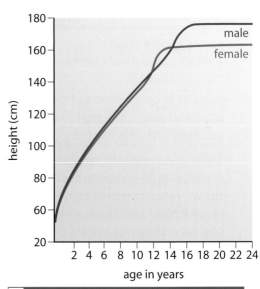

**B** Average height increases with age, with a growth spurt at puberty.

1 How does a zygote become a foetus?

2 What is meant by a growth spurt?

3 Look at graph B.
  a At what ages do girls grow fastest?
  b When do boys grow fastest?
  c Amy starts her growth spurt at age 9. This does not match the graph. How is this possible?

Each species has a minimum size and a maximum size. For humans, this is between 1.4 and 2.0 m in height. This is an average size range. There may sometimes be individuals above or below the range, but there are limits to this. For example, you won't find a person 10 m tall!

Height is a **continuous variable**. This means that there is a gradual variation in height across a population. Individuals can be any height within the range. If you have data from a large number of people, you will get a graph with a smooth bell-shaped curve. This is called normal distribution.

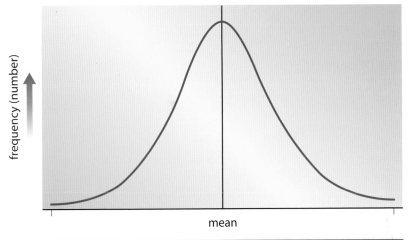

C A normal distribution curve shows that height is a continuous variable. A baby could grow to be any height within the range.

How tall you are depends on a number of factors. Environmental factors like better nutrition mean that children in Western Europe are now taller than children were fifty years ago. Children who are undernourished grow more slowly and for less time. Your genes are also important for your growth, as they control things like hormones. Growth hormone stimulates cell reproduction. Genetically engineered growth hormone can be given to children who don't produce enough of this hormone naturally.

4 What is continuous variation?

5 Some adults are much shorter than average, and some are much taller. Does this mean that they did not grow normally? Explain your answer.

6 Sarah and Raja are both tall. They think that this means their son Ben will be tall too. Are they right? Explain your answer.

7 Describe and explain how the pattern of growth changes in a human being from birth to age 18.

Summary Exercise

Higher Questions

**By the end of these two pages you should be able to:**

- explain what stem cells are and how they can be useful
- recall the scientific evidence for the potential benefits of stem cell research.

Cells do not live forever. They lose the ability to divide. In 1965 Leonard Hayflick discovered that cells can only divide a maximum number of 50 times. This maximum is called the Hayflick limit.

**Cancer cells** do not have a Hayflick limit. Sometimes mutations occur in the genes of a cell which cause the cell to keep dividing over and over again without limit. It has become a cancer cell and will develop into a tumour.

**Stem cells** also have no Hayflick limit. They can continue replicating. But these cells are not dangerous like cancer cells. They are naturally present in an embryo and perform an important job. They can become any type of cell in the human body. This is because stem cells are undifferentiated. The embryo starts out with stem cells, and these become specialised as the embryo grows into a foetus.

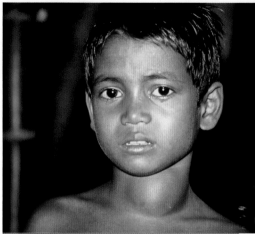

**A** Unlike normal cells, cancer cells keep on dividing, like in this thyroid tumour.

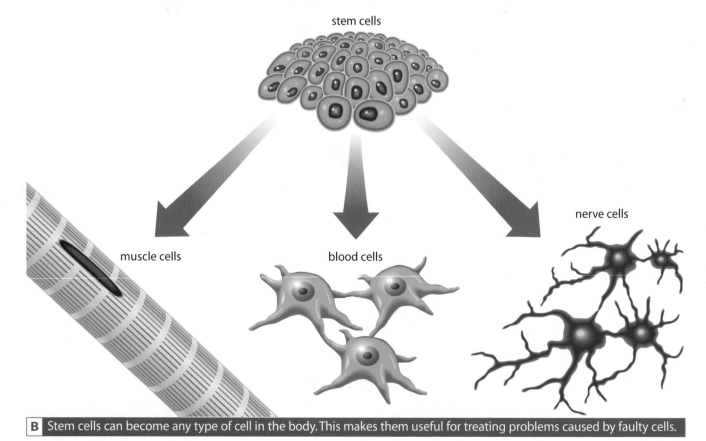

stem cells

muscle cells

blood cells

nerve cells

**B** Stem cells can become any type of cell in the body. This makes them useful for treating problems caused by faulty cells.

Most cells in the human body are highly specialised, like nerve cells and muscle cells. These cells can only divide to produce more of the same type of cell. A small number of stem cells stay undifferentiated in adulthood. These can still become different types of cell. But embryonic stem cells are easier to extract than adult stem cells, and some scientists say they are easier to change into the type of cell they need.

## Have you ever wondered?

What is a stem cell and why do scientists think it is so valuable?

There are several ways to get stem cells:
- from the cells of early embryos left over from fertility treatment
- from the umbilical cords of newborn babies
- from some types of adult tissue, such as bone marrow.

Stem cells can be used to grow new healthy cells to replace cells that have become damaged or faulty. Scientists hope that they could use this technique to cure many conditions, including Parkinson's disease, diabetes, arthritis and severe burns.

Some experimental treatments have successfully been used on humans. Doctors in Britain have used stem cells to repair damaged corneas. A cornea is the thin film at the front of the eye. Patients receiving this treatment have had dramatic improvements in their eyesight.

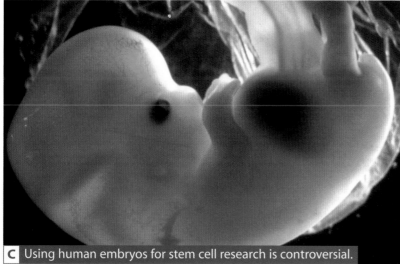

**C** Using human embryos for stem cell research is controversial.

Many people disagree with using human embryos for stem cell research. It depends on whether you consider embryos to be human beings with rights. Some people believe that life starts at the moment of fertilisation, so a fertilised cell should have the same status as a human being. Others argue that that an early embryo is just a ball of cells, so it cannot have any rights. This is a moral question, and there is no right or wrong answer.

**1** What is meant by the Hayflick limit?

**2** Why can cancer cells keep on dividing?

**3** What is a stem cell?

**4** Why are embryonic stem cells used for research more often than adult stem cells?

**5** Why do scientists think stem cells could help cure medical conditions like cancer?

**6** Why are many people against stem cell research?

**7** Write a newspaper article about the science of stem cell research. Include what stem cells are and how they could be used to treat medical problems.

**Summary Exercise**

**Higher Questions**

# 5. Science – some tough decisions

**By the end of these two pages you should be able to:**

- discuss the scientific basis of the laws regarding the termination of pregnancy
- discuss the use of growth factors to enhance performance in sport.

## Have you ever wondered?

How does scientific knowledge contribute to discussions regarding the termination of pregnancies?

In 2005, 186 400 pregnancies were terminated in the UK. A foetus takes approximately 40 weeks to develop from fertilisation to delivery. Different countries have different laws about when a pregnancy can be terminated. In the UK, **termination** is legal up to the 24th week of pregnancy. This limit was set in 1990. It is based on the **viability** of the foetus, or whether it can live outside the womb.

There are different views on when a foetus is viable. Improvements in medicine mean that some premature babies who would have died in the past can now survive. Babies born at 24 weeks have around a 39% chance of survival.

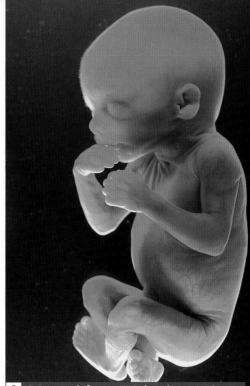

**A** A 24-week foetus. It is legal to terminate some pregnancies at this stage.

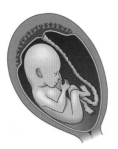

Week 12: some organs start to function and the bones begin to harden

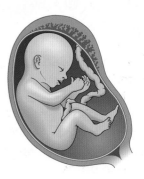

Week 20: the muscles are more developed and the foetus is more active

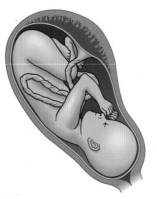

Week 24: the air sacs form in the lungs and the eyes are developed

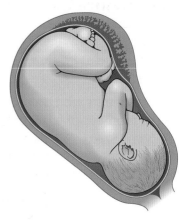

Week 36: the nervous system is developing rapidly and the lungs are nearly mature

**B** A foetus develops gradually during the pregnancy.

Whether a foetus is viable depends on how well developed it is at the time it leaves the womb. By week 24, most of the organs are functioning. However the lungs and nervous system are still very under-developed. All premature and some **full-term** babies require medical help.

Medical science cannot solve the controversy about termination. There is also an ethical side to the issue. Some people believe that a foetus at any stage has the right to life. The arguments about the termination of pregnancy are likely to continue long into the future.

## Have you ever wondered?

Why have the International Olympic Committee (IOC) banned certain chemicals?

**C** Some people take steroids to help build muscle, but there is a cost to their health.

Professional sports are very competitive. Many athletes are tempted to use **growth factors** to enhance their performance. These include drugs called **anabolic steroids**. Steroids are based on the male sex hormone testosterone. They work by increasing muscle growth. The same thing happens when boys go through puberty. Female athletes have also been known to take these drugs.

Steroids can have many dangerous side-effects, including:
- liver failure
- facial hair growth in women
- a deepening of the voice in women
- **impotence** and development of breasts in men.

There are also ethical concerns about steroids. Many people think these drugs give athletes an unfair advantage. They are no longer relying on their natural physical capabilities. For this reason, competitions ban athletes from taking steroids and other performance-enhancing drugs.

**Summary Exercise**

1 What is meant by a viable foetus?

2 Why is a 40-week-old foetus more viable than a 24-week-old foetus?

3 Explain how scientific evidence can be useful to people who make laws about the termination of pregnancy.

4 What advantage does taking anabolic steroids give to an athlete?

5 What are the health risks of taking anabolic steroids?

6 Why are these substances banned from sport?

7 Write a report on the use of growth factors, like steroids, in sport. Include a discussion of why most people think that using them is unethical.

**Higher Questions**

# 6. Plant growth and distribution

**By the end of these two pages you should be able to:**

- describe some of the factors that affect plant growth and distribution
- interpret data on these factors.

**A** **B**

The mammillaria cactus needs a hot dry environment in which to grow. The map shows, in green, where the cactus grows. These conditions would be hostile to many other plants.

All plants need certain conditions to grow. These include light, water, nutrients, temperature, carbon dioxide and oxygen. But these conditions can vary from place to place. This affects the **distribution** of plants.

## Have you ever wondered?

Why do 'weeds' always grow in the most awkward places?

Mineral salts in the soil are taken up in small amounts by plant roots to provide **nutrients**. If soil does not contain enough nutrients then some plants will grow poorly or not at all. Sandy soils are often low in nutrients. Plants that live in these soils are adapted to surviving on fewer nutrients. Gorse, heather, pine and birch are plants which grow well in sandy soils.

Plants also need light for photosynthesis. Photosynthesis is the chemical process used to make glucose. This is converted into all the other chemicals a plant needs for growth.

$$\text{water} + \text{carbon dioxide} \xrightarrow[\text{chlorophyl}]{\text{sunlight energy}} \text{glucose} + \text{oxygen}$$

Some plants need lots of light to grow. Others are adapted to low levels of light and like lots of shade. This can be clearly seen in the different layers of a rainforest.

1 Explain why the type of soil can affect how plants grow.

2 Why is light so important for the growth of plants?

| Layer | % light received | Plants that live there |
|-------|------------------|------------------------|
| emergent | 100 | the tops of the tallest trees, more than 35 m high |
| canopy | 99 | trees 25–35 m high forming a canopy where 90% of the organisms live |
| understory | 15 | thin trees about 20 m high covered in mosses, lichens, orchids and ferns |
| shrub | 3 | ferns and small shrubs |
| floor | 1 | a few small plants |

**C** Percentage of light penetrating each layer in a rainforest.

Photosynthesis is also affected by temperature. As temperature increases, photosynthesis gets faster. This is one reason why plants that live in cold climates, like conifers, grow more slowly. Photosynthesis will stop, and the plant will die, if the temperatures are too high or too low.

Plant cells can be damaged if the water in them freezes. Conifers produce oils which act like antifreeze. They are adapted to cold climates and high altitudes, such as in mountainous areas. But even conifers cannot survive extremely low temperatures. The edge of the area where trees can grow in cold locations is called the tree-line.

**D** Photosynthesis cannot take place where the temperatures are too low.

Most plants need air in the soil around their roots. If soil gets too wet it becomes waterlogged. Plant roots cannot get the oxygen they need, so the plant will die. Some plants are adapted to waterlogged soils. Mangrove trees have root-like structures that stick up out of the waterlogged soils so that the plants can take in oxygen.

**Summary Exercise**

3 Look at table C.
   a Describe how the plants that receive a small amount of light are different from those that receive a lot of light.
   b Explain why 90% of organisms that live in the rainforest are found in the canopy.

4 Explain how temperature can affect plant growth.

5 The table shows the height of the tree-line in different locations.

| Location | Approximate height above sea level (m) |
|----------|----------------------------------------|
| Sweden | 800 |
| Swiss Alps | 2400 |
| Yosemite National Park, USA | 3600 |
| Himalayas | 4400 |

   a The tree-line at Yosemite is around 3600 m above sea level. Explain this information in your own words.
   b Sweden is much further north than the Himalayas. Why might this affect the tree-line?

6 a What is waterlogged soil?
   b Why does it kill most plants?

7 Write a fact sheet about the factors that affect where plants can grow.

**Higher Questions**

**By the end of these two pages you should be able to:**

- explain that plant hormones affect their growth
- H discuss how artificial hormones can be used for fruit initiation.

## Have you ever wondered?

Why do plants need hormones?

Just as humans need **hormones** for growth, plants have hormones too. Plant hormones control things like flowering, fruit ripening, and the growth of roots, shoots, leaves and stems. There are five types of hormone produced by plants: gibberellin, cytokinin, auxin, ethylene and abscisic acid.

Each of these has particular jobs to do. Gibberellin promotes cell division and elongation. It also helps seeds to sprout. Cytokinin also promotes cell division. Higher levels of this hormone are found in areas that need the most growth, such as roots, young leaves and developing fruits and seeds.

Plant stems always grow towards the light. This growth is controlled by auxin. If plants receive light from one side they will grow towards it. The auxin is produced at the tip of a new shoot. It makes the cells elongate more on the shaded side of the shoot, so it bends towards the light.

**A** Plants grow towards the light because of their hormones.

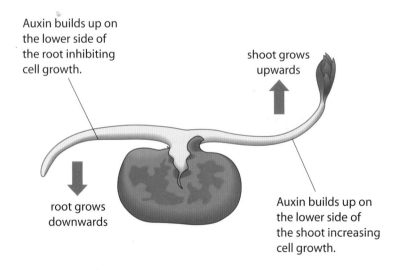

Auxin builds up on the lower side of the root inhibiting cell growth.

shoot grows upwards

root grows downwards

Auxin builds up on the lower side of the shoot increasing cell growth.

**B** The combination of light, gravity and auxin affect the direction in which shoots and roots grow.

1 Why do plants need more than one hormone?

2 Why is it an advantage for plants to be able to grow towards the light, instead of just straight up?

3 Explain how auxin controls this effect.

Auxin also makes the plant roots grow down into the soil. Gravity is an important part of this process. Auxin builds up on the lower side of the root and slows down growth on this side. This allows the upper side to grow much quicker. The force of gravity helps the root to bend downwards and grow deeper into the soil.

Sometimes plants also need to slow down their growth. This is the job of the hormone abscisic acid. This hormone slows down the plant's metabolism so that it doesn't grow during winter. If conditions become stressful, slowing down or stopping growth can help the plant to survive.

**H**

**C** Hormones produced in plant seeds cause the fruit to develop and ripen.

Hormones are also important for fruit growth. Fruit is the mature ovary of a flowering plant. It contains the seeds for the plant to reproduce. Auxin or gibberellin **initiates**, or stimulates, the development of the fruit. Ethylene helps it to ripen.

Hormones are produced by the developing embryo inside the seed. They stimulate seed growth and cause the ovary to develop into a fruit. Fruit growers sometimes spray artificial auxin onto the unpollinated flowers of fruit trees or tomato plants. This results in fruit with no pips. Seedless pears, grapes and satsumas are grown in this way.

**7** Explain how hormones cause fruit to develop.

**8** How has an understanding of plant hormones been helpful to gardeners growing fruit?

**4 a** Explain how gravity and auxin affect the way the roots of a plant grow.
  **b** Why is this important for the plant?

**5** Suggest some conditions that might be stressful for plants.

**6** Write a paragraph explaining how hormones affect plant growth.

P

P

Summary Exercise

Higher Questions

# 8. Artificial selection

**By the end of these two pages you should be able to:**

- discuss regeneration in animals
- explain how selective breeding is used to improve the quality of characteristics in plants and animals.

**A** Some animals can regenerate lost limbs. Humans can only regrow finger nails and small amounts of tissue.

Cut an earthworm in half and the head end will grow a new tail. This is called **regeneration**. Other animals can also regenerate body parts. A lizard can regrow a lost tail, and newts and salamanders can regrow limbs and many other parts, including eyes. A young spider can regenerate a lost leg. This is a special ability that only a few animals, and no mammals, have.

There is some evidence that these animals do this by reversing cell differentiation. When they lose a body part, the cells around the stump change their structure and become less specialised. These are joined by existing stem cells. The cells then differentiate again to produce all the different types of cell needed to grow a new limb. Stem cell research is looking at these animals to try to find a way to regenerate human body parts.

1 What is meant by regeneration?

2 Why are stem cell researchers interested in animals that can regenerate body parts?

**B** Many varieties of dwarf wheat are high yielding. They are also easier to harvest as they don't fall over in the wind like taller varieties.

**Selective breeding** is nothing new. Modern bread wheat **species** have been developed from wild emmer wheat. This was first cultivated 10 000 years ago. People carefully selected seeds from the highest yielding plants to plant the next year. This has gradually improved the crop.

Selective breeding means breeding from individuals that have the characteristics you most want. This increases the chance that more offspring will also have these characteristics. The selection and breeding process must normally be repeated over many generations. Selective breeding can improve resistance to disease, increase yield and make foods more attractive to consumers.

Agricultural scientist Norman Borlaug won the Nobel Prize for developing new varieties of dwarf wheat. He did this by cross-fertilising different strains of bread wheat. His new varieties give higher yields because more of the energy from photosynthesis goes into making grain, and less into making straw. They are also resistant to disease and drought.

**C** Sheep can be bred to produce more offspring.

Selective breeding is also used in animals. Dairy cows are selectively bred to produce higher quality milk, which contains more protein and butterfat. This milk is more profitable for farmers.

Sheep can be selectively bred to produce more lambs. These ewes can lamb twice a year instead of once, or they can be bred to have twins or triplets. This kind of breeding means that there is an almost constant supply of lambs all year round.

**Summary Exercise**

3 Explain what is meant by selective breeding.

4 The wheat that Norman Borlaug developed helped to save millions of people from starvation in the 1970s and 1980s. Explain how it could have achieved this.

5 Explain how cows could be selectively bred to produce higher quality milk.

6 What is the advantage of a year-round supply of sheep?

7 Explain how modern farmers have benefited from selective breeding. Use examples of plants and animals in your answer.

**Higher Questions**

# 9. Cloning mammals

**By the end of these two pages you should be able to:**

- explain how animals can be cloned
- discuss why advances in genetic modification can be beneficial but also raise ethical concerns.

A clone is a genetic copy of another single organism, or a group of cells. One method of artificial cloning is called cell nuclear transfer. The first mammal cloned in this way from adult cells was Dolly the sheep.

Body cells are diploid. This means they carry a full set of 46 chromosomes. Egg cells only contain half this number of chromosomes. In natural reproduction, the other half of the chromosomes would come from the sperm cells of the father. To produce a clone, a complete set of genetic information is needed from a single animal. Diploid body cells are used for this purpose.

**A** Professor Ian Wilmut created 'Dolly', the world's first cloned mammal in 1996. The research was conducted at the Roslin Institute in Edinburgh, Scotland.

Finn Dorset ewe
(sheep used for cloning)

Scottish Blackface ewe
(sheep supplying eggs)

diploid body cell

egg cell

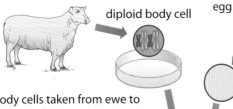

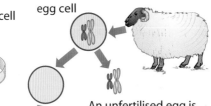

Body cells taken from ewe to be cloned. These are cultured to stop them dividing.

An unfertilised egg is taken from the ewe supplying the eggs. The nucleus is removed.

The body cell and egg are fused with an electric pulse.

A second electric pulse triggers cell division. An embryo develops after about 6 days.

The embryo is implanted into another Scottish Blackface ewe.

Dolly is born, genetically identical to the Finn Dorset parent.

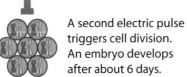

**B** How Dolly was cloned.

1 What stimulates the cell to divide?

2 Describe the process of cell nuclear transfer.

3 Why is it important to use body cells with diploid nuclei to produce the clone?

However a body cell cannot produce a new embryo on its own. An unfertilised egg cell is also needed. The nucleus is removed from the egg cell, and replaced with the nucleus of the body cell. These are fused together and the cell is stimulated to divide and grow into an embryo.

Cloning is not easy. It took 277 attempts, using new cells each time, to create the embryo that developed into Dolly the sheep. Few cloned embryos survive until birth. Many cloned animals are born abnormally large and with problems such as heart and lung disease. Research has improved the success rates of cloning, but there are still many problems to solve.

Cloning also raises ethical concerns. These are mainly about the cloning of humans. This is currently illegal in the UK and in most other countries. It is however legal to clone human embryos for stem cell research.

4 Outline the potential health problems that may be experienced by cloned animals.

5 Suggest why some people are against cloning.

Another type of research that causes controversy is **genetic modification**. Genes are manipulated and introduced into DNA in order to change the genetic characteristics of an organism.

Genetic modification has produced new vaccines and drugs such as human growth hormone and human insulin. Animals can be genetically modified to grow larger and to be immune to illnesses. Genes can be transferred from plants or animals into other organisms. These are called transgenic organisms. Transgenic animals can be genetically engineered to make their organs compatible for transplant into humans, or to produce milk with health benefits to us.

### Have you ever wondered?

Why do scientists want to modify cows?

There are ethical considerations with genetic modification. Some people believe it is unnatural. They argue that the products of transgenic animals may have side-effects that no-one knows about. Some people say that it is cruel to animals as it treats them as living factories. Others say the benefits outweigh the disadvantages, because so many people can be treated for illnesses.

C Cows can be genetically modified to produce enriched milk. The milk contains proteins that could help some human illnesses.

6 Describe some of the benefits of genetic modification.

7 Explain what is meant by an ethical dilemma. Use cloning and genetic modification as examples.

Summary Exercise

Higher Questions

P

H

**By the end of these two pages you should be able to:**

- consider whether gene therapy could stop diseases being passed on to the next generation
- explain how gene therapy could relieve the symptoms of inherited diseases like cancer.

Gene therapy is a new way of treating human disease. Some human diseases are caused by faulty genes, such as cystic fibrosis and haemophilia. The aim of gene therapy is to replace the faulty gene with one that works properly. It is hoped this will cure the disease. This technique is still at the experimental stage.

A

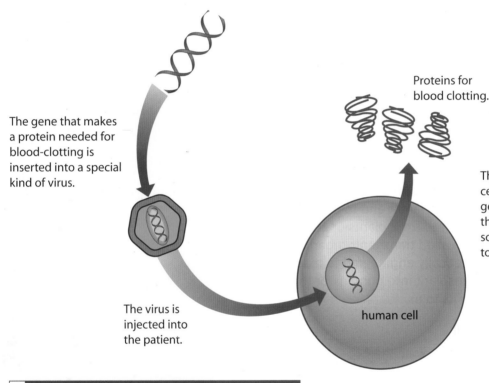

The gene that makes a protein needed for blood-clotting is inserted into a special kind of virus.

The virus is injected into the patient.

Proteins for blood clotting.

The virus 'infects' cells with the new gene. This replaces the faulty gene, so the cell starts to work.

human cell

**A** Gene therapy could be used to cure haemophilia.

One hope is that gene therapy could stop diseases from being passed on through **inheritance**. The gene could be inserted into a patient's reproductive cells. After that it would need to be incorporated into the chromosomes. The patient could then pass the introduced gene on to their offspring.

P

This procedure is particularly difficult, and has not yet been tried on humans. One problem is that once the gene is introduced into the reproductive cells, it would continue to be passed on to future generations. These generations would have had no choice in receiving the therapy. Another concern is that any long-term risks from this therapy are not yet known.

1 What is meant by gene therapy?

2 Write a newspaper article with the title 'Gene therapy – the end of inherited diseases?'

**H**

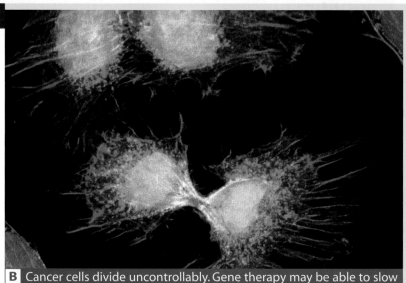

**B** Cancer cells divide uncontrollably. Gene therapy may be able to slow this down or stop this from happening.

## Have you ever wondered?

How can gene therapy help treat cancer sufferers?

Most researchers are working on the potential of gene therapy to treat patients currently suffering from disease. Some cancers are caused by faulty genes. It may soon be possible to treat some of these cancers by:

- inserting genes into the cancer cells to make them more sensitive to treatments such as chemotherapy
- inserting genes into cancer cells that make a toxin (poison) and then activating them to kill the cells
- using genes to stop cancer cells from making new blood vessels, which prevents the tumour from growing
- introducing genes into cancer cells so that the body's immune system identifies them as dangerous and destroys them
- inserting genes into normal cells so they can better withstand the side effects of treatment by radiotherapy and chemotherapy. This can reduce the patient's suffering and also make it possible to deliver higher doses of the treatments.

There are many difficulties to solve if gene therapy is to be successful. Targeting a gene to the correct cells is very important. If the gene is inserted into the wrong cells, the patient could have health problems. If the gene is accidentally inserted into reproductive cells, it could be passed on to offspring. The patient may also have an immune reaction to the virus used to deliver the new gene. In addition, many cells divide rapidly, so the new gene may not live in the body for very long. Patients may need many rounds of therapy.

**3** Describe how viruses can be used in gene therapy.

**4** Explain how gene therapy could be used to treat cancer.

**5** Explain why gene therapy isn't being used for these treatments yet.

**Summary Exercise**

**Higher Questions**

## Multiple choice questions

**1** Mitosis produces
- **A** plant hormones.
- **B** body cells for growth.
- **C** sex cells.
- **D** embryos.

**2** The characteristics of an organism are controlled by
- **A** genes.
- **B** cells.
- **C** gametes.
- **D** the nucleus.

**3** Cloning copies
- **A** all the characteristics of an organism.
- **B** half the chromosomes from a body cell.
- **C** a faulty gene.
- **D** the genetic material from a cell.

**4** Anabolic steroids
- **A** are used by some athletes to lose weight.
- **B** can cause hair loss in women.
- **C** are based on female hormones.
- **D** increase muscle growth.

**5** A zygote is
- **A** an ovum.
- **B** a cell implanted into the uterus.
- **C** a cell with no nucleus.
- **D** a fertilised cell.

**6** The Hayflick limit is
- **A** the number of times a cell can elongate.
- **B** the number of times a cancer cell can divide.
- **C** the number of times a cell can divide.
- **D** the number of times a cell can differentiate.

**7** Stem cells have
- **A** the ability to become any type of cell.
- **B** twice as many chromosomes as a normal cell.
- **C** the ability to increase growth.
- **D** different genes to a normal cell.

**8** Regeneration is the process of
- **A** repairing faulty genes.
- **B** multiplying cancer cells.
- **C** growing replacement body parts.
- **D** producing new stem cells.

**9** A viable foetus is one that can
- **A** survive without any medical assistance.
- **B** grow more quickly after birth.
- **C** survive outside the womb.
- **D** be carried to full-term.

**10** Plant stems always grow towards light. This is controlled by
- **A** genes.
- **B** hormones.
- **C** photosynthesis.
- **D** gravity.

**11** A haploid cell contains
- **A** 46 chromosomes in a human.
- **B** a complete set of chromosomes.
- **C** double the normal number of chromosomes.
- **D** half the normal number of chromosomes.

**12** Meiosis is important because it provides
- **A** new cells for growth.
- **B** genetic variation.
- **C** growth hormones.
- **D** diploid cells.

**13** Growers produce seedless grapes by
- **A** brushing pollen onto the unpollinated flowers of fruit trees.
- **B** spraying artificial auxin onto the unpollinated flowers of fruit trees.
- **C** dipping the plant roots into artificial auxin.
- **D** spraying ethylene onto the unpollinated flowers of fruit trees.

**14** Gene therapy may relieve the symptoms of cancer by
- **A** inserting genes into normal cells to make them more resistant to chemotherapy.
- **B** removing cancer-causing genes from cells.
- **C** inserting cancer-killing genes into reproductive cells to pass on to the next generation.
- **D** using radiation to destroy the cells that cause cancer.

**15** Meiosis is the division of a cell leading to the production of

**A** four haploid cells, each with a set of chromosomes that are not genetically identical to the original cell.

**B** two haploid cells, each with a set of chromosomes that are genetically identical to the original cell.

**C** four diploid cells, each with a set of chromosomes that are not genetically identical to the original cell.

**D** four haploid cells, each with a set of chromosomes that are genetically identical to the original cell.

**2 a** Describe the process of meiosis. State whether the cells are haploid or diploid at each step, and the reasons why.

**b** Explain how meiosis leads to genetic variation in a species.

**c** For each of the following processes, explain if they involve mitosis or meiosis, giving your reasons:
- cloning
- selective breeding
- genetic modification.

**H**

## Short-answer questions

**1** Seventy years ago, Danish scurvygrass was a small plant found only in coastal areas. In the 1970s local authorities started to spread salt onto main roads in icy weather.

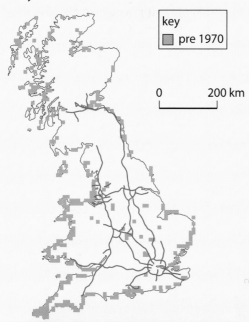

key
■ pre 1970

0      200 km

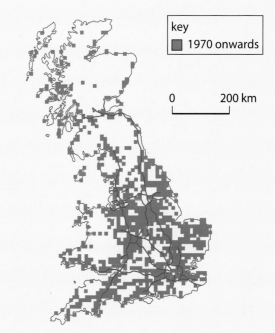

key
■ 1970 onwards

0      200 km

**A** The distribution of Danish scurvygrass before and after 1970.

**a** Describe the pattern in the distribution of Danish scurvygrass before 1970.

**b** Describe the pattern in the distribution of Danish scurvygrass after 1970.

**c** Explain the changes in the distribution of Danish scurvygrass after 1970.

**d** Describe what effect the salt would have on the plants that lived beside main roads.

**e** Suggest what would happen to the distribution of Danish scurvygrass if local authorities stopped putting salt onto roads in winter.

# 12. Glossary

**anabolic steroids** Hormones that promote cell growth and division, especially in muscle and bone tissue. Taken by some athletes to build muscle.

**\*cancer cell** A cell that divides uncontrollably due to faulty genes.

**\*cell division** The process through which one cell splits into two daughter cells.

**\*chromosomes** Long DNA molecules that carry genetic information.

**\*continuous variable** A variable that shows a gradual variation in data across a population. One example is height.

**\*differentiation** In cells, the process whereby new cells develop special characteristics to allow them to do their job.

**\*diploid** A cell that contains the full set of 46 chromosomes.

**distribution** The range of geographical locations in which a plant is found.

**dry weight** The weight of an object or organism (usually plant matter) that has had its water content removed.

**\*elongation** The increase in the length of plant cells when they absorb water during growth.

**\*embryo** The collection of cells that grows from a fertilised egg in animals. The next stage in development after the zygote.

**\*foetus** The name for an embryo after the eighth week of development in the womb.

**full-term** The end of a pregnancy, between 37 and 40 weeks after conception, when the baby is fully developed for life outside the womb.

**\*gametes** Sex cells, such as sperm, ova and pollen.

**\*genes** Sequences of DNA inside chromosomes that control the characteristics of an organism.

**\*genetic modification** Changing the genetic characteristics of an organism by manipulating genes and introducing them into DNA.

**\*growth** A permanent increase in the size or mass of an organism.

**growth factor** A substance that stimulates the growth of cells. Artificial growth factors may be used to enhance the way the body works.

**\*haploid** A cell that contains 23 (half) the full number of chromosomes. Produced by meiosis.

**\*hormones** Chemicals produced by a living organism which regulate growth, metabolism, and other important processes.

**impotence** The inability to produce offspring.

**\*inheritance** A term used to describe the passing of genes from parents to offspring.

**initiation** The process by which plants start to produce fruit.

**\*meiosis** A type of cell division that produces sex cells with half the full number of chromosomes.

**\*mitosis** A type of cell division that produces cells for growth, repair or the replacement of older cells.

**\*nucleus (pl nuclei)** In biology the part of both plant and animal cells that contain its genetic material (chromosomes and DNA). It directs and controls the activities of the cell.

**\*nutrients** The chemicals needed by an organism to grow.

**organ** A collection of different tissues working together to perform a particular function.

**\*ovum (pl ova)** An egg cell, found in females.

**\*regeneration** The special ability of some organisms to regrow parts of their bodies.

**\*selective breeding** Breeding plants or animals from individuals that have the characteristics you most want.

**\*species** A group of living things sharing the same characteristics.

**\*sperm** A male sex cell.

**\*stem cells** Cells that have the ability to become any type of cell in an organism. Found in large quantities in developing embryos.

**\*termination** Deliberately ending a pregnancy.

**tissue** A collection of similar cells that perform the same function.

**viability** The ability of a foetus to live outside the womb.

**wet weight** The weight of a living organism, including its water content.

**zygote** An ovum that has been fertilised by a sperm cell.

\*glossary words from the specification

# Energy flow

**A** This farm uses many different methods to get the best crop from each piece of land.

To get the best crops possible, farmers need to know what will make them grow best. This means understanding which minerals are needed from the soil and the best conditions for photosynthesis. This is the start of the food chains that lead to the nutrients you eat. Next time that you have your lunch, think how the energy in your food started as sunlight millions of miles from Earth.

Modern farming methods are able to produce large amounts of food but there are still people in the world who are starving. This topic will help you to find out about the way human activities are affecting the environment and how we can maximise food production to feed the increasing human population.

**In this topic you will learn that:**

- plants provide energy for all other organisms
- plants and animals are interdependent due to their use and production of oxygen and carbon dioxide
- energy flows through the biosphere and elements are recycled within it
- human activities are often unsustainable and there are many associated ethical considerations.

Put these statements into three groups:

I agree, I disagree, I want to find out more.

- Energy in my food comes from the energy in sunlight.
- Plant and animal cells contain the same structures.
- Respiration happens only in animals.
- Photosynthesis happens in all parts of a plant.
- There is enough food to feed everyone on the Earth.
- Global warming is being caused by human activities.

# 1. Cells

**By the end of these two pages you should be able to:**

- recall the structures of plant and animal cells
- describe how mineral salts are taken into roots by active transport.

Cells are the blocks that make up all living things. They are incredibly small and you need a microscope to see their detail. Cells are specialised to do different jobs. For example, in animals they make tissues like muscle, blood and skin. In plants they form leaves, stems, and **roots**. Robert Hooke (1635–1703) used one of the first microscopes to discover cells over 300 years ago. He looked at plant tissue and saw tiny compartments which reminded him of the cells that monks lived in. Modern microscopes can show a lot more detail.

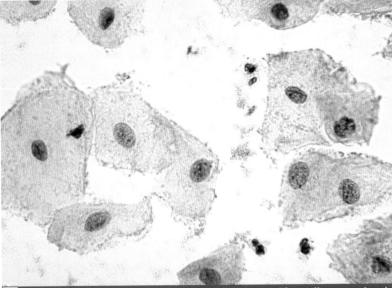

**A** Human cheek cells, seen through a microscope. The cells are stained with a dye to make it easier to see the structures.

Plant and animal cells have a similar structure. Both contain a **nucleus**, which holds the DNA as a set of chromosomes. The DNA is arranged into sections called genes, and each gene contains the information to make one protein. The nucleus controls cell activity. Reactions controlled by enzymes take place inside the jelly-like **cytoplasm**. This is where energy is produced through respiration. A flexible cell **membrane** forms a surface that covers the cell. In plant cells, the membrane is pushed against the inside of the cell wall and is difficult to see. The cell membrane contains many tiny channels which allow small molecules into and out of the cell. The membrane allows different things to either enter or leave the cell. Small molecules can pass through the channels but large ones cannot.

1 Put these structures in order of size (biggest to smallest):
   nucleus, protein, hover fly, cell, atom.

2 Explain why small molecules can pass through the cell membrane while large ones cannot.

**Plant cells** have some extra structures that are not found in **animal cells**. Most plant cells contain a large **vacuole**. This is like a bag inside the cytoplasm and it contains the cell sap. It controls the amount of water inside the cell. A **cellulose cell wall** forms a rigid outside cover for the cell. It gives the cell its strength and the plant its structure. **Chloroplasts** contain the chemical **chlorophyll** which makes plants green. Chloroplasts are found in the cytoplasm of cells in the green parts of a plant. **Photosynthesis** happens inside the chloroplasts. You would not find chloroplasts inside root cells because these are underground and do not photosynthesise.

**B** Plant cells contain some extra structures.

3 Describe what chloroplasts do and explain why they are mostly found in leaf cells.

4 What are the two main reactions that happen inside the cytoplasm of a plant leaf cell?

**H** Cells are specialised to do particular jobs. Hair cells in plant roots can absorb **mineral salts** from the soil by **active transport**. Their cell membranes contain molecular 'pumps' which force mineral salts, like nitrates and phosphates, into the cell. The energy needed for this process comes from respiration. This allows the roots to absorb and concentrate mineral salts efficiently.

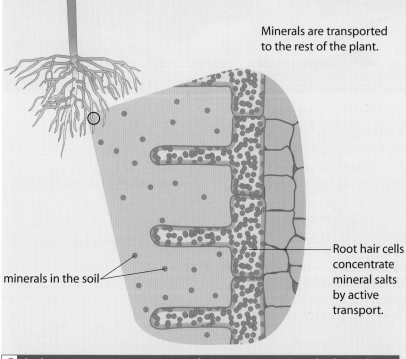

Minerals are transported to the rest of the plant.

minerals in the soil

Root hair cells concentrate mineral salts by active transport.

**C** Active transport uses energy and concentrates mineral salts in the roots.

5 Why is respiration needed for active transport to take place?

6 Copy and complete the table to compare the structure of plant and animal cells.
✓ = structure is present
✗ = structure is absent

|  | Plant cell | Animal cell |
| --- | --- | --- |
| Cell wall |  |  |
| Cell membrane |  |  |
| Cytoplasm |  |  |
| Vacuole |  |  |
| Chloroplast |  |  |
| Nucleus |  |  |

Summary Exercise

Higher Questions

# 2. Plants for food

**By the end of these two pages you should be able to:**

- explore how humans use plants, in particular for food.

**A** Many different uses of plants are shown here. See if you can identify them.

You may not realise it but you rely on plants for many things. Cotton fabric is made using fibres from cotton plants. Wood is used to make furniture and for fuel. Modern pharmaceutical companies research the chemicals found in plants to see if they can be used to make new medicines. The painkiller aspirin was developed from a chemical found in willow tree bark. Of course, plants are also essential for all of your food. Not only do you eat plants but if you eat meat, the animals you eat have also eaten plants.

Plants provide energy and nutrients to the humans and animals that eat them. This energy is needed for growth. All food chains start with plants or microscopic algae and the energy they contain is captured by photosynthesis.

Farming has helped us produce large quantities of food by planting crops suitable for the land and climate. Humans have learnt methods to increase the size of crops by controlling how the plants use energy. Farmers can make sure photosynthesis happens as quickly and effectively as possible.

1 List three ways in which humans use plants.

2 Suggest how the chemicals in plants may benefit humans.

Humans get energy and nutrients from the plants and animals they eat.

This cow grows using energy and nutrients in the grass.

Grass grows by capturing energy from sunlight by photosynthesis and taking minerals from the soil.

**B** Your food relies on energy from sunlight that is captured by photosynthesis.

**C** Using wood for energy is causing tremendous environmental damage in some areas.

In many poor areas, people depend on wood to provide the energy they need to cook their food. Trees are cut down for fuel quicker than they can grow and this causes **deforestation**. Gathering wood is often done by children. Imagine spending five or six hours each day collecting wood just to be able to cook your evening meal.

Energy in plants can also be used directly as a fuel. Vegetable oils or fermented sugar beet can be made into biodiesel or bioethanol for vehicles. These can help to tackle global warming because the plants absorb carbon dioxide as they grow. However, more demand for biofuels could lead to food shortages as crops may be used for fuel instead of food.

As the Earth's human population increases, there are more and more demands for food and other products from plants. Intensive farming can see huge areas of land covered by just one or two different types of plant. This reduces the biological diversity in the area and can have harmful effects on the environment. Some argue that intensive farming is necessary to increase **food production**. Others argue that it is better to try to conserve important habitats and produce food by organic methods. The best way to use our limited land and plant resources is an ongoing issue.

3 How has farming helped us make better use of plants?

4 Explain how plants are the source of all the energy in our diet.

5 What problems could be caused by using plants and trees for fuel?

6 Produce a spider diagram, or concept map, to show the various uses of plants by humans.

**P**

**P**

**Summary Exercise**

**Higher Questions**

# 3. How plants make food

**By the end of these two pages you should be able to:**

- recall that photosynthesis is a set of reactions that join carbon dioxide and water to make glucose (sugar) and oxygen.

Life on Earth could not exist without photosynthesis. Plants and green algae capture energy from sunlight. Photosynthesis makes **glucose** and oxygen. Glucose is needed for **respiration** and is used to make starch, fats and proteins. These are the start of the food chains that support all other living things. Oxygen from photosynthesis replaces the oxygen used by animals, plants and **microorganisms** during cell respiration.

Photosynthesis happens in the leaves of plants. It needs some specific conditions:

- *Chlorophyll* is the molecule that captures the energy from sunlight. It is found inside the *chloroplasts*. Palisade cells, on the upper side of a leaf, are packed full of chloroplasts to make photosynthesis as efficient as possible.
- *Sunlight* provides the energy that powers photosynthesis. Without a good level of light, photosynthesis cannot take place.
- *Carbon dioxide* is absorbed from the atmosphere and gets into the leaf through tiny pores in its surface.
- *Water* is joined to carbon dioxide to make glucose. It is transported from the roots to the leaves, where it is needed.
- The enzymes needed for photosynthesis require the right *temperature*. If it is too cold, then photosynthesis will slow down.

1 Give reasons why plants generally grow more quickly in the summer than in the winter.

2 How is carbon dioxide used in photosynthesis?

Water from the soil is transported to the leaves.

Cells in the leaf contain chloroplasts. These absorb energy from sunlight.

Carbon dioxide is taken into the leaf through tiny pores called stomata.

Oxygen is given out as a waste product of photosynthesis.

Glucose is made and transported to the rest of the plant to be used for growth and respiration.

**A** These strawberries are sweet because photosynthesis uses sunlight to convert carbon dioxide and water into glucose.

| Reactants | | | | Products | | |
|---|---|---|---|---|---|---|
| carbon dioxide | + | water | + | energy | → | glucose (sugar) | + | oxygen |
| $CO_2$ | + | $H_2O$ | + | energy | → | $C_6H_{12}O_6$ | + | $O_2$ |
| from the air | | from the soil | | in sunlight | | used in the plant cells | | released to air |

**B**

## Have you ever wondered?

Why it was once thought necessary to remove plants from hospital wards at night?

It is important to remember that plants respire all of the time. They are constantly using oxygen and producing carbon dioxide. During the day, photosynthesis is more active and plants generally produce more oxygen than they use. During the night, there is no sunlight for photosynthesis. Plants use more oxygen and produce carbon dioxide through respiration.

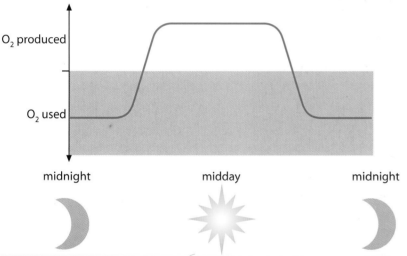

**C** Photosynthesis and respiration influence whether a plant takes in or gives out oxygen.

Photosynthesis provides glucose which is transported around the plant for respiration and growth. Glucose is also converted into starch which is then stored inside plant cells. This energy store is a good way of holding large amounts of glucose inside the plant cells. Starch does not dissolve in water and so it does not draw in water by osmosis. Potato tubers (the part that we eat) are specialised parts of the roots that are packed full of starch. We take advantage of this and grow potatoes for food. Without photosynthesis, there would be no food crops for humans and no food for the animals that we eat.

3 Look at the graph. Is the plant taking in more or less oxygen at midnight when compared to midday? Explain your answer.

**D** Potato plants store large amounts of starch in their tubers.

4 Photosynthesis makes glucose. Describe what glucose is used for in plants.

5 Explain how carbon dioxide and water produce glucose and oxygen through photosynthesis.

**Summary Exercise**

**Higher Questions**

### By the end of these two pages you should be able to:

- describe the factors that can slow down the rate of photosynthesis
- analyse data on these factors.

**A** Crops need the best conditions for photosynthesis so that their growth is maximised.

1 Explain what is meant by a limiting factor in relation to photosynthesis.

2 Describe why photosynthesis is slowed down at low light levels.

3 Suggest how a farmer could provide the conditions for plants to photosynthesise at night in a greenhouse.

Farmers want to get the biggest crops possible from their fields or greenhouses. To do this they need to make sure they have provided the best possible conditions for photosynthesis and growth. The **rate** (speed) of photosynthesis depends on the growing conditions. The best conditions produce the highest rate of photosynthesis. Some things can slow down the rate of photosynthesis. These are called **limiting factors**.

The most important limiting factor is the level of sunlight. If the light is too low, there is not enough energy to drive photosynthesis quickly. The temperature is also important. Enzymes in photosynthesis will not work properly if it is too hot or too cold. There needs to be chlorophyll in the leaf cells to carry out the photosynthesis. There must also be a good supply of water and carbon dioxide.

The graph shows the rate of photosynthesis of a plant in different light levels. In low light levels, there is not enough light to drive photosynthesis in all of its chlorophyll molecules. Low light is the limiting factor (section A). As the brightness of the light increases, more chlorophyll molecules are used. Eventually the rate of photosynthesis reaches its maximum (B). Increasing the light levels further has no effect because the plant is photosynthesising as fast as it can in this set of conditions (section C).

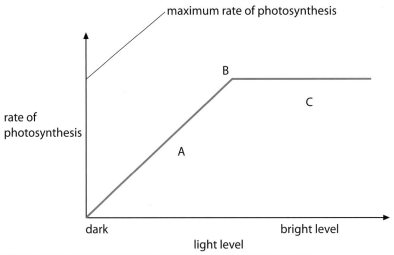

**B** The rate of photosynthesis changes with light levels.

The best way to measure photosynthesis is to look at how much oxygen is made by the plant in a set period of time.

Table D shows data gathered from an investigation using pondweed to measure photosynthesis in different conditions. To make a fair comparison between the conditions, the same piece of pondweed was used throughout the investigation.

| Conditions | Volume of $O_2$ produced in 10 minutes ($cm^3$) |
|---|---|
| bright light | 4.6 |
| dim light | 2.2 |
| bright light with ice added to water | 0.7 |
| bright light with sodium bicarbonate added to water | 6.1 |

**D** The effect of different conditions on photosynthesis.

**6** Look at table D.
**a** Describe the effect of light level on the speed of photosynthesis.
**b** Explain what happens to the speed of photosynthesis when ice is added to the water.
**c** Suggest why adding sodium bicarbonate to the water speeds up photosynthesis.

**7** Describe two ways in which you could investigate the factors that limit the rate of photosynthesis.

**4** Why is the first part of the graph a line that increases steadily?

**5** Explain why the graph levels off after point B as the light gets brighter.

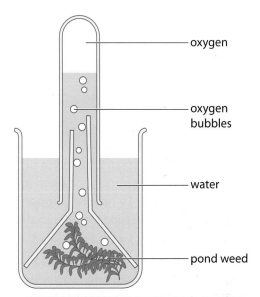

**C** The rate of photosynthesis can be measured using pondweed which gives off bubbles of oxygen that can be collected.

Summary Exercise

Higher Questions

# 5. Making more food

**By the end of these two pages you should be able to:**

- recall the factors that limit the rate of photosynthesis
- explain how food produced in greenhouses and fish farms captures energy efficiently.

**A** Tomatoes are grown commercially in large greenhouses.

**B** This aerial photograph shows whole fields covered with greenhouses.

Hundreds of square kilometres in southern Spain have been covered by greenhouses called polytunnels. They are used to grow crops like tomatoes, peppers, cucumbers and melons, which are exported to shops in the UK. Fruit and vegetables grown this way can be produced almost all year round.

The greenhouses are designed so that they produce crops in the most energy-efficient way. Their clear polythene walls allow through plenty of sunlight and keep in moisture. By removing the limiting factors that slow photosynthesis, the maximum sunlight energy is captured by the crops. The plants are fed with controlled levels of nutrients like phosphates and nitrates. This allows the crops to grow quickly and store the most energy possible. Intensive farming like this produces food efficiently, but some people argue that these methods harm the environment.

1 Explain how the polytunnels give good conditions for photosynthesis.

2 As the crops grow, they capture and store energy. What nutrients are supplied to help this happen efficiently?

## Have you ever wondered?

Why do some people put lights into greenhouses?

Some farmers use oil-burning heaters in their greenhouses to raise temperatures overnight and also increase carbon dioxide levels in the atmosphere. Adding artificial lights even allows the plants to photosynthesise at night when there is no natural light available. These methods mean energy can continue to be transferred to the plant to help it grow even faster.

Salmon farms are a good example of how animals can be intensively farmed. The salmon are fed concentrated food and kept in pens so they cannot move very much. This increases the amount of energy the salmon take in and reduces the amount of energy they lose through movement. The salmon grow bigger and faster than they would in the wild and they have fewer **diseases**.

| | Wild salmon | Farmed salmon | Comparison |
|---|---|---|---|
| Growth | 3–4 years to full size | 1 year to full size | Farmed salmon grow quicker than wild salmon. |
| Food | eat small fish in the open sea | fed on food pellets | More food is available for farmed salmon. |
| Food chain | human<br>↑<br>salmon<br>↑<br>herring<br>↑<br>zooplankton<br>↑<br>phytoplankton | human<br>↑<br>salmon<br>↑<br>food pellets | Lots of energy is lost in the wild salmon food chain. Farmed salmon have a short food chain which increases the energy transferred. |
| Movement | move to catch food and migrate long distances to reproduce | confined in cages and food is supplied in pellets | Wild salmon waste lots of their energy. |

**B** How a salmon grows in a fish farm compared to a wild salmon. The farmed salmon grows more efficiently and is less expensive but some people say that it does not taste as good as the wild salmon.

3 Why do wild salmon convert only a small amount of their food energy into growth?

4 What conditions allow farmed salmon to grow almost twice as quickly as wild salmon?

5 Explain how intensive farming methods like greenhouses and fish farms increase energy transfer in food production.

Summary Exercise

Higher Questions

# 6. Natural recycling – carbon

**By the end of these two pages you should be able to:**

- explain how carbon is recycled in nature
- interpret data on the carbon cycle.

Carbon is a very important element. It can be found in all organic materials. A diamond is pure carbon and so is the graphite in your pencil. Many molecules contain carbon, like fats and carbohydrates. These carry energy along the food chain. Carbon is a key element in other important biological substances like proteins, chlorophyll and DNA. Fossil fuels are the remains of pre-historic plants and animals and contain high levels of carbon. Without carbon, life on Earth would not be possible.

There is not an unlimited supply of carbon and you may think it would all get used up. Thankfully, carbon is naturally recycled and re-used. It's amazing to think that carbon atoms in your body could once have been part of a dinosaur or a giant tree from the Amazon rainforest.

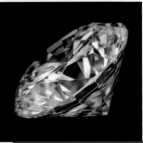

**A** Carbon is found in many natural and synthetic materials.

**1** If a plant had no carbon, which molecules would it be unable to make?

**2** Where does the carbon in fossil fuels come from?

Respiration by plants, animals and microbes produces carbon dioxide. Burning fossil fuels produces carbon dioxide.

Carbon passed on when animals eat animals.

Carbon, contained in carbon dioxide in the atmosphere.

Plants absorb carbon dioxide for photosynthesis.

 carbon dioxide

 Carbon-compounds like carbohydrates, fats and proteins.

Carbon passes to animals when they eat plants.

**B** The carbon cycle shows how carbon is recycled and re-used.

Plants capture carbon from the atmosphere during photosynthesis in the form of carbon dioxide. The carbon dioxide combines with water to produce glucose. This is used to make starch, fats, carbohydrates and proteins. When a plant is eaten, these molecules pass energy and carbon along the food chain. These molecules, especially carbohydrates and fats, provide fuel for cell respiration which happens in all living organisms. Carbon dioxide is then produced as a waste product of respiration. This returns to the atmosphere so that the cycle can continue.

When plants and animals die, their bodies are decayed by microorganisms. This also adds carbon dioxide to the atmosphere. When wood or fossil fuels are burned they release carbon dioxide into the air.

Photosynthesis captures carbon:

**carbon** dioxide + water + energy ⟶ glucose + oxygen
(contains **carbon**)

Respiration releases carbon:

glucose + oxygen ⟶ **carbon** dioxide + water + energy
(contains **carbon**)

Human activities are adding millions of tonnes of carbon dioxide to the atmosphere each year. Burning coal, oil and gas releases carbon that was trapped deep underground in fossil fuels. We are upsetting the balance of the **carbon cycle** because photosynthesis cannot take in carbon dioxide as quickly as human activities are producing it. **Combustion** of fossil fuels is a major cause of **global warming**.

The amount of carbon dioxide taken in by 1 hectare of growing forest (about the area of two football pitches) is 12.5 tonnes of $CO_2$ per year per hectare. The amount of carbon dioxide given out by a typical medium-sized car is 2.4 tonnes of $CO_2$ per year per car.

3 What processes return carbon dioxide to the atmosphere?

4 Explain why microorganisms are important in the carbon cycle.

5 How many cars produce the same amount of carbon dioxide that is taken in by 1 hectare of growing forest?

6 There are about 24 million cars in the UK. Calculate the amount of carbon dioxide put into the atmosphere by UK cars each year.

7 Describe how carbon is recycled in nature, starting and ending with carbon dioxide in the air.

Summary Exercise

Higher Questions

**By the end of these two pages you should be able to:**

- describe what nitrogen is used for in living organisms
- explain how nitrogen is recycled in nature
- describe the effects of using very large amounts of nitrogen fertilisers.

Nitrogen is an important element in living things. It is found in proteins and DNA. Plants get nitrogen in the form of nitrates which they get from the soil. The nitrogen can then pass into animals as they eat the plants. If the nitrates in the soil were not replaced, they would eventually run out and the soil would become infertile. This does not happen because nitrogen is naturally recycled in a similar way to the carbon cycle.

When plants and animals die, their bodies are broken down by decomposers. Proteins are digested into ammonia.

Animals eat plant proteins.

animal waste

Plants absorb nirates to make proteins and DNA.

Nitrogen gas in the atmosphere.

Lightning can convert nitrogen into nitrates.

Denitrifying bacteria remove nitrates from waterlogged soil.

Decomposers: bacteria and fungi.

soil

nitrogen

Nitrogen-fixing bacteria in the roots of peas and beans.

nitrates in soil

ammonia    nitrates

nitrites

nitrifying bacteria

**A** The nitrogen cycle.

Nitrogen is mainly recycled by microorganisms in the soil. **Decomposers** break down dead organisms and animal waste (manure and urea) into ammonia, which contains nitrogen. **Nitrifying bacteria** then use a series of reactions to convert the ammonia into nitrates that plants can absorb. In areas where the soil is waterlogged, **denitrifying bacterial** break down nitrates and release nitrogen into the atmosphere.

Some plants, such as peas, beans and clover, have **nitrogen fixing bacteria** living in their roots. This means they can take nitrogen from the atmosphere and convert it directly into nitrates. The bacteria provide the plant with nitrates and, in return, the plant supplies the bacteria with nutrients. Organic farmers may grow these plants, called legumes, in a field to act as a natural fertiliser. The plants are ploughed back into the soil to add nitrogen in the form of nitrates.

Modern agriculture is extremely intensive. The natural **nitrogen cycle** cannot replace nitrates as quickly as they are removed, so farmers add industrially made nitrate **fertilisers**. This can cause problems if the nitrates get washed from the soil and into local water supplies.

Organic farmers use a different approach. They add manure to fields or grow clover to replenish the soil with nitrates.

## Have you ever wondered?

How do fertilisers harm the environment?

Adding too much nitrogen fertiliser to a field can cause problems. If nitrates are washed into local lakes they provide nutrients which encourage algae in the water to grow quickly. Algae cover the surface and block out sunlight needed by plants in the lake. Plants die, the food chain is broken and oxygen is taken out of the water as they decompose. Fishes and insects cannot survive so that eventually only algae and certain bacteria are able to live in the lake. This process is known as eutrophication and the lake becomes stagnant.

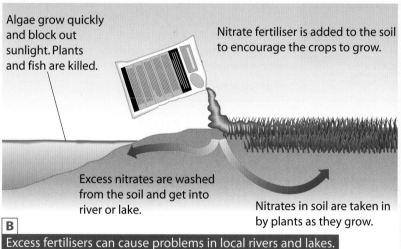

Algae grow quickly and block out sunlight. Plants and fish are killed.

Nitrate fertiliser is added to the soil to encourage the crops to grow.

Excess nitrates are washed from the soil and get into river or lake.

Nitrates in soil are taken in by plants as they grow.

**B** Excess fertilisers can cause problems in local rivers and lakes.

Algal blooms cover the water surface and block out sunlight.

1 Nitrogen makes up nearly 80% of the atmosphere. Which plants are able to take advantage of this nitrogen? Explain how they can do this.

2 How do animals get the nitrogen that they need for growth?

3 What would happen if decomposers did not break down dead plants and animals?

4 How do organic farmers add nitrogen to their fields?

5 Are the benefits of using chemical fertilisers worth more than the problems they may cause? Explain your answer.

6 Explain how nitrogen gets into the soil and from there into animals before being returned to the soil. How can nitrogen get from the soil into the atmosphere?

**Summary Exercise**

**Higher Questions**

# 8. Population problems

**H** *By the end of these two pages you should be able to:*

- describe how the increasing human population can lead to environmental damage, such as deforestation.

The world population is currently around 6.5 billion people and it is increasing rapidly in many countries including India, Pakistan, China and the African continent. Everyone will need food, water, shelter, medical care and energy. People also want things like mobile phones, cars, televisions and other luxuries. Meeting these demands is already having dramatic effects on the environment.

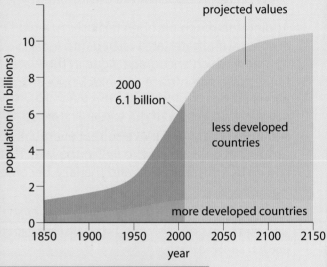

**A** Large areas of forest are burned to create land for farming to feed an increasing human population.

One consequence of population increase is deforestation. Large areas of forest are cut down in developing countries to produce wood for sale and to clear land for farming. Burning the forest adds carbon dioxide to the atmosphere and removes trees that would absorb it by photosynthesis. Both actions add to the problem of climate change.

Once the trees are removed, the soil can quickly become poor and dusty. Soil erosion increases the risk of landslides and areas becoming deserts. So farmers move on and clear a new area of forest. Deforestation destroys habitats and reduces the range of plants and animals that can live in an area. Once a species is extinct, it can never come back again.

3 Explain how an increasing population can lead to deforestation.

4 Land cleared for farming often becomes infertile after just a few years. Suggest why these farmers can not just use chemical fertilisers to improve the soil.

1 Look at the graph of world population.
  a What is the estimated population in 2050?
  b What percentage increase will occur between today and 2050?

2 List some of the needs of this increasing population and suggest some of the problems these might cause.

If humans kill one type of animal, could we ever get them back?

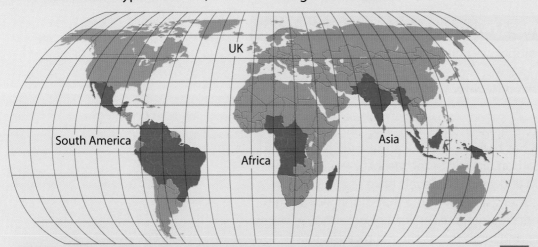

B Deforestation happens mostly in the tropical areas of the world.

Areas of deforestation

Deforestation and protecting the environment is a complex issue. Developing countries are poor and need to exploit their natural resources. Cattle farming, palm oil and timber production often provides incomes for local people in poor areas. Much of our meat for burgers, wood for furniture and oil for cosmetics and detergents comes from land cleared in rainforests.

Industries often use up natural resources more quickly than they are replaced. This is not sustainable. In some areas, over-fishing has reduced fish stocks to dangerously low levels. Mining can cause environmental damage and fossil fuels are becoming more scarce.

Have you ever wondered?

Why is there a global ban on whaling?

Sustainable development tries to use natural resources so that they will not run out. Reducing waste and recycling resources helps sustainable development to provide jobs for people without damaging the environment for future generations. You can be part of the solution by choosing food from sustainable sources and furniture that uses wood from sustainable forests.

**Soil Association**

C Organisations like the Forest Stewardship Council and the Soil Association are helping to reduce damage to the environment and help local farmers.

5 What types of things that you buy may have come from areas where deforestation is a problem?

6 Modern fishing ships can remove huge amounts of fish each time they go to sea. Suggest how this could damage levels of fish stocks.

7 Explain how sustainable development tries to conserve natural resources.

8 Explain some of the environmental effects of population increase and how we can tackle these problems.

Summary Exercise

Higher Questions

**By the end of these two pages you should be able to:**

- describe how global warming is threatening the human population
- collect and summarise information on global warming.

It is now widely accepted that the Earth is getting warmer. Since 1990, the UK has had ten of the warmest years on record. Current levels of carbon dioxide in the atmosphere are at their highest in over 400 000 years. Sea levels have risen by 20 cm in the last 100 years. Scientists now agree that global warming is a reality. The evidence points to emissions of greenhouse gases like carbon dioxide and methane, as the main cause.

## Sea levels rise – London flooded

## Severe winter storms – electricity cuts as power cables damaged

## Record droughts cause Amazon rainforest to die

## Food prices increase as drought hits crops

## Summer temperatures sizzle – cars banned from town centre

## Hurricane wrecks oil fields – petrol rationed

**A**

Estimates suggest that the Earth's temperature will rise between 2 °C and 5 °C over the next 50 years. That could be enough to upset the natural balance of the Earth's climate and have a big effect on global weather systems. In the UK, winters will become wetter with more violent storms. Summers will be hotter and drier, and water shortages are likely.

As the polar ice caps melt, tremendous amounts of water are released into the world's oceans, causing sea levels to rise. These rising sea levels will threaten coastal areas and London will be at a greater risk of flooding.

On a global scale, global warming could affect food production because rainfall patterns will change and billions of people may need to move from coastal areas as the sea floods their land. Developing nations that are least able to cope with climate change will probably be affected the most.

## Have you ever wondered?

Should I travel on buses rather than take the car?

1 What is the main cause of global warming?

2 Give three ways in which climate change might affect the UK.

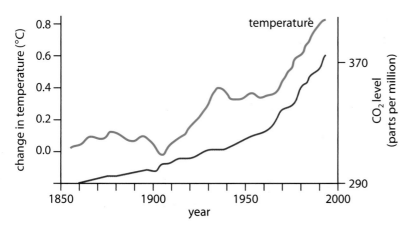

**B** As carbon dioxide in the atmosphere has increased, so have global temperatures.

The Internet can be an excellent source of information and data on climate change. Choose reliable sites such as ones from the BBC, NASA and the Meterological Office. Table C shows data from the Meteorological Office.

| Year | Maximum temperatures in June (°C) | Rainfall during June (mm) |
|------|-----------------------------------|---------------------------|
| 1915 | 18.6 | 62.0 |
| 1925 | 18.9 | 2.1 |
| 1935 | 18.7 | 79.0 |
| 1945 | 17.7 | 72.7 |
| 1955 | 16.4 | 46.7 |
| 1965 | 18.2 | 58.7 |
| 1975 | 19.0 | 18.4 |
| 1985 | 15.7 | 47.8 |
| 1995 | 17.6 | 11.0 |
| 2005 | 19.3 | 35.8 |

**C** Rainfall and temperature for Bradford, UK, from 1915 to 2005.

3 Use the data in table C and a spreadsheet to draw two graphs to show the changes in rainfall and temperature since 1915.
 a What are the trends that you can see in the two sets of data?
 b What could help you to make a more reliable conclusion on the trends?

4 Go to the Meteorological Office website and search for historic data from the Bradford weather station.
 a Use a spreadsheet to find the average yearly temperatures for 2000 to 2005 and plot these on a graph.
 b What is the trend for the years 2000 to 2005?

5 Write a fact sheet about how global warming might affect the people on Earth. Include data in your work.

Summary Exercise

Higher Questions

# 10. Food production

**By the end of these two pages you should be able to:**

- discuss the difficulties of making enough food for everyone
- explore whether a biosphere could be built on Mars
- describe how to achieve the best conditions for food production.

The United Nations has estimated that 800 million people across the world do not have enough food, while in the UK nearly 75% of people are overweight.

There is enough food produced in the world to feed everyone, but some people have plenty while others starve. This imbalance could be caused by factors like climate change, drought, poverty, wars and unfair world trade rules.

Many developing countries have borrowed money from richer, developed nations. They need to sell lots of their resources just to repay what they owe. This third world debt is one of the reasons why these nations remain poor. Some politicians and campaigners see this as exploiting the poorer countries. They are working to get the debts wiped out so that the countries can help themselves and grow enough food to feed their people.

1 Do you think it is best to give food to developing nations? Or should they be helped to grow enough to feed their people?

2 Do you think that banks in developed countries should write off the loans they have given to developing countries?

**A** **B** Should people with plenty of food donate food to people who are starving?

## Have you ever wondered?

We can feed the world, but how exactly?

**C** Greenhouses are examples of intensive food production.

**D** This farmer is ploughing a field using oxen. Farmers in developing nations cannot afford the technology needed for intensive farming.

**H** Growing food more efficiently could be one solution to food shortages. Intensive farming means that many developed nations have the ability to produce more food than they need. Fish farms provide conditions for maximum growth by limiting the movement of the fish, feeding them with high energy food pellets and controlling the threat from **predators**. Greenhouses provide plants with plenty of light and warmth. Fertilisers provide nutrients for growth and chemical pesticides prevent damage by insects.

Some groups suggest that technologies like genetically modified foods, pesticides and chemical fertilisers can increase food production in developing nations. However, these intensive methods are all expensive and most farmers in developing nations cannot afford them.

**3** How do greenhouses provide good conditions for the growth of crops?

**4** Suggest why intensive farming methods are not used in many developing nations?

**C** This biosphere in the Arizona desert tried to create a self-sustaining environment.

### Have you ever wondered?

Can we set up a biosphere on Mars?

One radical solution to our population and food problems could be to colonise Mars. For people to live and produce food on this hostile planet, they would need to use **biospheres**. These are self-contained environments that can sustain life.

In September 1991, eight people sealed themselves inside a biosphere in the Arizona desert. There was no contact at all with the outside world and it contained all the plants and animals necessary to sustain human life. The experiment lasted for over two years before oxygen levels became dangerously low and the people had to leave. Scientists would need to do a lot more research before such biospheres could be real options.

**5** What is a biosphere?

**6** What are the essential things that would need to be self-sustaining in a biosphere?

**7** Discuss some of the problems there are in feeding all the people on the Earth.

**Summary Exercise**

**Higher Questions**

# 11. Questions

## Multiple choice questions

**1** What structure is found in a plant cell but *not* in an animal cell?

  **A** nucleus     **C** cell wall

  **B** cytoplasm   **D** cell membrane

**2** What nutrients are found in plants?

  **A** proteins     **C** fats

  **B** starch      **D** all three (A, B & C)

**3** What two compounds are needed for photosynthesis?

  **A** carbon dioxide and oxygen

  **B** oxygen and water

  **C** oxygen and glucose

  **D** carbon dioxide and water

**4** Which conditions would give the fastest photosynthesis?

  **A** bright sunlight

  **B** low level of sunlight

  **C** complete darkness

  **D** low level of artificial light

**5** What would allow farmers to grow fruits nearly all year round?

  **A** growing the crops in large sheds to keep them warm

  **B** watering the crops during a dry summer

  **C** adding extra fertiliser in the winter

  **D** growing the fruit plants in a greenhouse with artificial lights

**6** What process removes carbon dioxide from the atmosphere?

  **A** respiration

  **B** photosynthesis

  **C** active transport

  **D** nitrifying bacteria

**7** How do plants take in nitrogen?

  **A** They absorb nitrogen directly from the air.

  **B** They absorb ammonia from animal waste.

  **C** They digest bacteria living in the soil.

  **D** They absorb nitrates from the soil.

**8** What is the current human population of the world?

  **A** 1 million    **C** 4.5 billion

  **B** 89 million   **D** 6.5 billion

**9** What is the cause of global warming?

  **A** carbon dioxide from respiration

  **B** gases from human activities

  **C** excessive fertilisers added to farmland throughout the world

  **D** photosynthesis

**10** Which part of the world has the most food shortages?

  **A** United States of America

  **B** United Kingdom

  **C** Africa

  **D** Australia

**11** How do plant root cells take up mineral salts?

  **A** osmosis

  **B** diffusion

  **C** passive transport

  **D** active transport

**12** Wood is an important fuel in many developing nations. What is one of the problems of using wood for fuel?

  **A** deforestation

  **B** food shortages

  **C** increasing price of wood

  **D** health problems

**13** What is meant by sustainable development?

  **A** development of industries in new areas of the world

  **B** development of industries that use only local resources

  **C** development that does not harm the environment for future generations

  **D** development to provide jobs for both now and the future

**14** How do greenhouses provide conditions for good crop growth?

  **A** Greenhouses provide shelter from the rain in summer.

  **B** Greenhouses provide light and warmth for maximum photosynthesis.

  **C** Greenhouses keep pests, like insects, away from the crops.

  **D** Greenhouses are made of glass which absorbs harmful ultraviolet radiation in the sunlight.

**15** Why does a fish farm transfer energy efficiently?

  **A** Fish are confined in pens so their movement is reduced.

  **B** Fish are already large when they are put into the fish farm.

  **C** Fish growth is increased because they are kept at the right temperature.

  **D** The fish are checked regularly to monitor their weight.

## Short-answer questions

**1** The graphs show a comparison of the climate in London and the South of Spain.

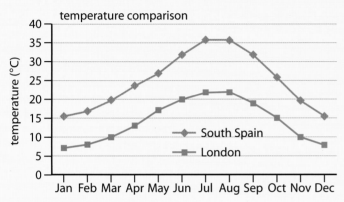

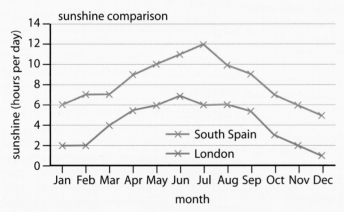

**a** What are the maximum hours of daily sunshine in London and the South of Spain?

**b** What are the maximum temperatures in London and the South of Spain?

**c** Explain why farmers in Southern Spain can grow fruit and vegetables in February and March that cannot be grown around London until the middle of the summer.

**d** What would farmers in the UK need to do to be able to grow fruit and vegetables at the same time as growers in Spain? How would this affect the price of crops grown by UK farmers?

**2** The graph shows the amount of oxygen either taken in or given out by a plant over a 24-hour period.

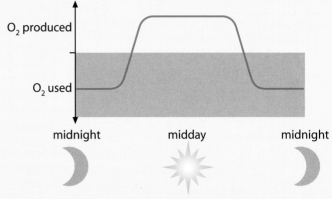

**a** Explain why the graph shows that the plant was producing oxygen at midday.

**b** Explain why the graph shows that the plant is using oxygen during the night.

**c** This graph was taken during the summer months. Sketch how you think the graph would look for readings taken in the winter. Explain your answer.

**d** Draw a flow diagram to show how carbon is recycled in nature.

**3** The table shows results of an investigation into the growth of vegetables. It compares the amounts (yield) from a greenhouse and an open field. **H**

| Crop | Greenhouse (tonnes per hectare) | Field (tonnes per hectare) |
|---|---|---|
| broccoli | 13.2 | 3.4 |
| cucumbers | 52.7 | 4.9 |
| lettuce | 39.5 | 6.8 |

**a** Draw a graph to compare the yield of vegetables grown in greenhouses and open fields.

**b** List the conditions which are controlled in the greenhouse that cannot be controlled in the open field.

**c** Explain why the greenhouse gives a higher yield than vegetables grown in an open field.

**d** Greenhouses can produce crops for longer periods of the year than can be grown in an open field. However, greenhouse crops are often more expensive to buy.

  **i** What would a farmer need to do to grow crops in a greenhouse during the winter?

  **ii** Suggest why this would add to the expense of the vegetables grown by this method.

# 12. Glossary

*active transport  Movement of molecules into the cell using energy from respiration. It allows the cell to build up a high concentration of the molecules inside the cell. For example, the way that plant root cells take in mineral salts from the soil.

*animal cell  Cell containing a cytoplasm, nucleus and cell membrane. Found in animals.

*biosphere  A self-contained structure that holds all the plants and animals needed for a sustainable environment. The Earth is also called a biosphere as it is self-contained in space.

*carbon cycle  The use and recycling of carbon through photosynthesis and respiration.

*cellulose cell wall  Rigid outer wall of a plant cell. It gives the cell strength.

*chlorophyll  Protein in a plant cell that captures energy from sunlight. Found in chloroplasts.

*chloroplast  Structure found inside plant cell cytoplasm where photosynthesis happens.

*combustion  Burning of things like fossil fuels (coal, oil and gas). It adds carbon dioxide to the atmosphere.

*cytoplasm  Jelly-like part of plant and animal cells.

*decomposer  Microorganisms, like bacteria and fungi, that digest and break down the bodies of dead plants and animals.

*deforestation  When large areas of trees are cut down for wood or to create space for humans. A typical example is the cutting down of rainforests in South America.

*denitrifying bacteria  Bacteria in the ground that break down nitrates and convert them into nitrogen gas. Usually found in waterlogged soil.

*disease  An illness caused by an infectious organism.

*fertiliser  Substance added to soil that contains nutrients for plant growth. Common fertilisers contain nitrate, phosphate and potassium mineral salts.

food production  Farming or fishing to produce food for humans.

*global warming  The increase in the Earth's temperature that is caused by excessive greenhouse gases, such as carbon dioxide, in the atmosphere.

*glucose  A simple sugar that is broken down in cells to release energy. It is also produced during photosynthesis.

limiting factors  Things that slow down the rate of photosynthesis.

*membrane  Thin and flexible covering to cells.

*microorganism  A very small organism that can only be seen through a microscope. Bacteria, fungi and viruses are examples of microorganisms.

*mineral salt  Nitrate and phosphate salts required by plants for healthy growth.

*nitrifying bacteria  Bacteria found in soil that convert ammonia into nitrate salts.

*nitrogen cycle  The use and recycling of nitrogen through plants and animals.

*nitrogen fixing bacteria  Bacteria that live in the roots of some plants (peas, beans and clover). They directly convert nitrogen gas into nitrates.

*nucleus  In biology the part of both plant and animal cells that contains its genetic material (chromosomes and DNA). It directs and controls the activities of the cell.

*photosynthesis  Process carried out in the green parts of plants. Carbon dioxide and water are joined to form glucose. This uses energy from sunlight.

*plant cell  The building block of plants. Contains a cell wall, cell membrane, cytoplasm, nucleus and a vacuole. Green parts of the plant also contain chloroplasts.

predator  An animal that kills and eats other living animals for survival.

rate  The speed of something. The rate of photosynthesis depends on the growing conditions.

*respiration  The chemical reaction occuring in all living cells. Glucose is broken down into carbon dioxide and water to release energy.

*root  Part of the plant that anchors it into the ground and absorbs water and mineral salts.

*vacuole  Sac-like structure in plant cells that controls the amount of water in the cell.

*glossary words from the specification

# Interdependence

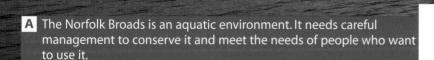

**A** The Norfolk Broads is an aquatic environment. It needs careful management to conserve it and meet the needs of people who want to use it.

The Norfolk and Suffolk Broads is home to some of Britain's rarest plants and animals. It is also very popular with tourists and people who like boating. The Broads Authority has to manage this environment. It has to keep the tourists and boaters happy, but also conserve the natural environment.

To understand how this management works, you need to know more about how interdependence affects the distribution and numbers of organisms in an environment. You also need to know more about the effect people have on the environment.

## In this topic you will learn that:

- organisms compete with each other for resources
- organisms are interdependent, which affects their distribution and population size
- extreme environments often promote unusual organisms with unusual strategies
- human impact on the environment and conservation measures need management.

Look at the following statements and sort them into the following categories:

I agree, I disagree, I need to find out more.

- The more carbon dioxide that is produced by plants the better it is for the environment.

- Biodiversity is when there are too many species in one area.

- The population of one animal can affect the population of another.

- Conservation of animals and plants is vital for the future of humans.

- Recycling could solve the problem of waste disposal.

- The Sun provides all of the energy needed for life on Earth.

- It is beneficial to introduce new animals into the environment.

# 1. Extreme environments

**By the end of these two pages you should be able to:**

- explain what an extreme environment is
- give examples of extreme environments.

Some **environments** can be extreme, but **organisms** still live there. Emperor penguins have to survive continuous darkness and temperatures that drop to −70°C in the Antarctic winter. The ocean is so deep that no light ever reaches there, yet even here there is life. The organisms have become adapted to their **extreme environment**.

Organisms need several conditions if they are to survive, wherever they live:

- they need a source of energy or food
- they need water
- they need a suitable temperature
- just about every organism needs oxygen.

Black smokers look like chimneys. They are hydrothermal vents that were discovered on the ocean floor in 1977. The water around these vents is very hot and acidic. Scientists had believed that conditions in these areas were too severe for organisms to exist. Then an expedition to the Galapagos Islands found crabs and shrimps, and worms that were 2 m long, living near to these vents on the ocean floor.

**A** A black smoker is an extreme environment.

1 What is the source of energy for green plants?

2 How do animals get their energy?

3 What conditions do you need if you are going to survive?

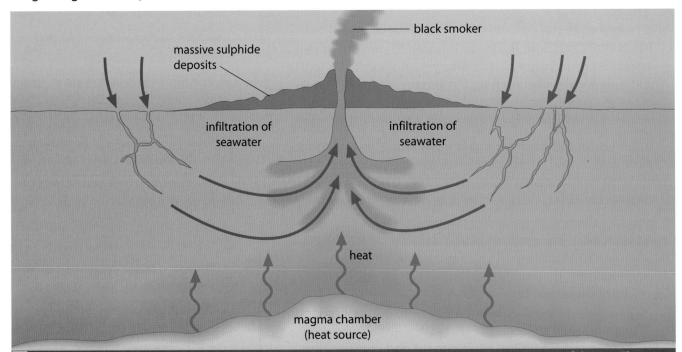

**B** Sea water is heated by the very hot rocks and dissolves minerals. The very hot sea water pours out of the top. The minerals precipitate out of the solution.

There is no light here so photosynthesis is impossible. Energy does not come from the Sun, but from the minerals that pour out of the black smokers. Bacteria use these minerals to manufacture the chemicals they need for growth. Other organisms feed on the bacteria, creating a food chain. The organisms have adapted to the environment by using a different source of energy.

## Have you ever wondered?

Why deep-sea fish have cylindrical eyes and not eyeballs?

The Antarctic is another extreme environment. Winter arrives in March and ends in September. The Sun never rises and temperatures can fall to −70 °C. Emperor penguins are adapted to this harsh environment. They have oily, water-resistant feathers. Underneath is a layer of soft down feathers and under that a thick layer of fat. This insulation keeps the penguins so warm they need to fluff their feathers to release heat in order to cool down.

Some organisms, such as the snow leopard, live at high altitudes – over 3000 metres above sea level. Atmospheric pressure is lower and there is much less oxygen. Temperatures can be very low, and there are high levels of ultraviolet radiation. Organisms living in extreme environments have to be specially adapted to live where they do. Studying them can tell us about the way organisms evolve. This knowledge can also help humans to survive in extreme environments.

C The male penguin keeps the egg warm by balancing it on the top of his feet while lowering his body over the top of the egg as a blanket. Male penguins huddle together as they look after the eggs to keep warm.

4 Suggest why penguins have oily, water-resistant feathers.

5 Why do you think the penguins carry their eggs on their feet?

D The snow leopard is perfectly adapted for its extreme environment.

6 The snow leopard warms the air it breathes in before the air gets to its lungs. Suggest a reason for this.

7 Why do most humans feel breathless and sick at such high altitudes?

8 Give three examples of extreme environments. For each one, explain how organisms have adapted to living there.

**Summary Exercise**

**Higher Questions**

# 2. Interdependence and adaptation

**By the end of these two pages you should be able to:**

- explain the principles of interdependence and adaptation
- explain how adaptation enables organisms to live in an environment.

**A** The Norfolk Broads – an aquatic environment.

The Norfolk and Suffolk Broads is one of the UK's national parks. Peat in the area was dug up for fuel between 1000 and 500 years ago. The total area, dug by hand, is more than 4000 football pitches in area. Once the peat digging stopped, the dug-out areas flooded to form lakes.

The Norfolk Broads has several different **aquatic**, or water-based, habitats. There are also **terrestrial**, or land-based, habitats. Each habitat has a community of plants and animals that depend on each other for what they need, such as food and energy. They are **interdependent**. Plants provide oxygen for other organisms, and can also provide shelter for some. When organisms die, the minerals they contain are released so that other organisms can use them.

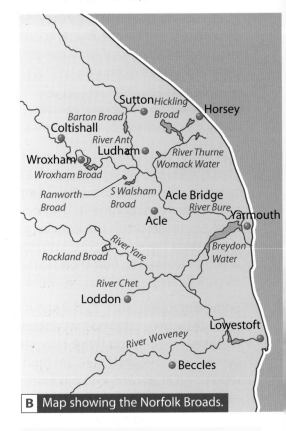

**B** Map showing the Norfolk Broads.

1 What is meant by:
   a interdependence
   b an aquatic environment
   c a terrestrial environment?

2 Why do animals need food?

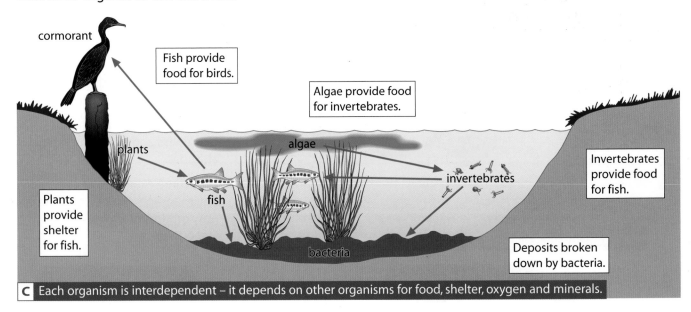

Fish provide food for birds.

Algae provide food for invertebrates.

Invertebrates provide food for fish.

Plants provide shelter for fish.

Deposits broken down by bacteria.

cormorant · plants · algae · fish · invertebrates · bacteria

**C** Each organism is interdependent – it depends on other organisms for food, shelter, oxygen and minerals.

Every organism within a habitat is adapted to living in that habitat. This means that they have evolved **adaptations** to survive the particular conditions, or **environmental factors**. These factors include water, light, oxygen, temperature and the other living organisms in the habitat.

If one of these factors changes, it will affect some of the organisms more than others. If less light reaches the bottom of a lake, some plants will no longer be able to live there and will die out. This will affect any type of animal that feeds on these plants. The **population** of these animals may decrease, or they may adapt and start feeding on another plant. This will affect the numbers of yet another type of animal.

Any organism that cannot adapt to changes in its environment is likely to have a smaller population. They may die out altogether and become extinct.

## Have you ever wondered?

Why did dinosaurs become extinct?

The bittern is a bird found in the Broads and similar wetland environments. It was once common but is now very rare. Bitterns need reed beds to live in and areas of water to catch fish. Humans use reeds for thatching houses, but there is no longer much demand for thatching. Many reeds beds have since dried out and been lost, or have been ploughed for agriculture. The bittern has been unable to adapt to these changes, so the population of bitterns has dropped. In 1997 there were just seven males left in Britain. New reed beds have now been created and this is helping to increase the bittern population.

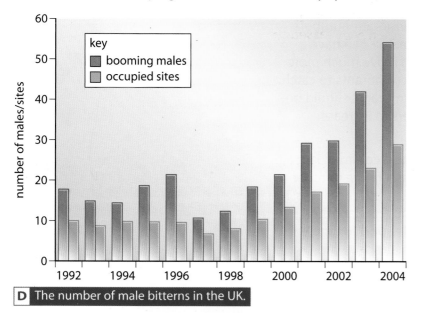

**D** The number of male bitterns in the UK.

3 Explain why a drop in numbers of water fleas in a pond can affect other organisms in the same habitat.

4 What is meant by adaptation?

5 What has caused the number of bitterns in the UK to fall so low?

6 a Describe how the population of otters in an aquatic environment like the Broads could be affected by other organisms in this environment.

b Describe the ways in which otters need to be adapted to their environment.

Summary Exercise

Higher Questions

P

**By the end of these two pages you should be able to:**

- explain the principles of predation
- explain how predation affects the population of other organisms in an environment.

V

**A** A cormorant is a predator of fish on the Broads.

**Predation** causes changes in the numbers of both the predator and the prey. There are usually only a few predators and far more prey.

Heron and cormorants can often be seen beside the water on the Broads. They feed on fish. In winter cormorant numbers increase as they move inland from the sea. This can have a serious impact on the number of fish. Fish move much more slowly in winter and so are easier for the cormorants to catch. Some people say that the numbers of cormorants should be reduced. This would allow the fish numbers to increase. Fishermen would have more to catch.

Some fish are predators. The pike is the most common large predator and will eat many fish. It also eats a range of other animals, including insect larvae, frogs, water rats and ducks. The zander is an introduced fish. It was brought from another country and released into rivers to provide sport for anglers. It kills and eats smaller fish and can have an effect on the numbers of young fish.

P

P

1 What is meant by predation?

2 Suggest reasons for and against the argument that cormorant numbers should be reduced.

3 Why does the number of predators always increase after the numbers of prey have increased?

Introducing a species into an area where it does not normally live can be dangerous. If that species has no natural predators then its numbers can grow to high levels. The American mink was introduced into the UK for its fur, and was kept on fur farms. Some escaped and others were released by anti-fur activists. They are now wild in the UK countryside. The mink is a predator and has caused the decline of the water vole and other animals in the Broads.

**B** The mink is an introduced predator and eats a range of prey.

**C** The coypu was introduced to the UK. It had no natural predators and so the population grew.

## Have you ever wondered?

Why are rabbits such a pest in Australia?

**Summary Exercise**

4 Zander were introduced to rivers for anglers. What are the advantages and disadvantages of doing this?

5 Animal rights protestors released mink from farms because they believed it is wrong to farm animals for their fur. Suggest why many people feel it is wrong to release these animals into the wild.

6 A virus called myxomatosis was introduced in Britain from Brazil in the 1950s to control the very large numbers of wild rabbits. The numbers of rabbits dropped rapidly.
   a What are the advantages of controlling the population in this way?
   b What are the advantages of using natural predation instead?

7 Explain how predation can affect populations of different organisms in a water-based environment like the Broads.

**Higher Questions**

# 4. Competition

**By the end of these two pages you should be able to:**

- explain the principles of competition
- explain how competition can affect the numbers and spread of organisms in an environment.

**A** If left unmanaged the Broads will eventually become woodland with the trees out-competing other plants.

**B** One plant can out-compete all the rest.

Plants need light so they can carry out photosynthesis. There is always **competition** between plants to get the most light. Plants have all sorts of adaptations to help them do this. Some climb up other plants. Some grow earlier in the year than others. Some store up energy in underground reserves, so they get a head start when the growing season begins. Plants that are very good at obtaining the **resources** they need will increase in number, while the population of plants that cannot compete so well will decrease.

The reed beds in the Broads slowly change. Mud builds up and other plants start to grow. These compete with the reeds for space and nutrients. The ground slowly dries out, making the environment less suited to the reeds. As trees start to grow, they compete with the reeds and other plants. They take more space, water and nutrients. As they get bigger they take more of the light. As a result of all this competition the trees will win and the area will become woodland.

1 Why do plants compete with each other for light?

2 What will happen to the population of a plant that competes better?

3 Describe two ways in which plants can adapt to help them compete better with other plants.

## Have you ever wondered?

If animals fight over land and mating partners, what do plants fight over?

Birds are very good examples of animals that compete for territory and for a mate. The male robin has a red breast and a song it sings in the breeding season. He uses these to attract a mate. If a rival robin enters the territory, the robin sings a different song and shows his red breast to the intruder. If this does not warn off the intruder, there may be a fight. Robins are very aggressive, and a fight will often lead to the death of one of the birds. If a robin cannot defend his territory he will not find enough food and is unlikely to breed. Successful robins have a big territory and plenty to eat, so they can find a mate and breed.

**C** A robin defending his territory.

Cormorants move into the Broads in winter because it is easier to catch fish than at sea. They are also very good at catching fish. If there are large numbers of them they will catch so many fish that other birds and animals will not have enough food. The cormorants out-compete the other birds and animals, and these populations may decrease. They may die out altogether and this will reduce **biodiversity**. If the cormorants eat too many fish in one area, they can fly somewhere else to catch food.

## Have you ever wondered?

Why is there a variety of birds in the park and not just one species?

## Have you ever wondered?

Why territory is so important for animals?

**Summary Exercise**

**4** Why do animals compete for territory?

**5** Why does the male robin have a red breast?

**6** Explain how competition can mean that reed beds eventually disappear.

**Higher Questions**

P

# 5. Human activity and air pollution

**By the end of these two pages you should be able to:**

- describe how air can become polluted and the effects of these pollutants
- H explain how economic and industrial conditions can lead to effects on the environment and changes in populations.

Air **pollution** is caused when gases and tiny particles of materials like soot get into the atmosphere. Volcanoes cause natural pollution by throwing sulphur dioxide, carbon dioxide and dust into the atmosphere. But pollution of the atmosphere is also caused by human activity. Burning fossil fuels creates carbon dioxide, which is a greenhouse gas and is one of the factors affecting global warming.

Methane is over 20 times more potent than carbon dioxide as a greenhouse gas. Methane is produced by rotting vegetation, the digestive systems of herbivores like cows and from landfill sites.

Sulphur dioxide is produced when sulphur-containing fuels like oil and coal are burned. Sulphur dioxide dissolves in moisture in the atmosphere and returns as acid rain. It reacts with minerals in the ground so that trees can no longer use them. Acid rain affects the organisms in lakes. Some are killed, others grow more. The balance of biodiversity in the lake is changed.

**A** Air pollution affects all living organisms.

**B** Acid rain can corrode limestone buildings and statues as well as affecting natural environments.

1 Explain how air pollution can be both natural and produced by humans.

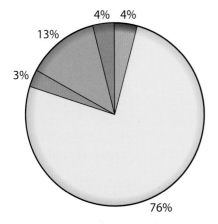

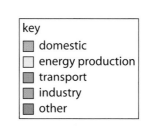

key
- domestic
- energy production
- transport
- industry
- other

4% 4%
13%
3%
76%

**C** Sulphur dioxide emissions in the UK, 2003. They are one of the main causes of acid rain. Much of this comes from homes, power stations, factories and vehicles.

Carbon monoxide is formed when fuels containing carbon are burned without enough air. Cars produce carbon monoxide. Faulty gas, coal and wood fires can also produce carbon monoxide if they are not serviced properly. Carbon monoxide can increase **ozone** at ground level. This can be very damaging for plants and animals, and causes breathing problems in people. Carbon monoxide is also a greenhouse gas.

**H** Much of the pollution in the world today is a result of industrialisation in both developed and developing countries. People want a high standard of living, which means they need a lot of energy for their homes, cars and factories. The environment is affected by the methods we use to obtain the fuels for this energy, and also by the substances released when energy is produced and used.

For example, there are plans to build over 500 coal-fired power stations in China to provide energy for the huge population as the country becomes more industrialised. Coal mines can damage the land and the power stations release polluting gases into the atmosphere.

Industrialisation also affects the populations of certain species. Towns and cities increase in size as people's economic conditions improve. Some species may lose their natural habitats or may suffer the effects of pollution. These factors can decrease biodiversity and threaten the continuation of some species.

4 Suggest what effects industrialisation in China might have on the environment.

5 Explain how industrialisation can lead to changes in animal populations.

2 Explain how the following gases pollute the air and describe their effects.
**a** sulphur dioxide
**b** methane

3 What is the main source of the chemicals that cause acid rain?

6 Explain why carbon monoxide is a polluting gas. **P**

7 Describe the different forms of air pollution caused by human activity, and their effects on the atmosphere. **P**

**Summary Exercise**

**Higher Questions**

# 6. Human activity and water pollution

**By the end of these two pages you should be able to:**

P

- describe how water can become polluted and the effects of these pollutants

H

- explain how economic and industrial conditions affect the environment and lead to changes in population.

V

**A** The challenge is to get water quality in the Broads back to where it was 100 years ago. Boats are no longer allowed to dump sewage into the water.

**B** The first steps to clean water and increased biodiversity.

One hundred years ago, the water in the Norfolk Broads was clean and clear. There was good biodiversity, as the water was unpolluted. Then pollution started to become a problem. **Sewage** from homes and businesses was discharged into the rivers, and boats dumped their sewage straight into the water. Fertiliser was put onto the surrounding fields to increase crops. The Broads is the lowest point in the area, so some of the fertiliser ended up in the water as run-off from the fields.

H Many of these changes are due to increasing affluence in Britain in the last 100 years. People have more time and money for holidays and leisure activities. The Broads became very popular and the number of boats and homes increased. As the population grew there was more pressure on the environment. The result was a damaged environment which affected the populations of many animals and plants.

Barton Broad is a good example of how pollution can affect the environment and biodiversity. Sewage and fertilisers found their way into the water. Tiny single-celled plants called algae grew very fast and the water turned green. This process is called **eutrophication**. This cut off the light to plants growing in the Broad, so they died. The number of animals in the water decreased. Layers of smelly mud built up.

1 What is meant by eutrophication?

2 What was the effect of the pollution on Barton Broad?

fertiliser
run-off

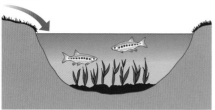 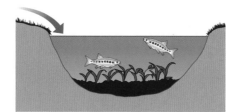 

1. The fertiliser makes the algae grow fast. The increased algal growth cuts out sunlight and uses up oxygen.

2. The plants do not get enough sunlight and they die. Dead plants and algae build up on the bottom.

3. The dead plants and algae rot, using up oxygen in the water. There are fewer animals in the water.

**C** Eutrophication takes place when nitrates and phosphates let algae grow really fast.

The algae in the water and the mud needed to be removed. A natural way to do this was with the tiny water flea *Daphnia*. It eats algae and can multiply quickly. However, water fleas are the favourite food of many fish. So to give the water fleas a chance to do their job the fish had to be kept away. Areas of Barton Broad were separated off with fish-proof barriers. Gradually the quality of the water has started to improve and biodiversity is increasing.

3 Why are boats not allowed to put sewage into the water?

4 a Describe the pattern of changes in the levels of phosphate in the River Ant between 1980 and 2005.

   b Suggest reasons why these changes have taken place, and what the effect would be on the environment.

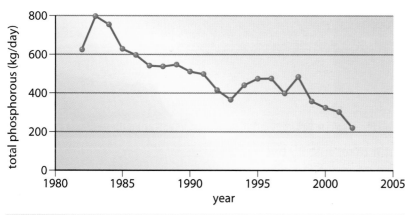

**D** Phosphates are now more carefully regulated. The graph shows levels of phosphate in the River Ant between 1980 and 2005.

The chemicals that caused this problem are nitrates and phosphates. **Nitrates** come mainly from farm fertiliser. **Phosphates** come mainly from sewage. The levels of these chemicals can be reduced. Farmers can use different types of fertiliser, or try alternative ways to increase the yields of their crops. Phosphates can be reduced in sewage works. Phosphates also leach into the water from mud, so removing the mud is another approach.

Development in the Broads is now strictly controlled, but more work needs to be done to repair the damage already caused.

5 What are the main sources of nitrate and phosphate pollution on the Norfolk Broads?

6 How can water fleas help to reverse the effects of eutrophication?

7 Write a fact sheet about water pollution in the Broads. Include information about how humans have contributed to the problem.

Summary Exercise

Higher Questions

93

# 7. Recycling

**By the end of these two pages you should be able to:**

- explore whether recycling reduces the demand for resources
- explore whether recycling reduces the problem of waste disposal.

**A** Rubbish or resource?

**B** A fleece made from recycled plastic.

Next time you wear a fleece remember that it takes just 25 two litre plastic drinks bottles to make one fleece garment. Plastics make up about 7% of our household waste. That is nearly 3 million tonnes every year in the UK. A lot of this is plastic bottles and most end up in landfill. Here they take up space and do not biodegrade.

## Have you ever wondered?

Why is recycling of materials encouraged?

**Recycling** has many benefits. If all the glass, metals, plastic and paper in our dustbins were recycled that would be nearly half the contents of the average bin. This could reduce the problem of **waste disposal** and landfill sites that are getting full. Recycling also uses less energy and produces less damaging carbon dioxide than manufacturing new materials. For example, recycled steel uses 75% less energy and produces only 15% of the carbon dioxide produced when steel is made from iron ore.

1 How many plastic bottles are needed to make one fleece?

2 Give two advantages of recycling.

Most people agree that recycling is beneficial to the environment. But not all the materials that the UK could recycle are being recycled. Part of the reason is that many more facilities are needed to deal with the amount of waste we produce. The UK is particularly poor at recycling compared with other EU countries.

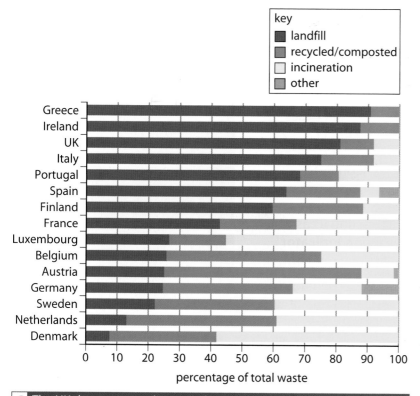

key
- landfill
- recycled/composted
- incineration
- other

percentage of total waste

**C** The UK does not recycle as much as many other countries in Europe.

Not everything can be recycled and some materials are more difficult to recycle than others. Plastics have to be sorted by hand and many types are not suitable for reuse. Paper can only be recycled about five times before the fibres become too short and weak. Refrigerators are a particular problem because of the harmful gases they contain.

Although recycling uses less energy and resources it is still an industrial process. Some materials need a lot of cleaning and reprocessing. Where materials are difficult to recycle it can be easier and cheaper to make new products. Even when it is possible to recycle waste, many of us do not because of the effort involved if facilities are not convenient. In addition, some people do not like the idea of recycled products, as they worry they might be contaminated or do not look as good as new. This means that there is always a demand for new products. Tougher laws may be needed to improve recycling in the UK and help us catch up with our European neighbours.

**3 a** Describe the pattern of recycling across Europe.
  **b** Suggest reasons for the pattern.

**4** Which countries do you think manage their waste disposal best? Explain your answer.

**D** The UK only has 10% of the capacity it needs to recycle these old fridges. Other countries like The Netherlands can recycle all of theirs.

**5** Suggest why the UK does not recycle as much as other EU countries.

**6** Give reasons why people might not recycle as much as they would like to.

**7** Would effective recycling:
  **a** solve the problem of waste disposal
  **b** reduce the demand for resources?
Explain your answers.

Summary Exercise

Higher Questions

**By the end of these two pages you should be able to:**

- interpret data on the impact of human activity on the environment
- give examples of how living and non-living things can be used to show this impact
- **H** • interpret data on environmental change.

Human activity can have negative effects on the environment. Some of these effects can be measured. Manufactured gases called CFCs have damaged the ozone layer in the upper atmosphere. Ozone filters out much of the ultraviolet radiation from the Sun, which can damage your skin. Sometimes this damage can lead to **skin cancer**. The number of cases of skin cancer has more than doubled in the UK in the last 20 years. This is one sign that the ozone layer is not protecting us as well as it used to. So skin cancer can be used as a **living indicator** that shows the effects of human activity on the environment.

However, skin cancer may not be directly caused by damage to the ozone layer. Plants called lichens are better indicators of our impact on the environment. They are very sensitive to air pollution, especially sulphur dioxide. An accurate picture of air pollution can be made by doing a lichen survey.

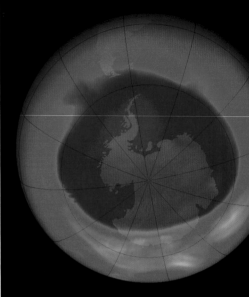

**A** Human activity can have a serious impact on the environment. This hole in the ozone layer is caused by human activity.

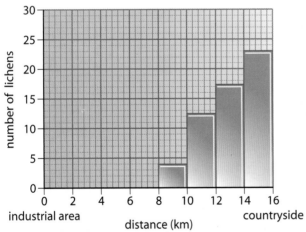

**B** To do the survey the number of lichens found on twigs were counted at 2 km intervals from an industrial area.

Mayfly larvae are found only in very clean water with lots of oxygen. They are used as living indicators to monitor water quality in streams. Lots of mayfly larvae means that a stream has high water quality.

Non-living indicators can also be used to show the human impact on the environment. One example is the rise in **global temperature**. Most scientists agree that greenhouse gases like

1 What is meant by a living indicator?

2 Look at the lichen survey results.
   a How many lichen plants were found 4–6 km from the industrial area?
   b How many lichen plants were found 12–14 km from this area?
   c What does this tell you about the air quality? Explain your answer.

3 If there are few mayfly larvae in a stream, what could you conclude about the water quality?

carbon dioxide are the main cause. Data shows that as the amount of carbon dioxide has increased over the last 100 years, the temperature of the Earth has risen.

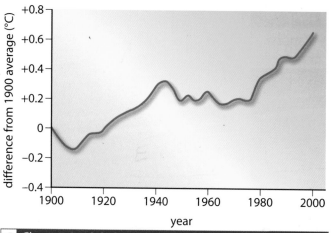

C Changes in global mean surface temperature 1900–2000.

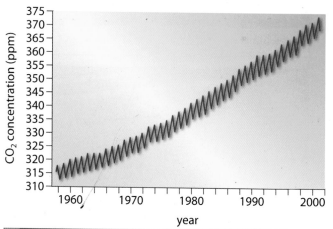

D Changes in global carbon dioxide levels 1958–2001.

**H** Global temperature has to be measured over a long period of time – even hundreds of years – before scientists can confidently claim that the climate is changing. The effects may not always be hotter summers and milder winters. Climate change can also result in more severe and unpredictable weather. The incidence of hurricanes has increased in the last few years, and storms seem to be more severe.

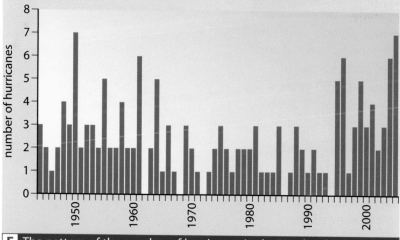

E The pattern of the number of hurricanes in the North Atlantic from 1944 to 2004.

7 Describe the pattern in the number of hurricanes each year between 1944 and 2004.

8 **a** Do these data provide evidence that global warming is increasing the number of hurricanes? Explain your answer.
  **b** What further evidence would be needed to see if there is a link?

4 Look at graph C. How did the surface temperature change between 1960 and 2000?

5 Look at graph D. What happened to the carbon dioxide levels during the same period?

6 Explain how this data supports the claim that humans have had an impact on the environment.

9 What is a non-living indicator?

10 What is causing the Earth to heat up?

11 Explain how different pollution indicators can be used to show the effect people are having on the environment.

**Summary Exercise**

**Higher Questions**

**By the end of these two pages you should be able to:**

- explain why it is important to protect natural populations.

**A** The population of this rare butterfly is protected.

The Broads is home to some of the rarest animals and plants in the UK. The bittern, the swallowtail butterfly, the fen orchid and the Norfolk hawker dragonfly are all species on the edge of extinction. Changes to their habitats over the last 100 years made it harder for them to exist. In 1997 there were just seven male bitterns left in the UK.

Most people will never see any of these four organisms. Yet a lot of effort and money goes into protecting them. The protection of natural populations is very important. Every time a species becomes extinct, biodiversity is reduced. Careful management of the environment is called **conservation**.

Conservation measures have brought the bittern back from the edge of extinction. Bitterns rely on reed beds. As these beds are delicate and can dry out, this habitat can easily be lost. Old reed beds have been cleaned and improved and new reed beds have been created by making shallow lagoons. There are now 30 breeding pairs of bitterns in the UK, ten of them in Norfolk.

The swallowtail butterfly is the UK's largest butterfly and is a protected species. It is now only found in Norfolk. Its caterpillars feed on milk parsley. This is a plant common in the Broads but not elsewhere. Careful management of the plant has meant that numbers of the butterfly are increasing in this area.

1 Why are numbers of swallowtail butterflies starting to increase again?

2 What is being done to increase the numbers of bitterns?

3 Why is conservation important in maintaining biodiversity?

**B** **C** A panda and the Fen Orchid. Both protected and equally rare but only one is famous.

The giant panda also needs to be protected. It lives in mountainous regions of south-west China. Logging, farming and road building have divided up the area the pandas live in, so their habitats are becoming smaller. There are now efforts to put back the forest so that the different areas are linked up again.

The World Conservation Union monitors populations of all natural species. In 2006 it published the Red List of Threatened Species. This showed that two out of every five species on the planet that have been assessed by scientists face extinction. The main cause of extinction is people. As human populations grow and need more and more resources, many other species are pushed out, as they are unable to compete.

**4** Why are pandas an endangered species?

Conserving all species – even flowers or insects, which may seem unimportant – in order to maintain biodiversity is important because of interdependence. The extinction of one species threatens others, because that species might be a food source or a predator. If biodiversity is lost, scientists will also find it harder to find out how organisms adapt and evolve.

**5** How do scientists know which species might be at risk?

**6** What is meant by conservation?

**7** Why is it important that natural populations are protected?

**Summary Exercise**

**Higher Questions**

# 10. Conservation management

**By the end of these two pages you should be able to:**

- explain some conservation management techniques
- discuss how conservation can lead to greater biodiversity.

**A** Conservation management techniques can lead to greater biodiversity.

The Norfolk Broads is an area of wetland produced by the interaction between people and the environment. Left to itself, the whole area would gradually dry out and become woodland. This is an entirely natural process called **succession**.

Conservation management means intervening in this process. Natural succession is stopped by careful management. This is because people like the Broads the way they are. Important organisms like the bittern and the swallowtail butterfly would be lost.

Some areas are allowed to re-grow into woodland. Others are kept as open water. The result is a wide variety of habitats. Different animals and plants are adapted to each of these habitats. This means there is greater biodiversity in the Broads.

People living in the Broads used to harvest the reed and sedge to provide animal feed and bedding and to use as thatch for houses. Now these resources are being used again. As oil has become more expensive scientists have looked for alternative fuels. Reed and other fen products make good biofuels. They can be chopped, dried and burnt to produce heat and electricity, or can be formed into briquettes suitable for a domestic open fire.

1 Give an example of succession in the Norfolk Broads.

2 How can the Norfolk Broads be used to produce biofuels?

3 Why did reed harvesting die out in the last century?

4 What will happen to any wetland if it is not managed?

**B** Effective management can provide useful crops as well as conserving the environment.

**C** New technology has made the harvesting easier. The fen harvester is a machine that can do the job quickly and cheaply.

**Coppicing** is a technique where trees like hazel and willow are cut near the base of their trunk. From this base they grow lots of new branches very quickly. A well-managed coppice wood has trees at different stages, so that there is a harvest every year. No trees are destroyed in the process and it actually makes the trees live far longer. Coppicing also opens up woodland letting in more light. This leads to greater biodiversity.

## Have you ever wondered?

Why are all conservation initiatives not equally successful?

**Reforestation**, or planting trees, is another conservation management technique. Thousands of years ago much of the UK was covered in forest. Now less than 12% of the UK is woodland. Trees store carbon, make oxygen, reduce flooding, stabilise the soil and help to improve air quality. They provide us with renewable resources and a habitat for all sorts of animals and plants.

**Replacement planting** is slightly different. This means that if a tree or shrub is removed it is replaced by a plant of the same species. Sometimes trees have to be removed, so it is important that each one cut down is replaced by one of the same species nearby. This helps to maintain the biodiversity of the area, but it takes a long time for many species to grow.

5 Why does coppicing mean that trees do not have to be replaced?

6 What is meant by replacement planting of a tree?

7 How does reforestation help to improve biodiversity?

8 Write a short newspaper article about how conservation management is being done in the Norfolk Broads.

Summary Exercise

Higher Questions

# 11. Questions

## Multiple choice questions

**1** Bacteria in a hydrothermal vent get their energy from
  **A** sunlight.
  **B** hot water.
  **C** minerals.
  **D** photosynthesis.

**2** Coppicing is a conservation management technique which involves
  **A** replanting trees to increase the number of trees.
  **B** cutting trees and shrubs to ground level to encourage rapid new growth.
  **C** replacing a tree or shrub that is removed by planting another of the same species.
  **D** keeping a habitat the same as environmental conditions change.

**3** To survive particular conditions in a habitat, organisms are
  **A** interdependent.
  **B** extinct.
  **C** adapted.
  **D** evolved.

**4** Ozone depletion is caused by
  **A** carbon dioxide.
  **B** global warming.
  **C** CFCs.
  **D** methane.

**5** If the numbers of predators increase the number of prey will
  **A** increase.
  **B** stay the same.
  **C** decrease.
  **D** reproduce.

**6** Plants compete with each other for light for
  **A** photosynthesis.
  **B** food.
  **C** respiration.
  **D** competition.

**7** Organisms that compete better will
  **A** grow bigger.
  **B** increase their population.
  **C** become extinct.
  **D** become predators.

**8** Paper in landfill sites rots and produces
  **A** carbon monoxide.
  **B** acid rain.
  **C** methane.
  **D** ozone.

**9** Phosphate pollution in rivers comes mainly from
  **A** fertilisers.
  **B** sewage.
  **C** acid rain.
  **D** fish.

**10** Nitrate pollution in rivers comes mainly from
  **A** mud.
  **B** sewage.
  **C** acid rain.
  **D** fertilisers.

**H 11** People want a high standard of living. This results in a huge increase in demand for
  **A** pollution.
  **B** energy.
  **C** food.
  **D** biodiversity.

**12** Industrialisation can have serious effects on natural habitats and can increase pollution. These factors can decrease
  **A** competition.
  **B** environment.
  **C** conservation.
  **D** biodiversity.

**13** Increased affluence means
  **A** requiring more food.
  **B** increasing water pollution.
  **C** having more money for luxuries like holidays.
  **D** recycling more waste materials.

**14** Data collected since 1995 suggests that there has been an increase in the number of hurricanes. Some people argue that this is being caused by global warming. Why is this conclusion unjustified, based on this evidence?
  **A** This evidence is primary data.
  **B** Evidence needs to be checked by other scientists.
  **C** This evidence is secondary data.
  **D** Data is needed over a much longer period of time.

**15** Global temperature is
   **A** the effect of global warming.
   **B** average temperatures measured across the whole surface of the planet.
   **C** how much temperatures have been increased by global warming.
   **D** the effect of increasing amounts of carbon dioxide in the atmosphere.

## Short-answer questions

**1** The graph shows the change in incidence of skin cancer from 1975 to 2001.

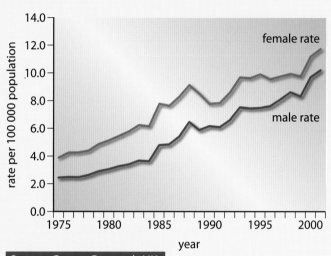

Source: Cancer Research UK.

**a** Describe the pattern in the incidence of skin cancer cases for both males and females since 1975.
**b** Suggest reasons for this pattern.
**c** Suggest reasons why the incidence for females is higher than that for males since 1975.

**2** The graph shows the change in the amount of ozone in the upper atmosphere from 1955 to 1995.

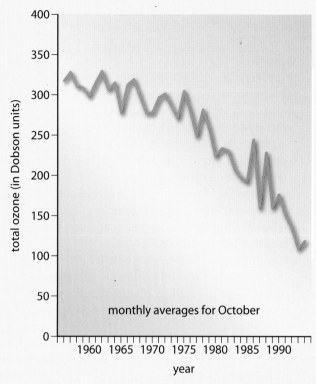

*A Dobson unit is a measure of ozone depth.

**a** Describe the pattern in the changes in amount of ozone in the upper atmosphere from 1955 to 1995.
**b** This pattern illustrates ozone depletion. Explain how ozone depletion takes place.

**3 a** Skin cancer can be used as a living indicator to show the impact of human activity on the environment. Use the two graphs above to help you to explain what this means.
**b** The two graphs could be used to argue that changes in ozone have caused changes in skin cancer. Discuss whether the evidence is sufficient to make this claim.

**\*adaptation**  Changing to suit the environmental conditions.

**\*aquatic**  Living in water.

**\*biodiversity**  A variety of species of plants and animals.

**\*competition**  The battle between different types of organism over the same resource.

**\*conservation**  Keeping a habitat the same as environmental conditions change.

**\*coppicing**  Cutting trees and shrubs to ground level to encourage rapid new growth.

**\*environment**  A particular set of conditions, including water, temperature, light and air.

**environmental factors**  The living and non-living factors which affect organisms.

**eutrophication**  The process where fertilisers and sewage build up in water, over-encouraging algal growth which leads to light and oxygen supplies being depleted. This in turn leads to other organisms in the water dying off.

**\*extreme environment**  Conditions that are far outside the boundaries where humans can live comfortably.

**\*global temperature**  Average temperatures measured across the whole surface of the planet

**\*interdependence**  The mutual dependence of one organism with another.

**living indicator**  Evidence of the effects of human activity on the environment shown on a live organism.

**\*nitrate**  Chemicals used as fertilisers to make crops grow better.

**\*organism**  Living creatures such as animals, plants or insects.

**\*ozone**  A gas found in the upper atmosphere.

**\*phosphates**  Chemicals that act as fertilisers which are also found in sewage.

**\*pollution**  Contamination of the environment.

**\*population**  A group of individuals of the same species living in the same habitat.

**\*predation**  Killing and eating other animals for food.

**\*recycling**  Reusing materials instead of the original resource.

**\*reforestation**  Planting trees to increase the number of trees.

**\*replacement planting**  Replacing a tree or shrub by planting another of the same species.

**\*resource**  Material or energy used by living things.

**\*sewage**  Solid waste from humans and other animals.

**\*skin cancer**  A tumour of the skin, usually caused by too much UV-B radiation.

**succession**  The gradual change of a habitat to become woodland

**\*terrestrial**  Living on land.

**\*waste disposal**  Getting rid of things we no longer need.

\*glossary words from the specification

# Synthesis

**A** An oil refinery seen at night.

Organic chemistry deals with compounds that contain carbon. Organic compounds are the basis of life, but we can make many substances that are not found in nature.

Crude oil is a complex mixture of organic compounds. It gives us fuels such as petrol and diesel to power our cars and lorries. It is also a very useful raw material for making new substances such as polymers and medicines. But oil is a non-renewable resource. It is important that we use oil wisely.

There are often several ways to make the same substance, but some are more efficient than others. Modern industrial processes try to use as little energy and produce as little waste as possible.

## In this topic you will learn that:

- organic chemicals are based on the element carbon and mainly originate from living things
- many new chemicals are made from oil
- polymers are large molecules which can be formed by a combination of many smaller molecules
- disposing of some plastics is an environmental problem
- raw materials are converted into new and useful substances by chemical reactions
- the amount of reactant needed to get a desired quantity of product can be calculated
- the theoretical yield often differs from the actual yield and this has financial implications.

Look at these statements and decide whether you think they are true or false.

- Organic chemicals are things like food, grown without artificial fertilisers.
- Hydrocarbons are compounds that contain only hydrogen and carbon.
- All polymers are plastics.
- Plastics take thousands of years to rot.
- Runny oils are polyunsaturated and hard fats are saturated.
- Making new substances is mostly a matter of trial and error.
- You can work out a chemical formula using an experiment.

# 1. The basics of organic chemistry

**By the end of these two pages you should be able to:**

- explain that there are many organic compounds because carbon atoms can form four bonds
- recall the formulae of methane, ethane, propane, ethene and propene, and draw the structures of their molecules.

If you see the word 'organic' you will probably think of food grown without the use of artificial chemicals. But a chemist will think of a huge number of fascinating organic compounds that all have one thing in common. They contain carbon, the non-metal that is the basis of life.

Carbon is unusual because it forms four chemical bonds with other non-metals, including itself. Most other non-metals can only form one, two or three bonds. This ability means that carbon atoms can form chains, branches, rings and other complex shapes. Some organic substances are simple, like methane. Others contain many atoms, like sugars, fats, proteins and DNA. Organic compounds that contain just hydrogen and carbon, like methane, are called **hydrocarbons**.

There are two main families of hydrocarbons which have similar structures and properties. These are the **alkanes** and **alkenes**. Alkanes are found in natural gas and crude oil. Methane only has one carbon atom in its molecule. But the carbon atoms in all other alkanes are joined to each other by single chemical bonds to form chains. Ethane has two carbon atoms joined together, and propane has three carbon atoms.

**1** Which element do organic substances have in common?

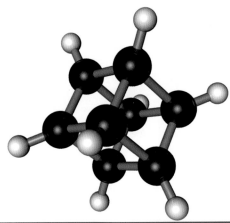

**A** This organic compound is cubane. It has eight carbon atoms (shown in black) arranged in a cube. There is a hydrogen atom (shown in white) at each corner.

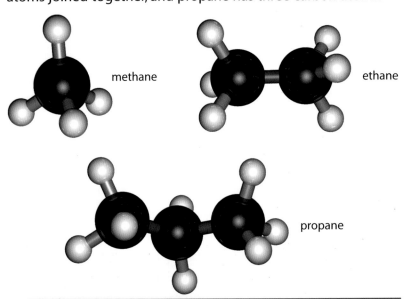

methane

ethane

propane

**B** Molecular models of methane, ethane and propane. The carbon atoms are shown in black and the hydrogen atoms are shown in white.

**2** How many bonds can a carbon atom form?

**3** What is a hydrocarbon? Give an example in your answer.

**4** How many carbon atoms are there in methane, ethane and propane?

You can draw simple diagrams of the alkanes to show their structure. You do not need to draw any circles, you can just use a C for each carbon atom and an H for each hydrogen atom. A type of bond called a **covalent bond** joins the atoms together. These are drawn as straight lines. Methane is easiest to draw. A diagram like this is called a **displayed formula**.

C   C   C

C—C—C

**1** Write the correct number of Cs in a line.

**2** Draw a bond between each C.

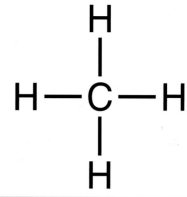

C The displayed formula of methane. Hydrogen atoms can only form one chemical bond.

**3** Add enough bonds so that each C has four.

**4** Write an H on the end of each empty bond.

D How to draw a longer molecule such as propane.

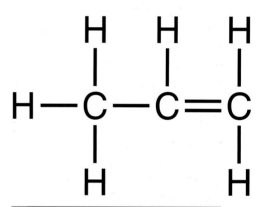

E The displayed formula of propene.

Sometimes it is enough just to know the **molecular formula**. This tells you how many carbon atoms and hydrogen atoms there are in the molecule but not how they are joined together. The molecular formula of methane is $CH_4$. The molecular formula of ethane is $C_2H_6$. Notice that the number of hydrogen atoms is twice the number of carbon atoms plus two.

**5** Draw the displayed formula of ethane.

**6** What is the molecular formula of propane?

A second family of hydrocarbons is called the alkenes. In alkanes, all the bonds are single. But in alkenes, there is a **double bond** between two of the carbon atoms. A double bond looks like a long equals sign.

The simplest alkene is ethene. The molecular formula of ethene is $C_2H_4$. The number of hydrogen atoms is exactly twice the number of carbon atoms.

**7** Draw the displayed formula of ethene.

**8** What is the molecular formula of propene?

**9** Give three similarities and three differences between propane and propene. Include their molecular **formulae** and diagrams of their structural formulae in your answer.

Summary Exercise

Higher Questions

# 2. A cracking lesson

**By the end of these two pages you should be able to:**

- describe the process of cracking
- recall that when alkanes are cracked, mixtures of alkanes and alkenes are formed
- explain the differences between alkanes and alkenes
- describe how bromine water is used to show if something is an alkane or an alkene
- **H** explain how ethene can be reacted with water to make ethanol.

## Have you ever wondered?

Only a small part of crude oil is petrol, so how do we make enough for all the cars in the world?

Crude oil is a mixture of many different hydrocarbons. **Fractional distillation** is used to separate different parts of the oil, called **fractions**. The supply of fractions with large molecules, like bitumen, is greater than the demand for them. But the supply of fractions with small molecules, like petrol, is less than the demand for them. Large hydrocarbon molecules need to be turned into smaller ones, so that we can supply enough petrol for our needs. A **chemical reaction** called **cracking** lets us do this.

In cracking, oil fractions are heated very strongly so that some of the carbon–carbon bonds in the molecules break. Smaller hydrocarbon molecules form as a result. Some of them are alkanes, which can be used to meet the demand for petrol. Some of them are alkenes, which are used to make polymers.

For example, decane is a large hydrocarbon that can be cracked to form two smaller hydrocarbons, octane and ethene. The balanced formula equation for the reaction is:

$$C_{10}H_{22}(g) \rightarrow C_8H_{18}(l) + C_2H_4(g)$$

The (g) after a formula is called a **state symbol**. It shows that the substance is a gas. There are three other state symbols: (s) means solid, (l) means liquid and (aq) means aqueous or dissolved in water.

1 **a** What is cracking?
  **b** Why do we need it?

2 Complete this equation for the cracking of hexane into butane and ethene:

$$C_6H_{14}(l) \rightarrow C_4H_{10}(g) + ?$$

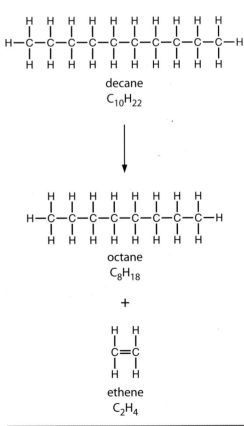

decane
$C_{10}H_{22}$

octane
$C_8H_{18}$

+

ethene
$C_2H_4$

**A** Cracking breaks down larger alkanes into smaller alkanes and alkenes.

Alkanes are **saturated hydrocarbons**. They only have single covalent bonds between their carbon atoms and no more atoms can add onto the molecule. Alkenes are **unsaturated hydrocarbons**. They have a double covalent bond between two of their carbon atoms, so more atoms can be added to the molecule without breaking the chain of carbon atoms.

Bromine water is made by dissolving bromine in water. You can use this to test whether a hydrocarbon is an alkane or an alkene. To do this, add a small volume of bromine water to a test tube containing a hydrocarbon, then shake it. If the hydrocarbon is an alkene, the bromine water changes from brown to colourless. If the hydrocarbon is an alkane, it stays brown.

Spare bond.

**B** The double bond in alkenes allows more atoms to join on. In this example, bromine atoms add to a butene molecule.

3 What is the difference between a saturated hydrocarbon and an unsaturated hydrocarbon?

4 What would you see when bromine water is shaken with:
   **a** ethane
   **b** ethene?

5 Paraffin oil does not affect bromine water. If paraffin oil is cracked, one of the products is a gas that makes bromine water colourless. Explain these results.

**C** Bromine water stays brown when mixed with an alkane but the colour disappears with an alkene.

**H** Ethene that is produced by cracking can be used as a fuel. But, as it contains a double bond, it is much more useful as a raw material in the chemical industry. Ethanol is one of the useful substances that can be made from ethene. It is the alcohol in alcoholic drinks. Ethanol is also a solvent for ink, glue, perfume and aftershave. It can be made by reacting ethene with steam at high temperature and pressure:

| ethene | + | steam | → | ethanol |
|--------|---|-------|---|---------|
| $C_2H_4(g)$ | + | $H_2O(g)$ | → | $C_2H_5OH(l)$ |

**D** Ethene and steam react to produce ethanol.

6 Will bromine water go colourless when mixed with ethanol? Explain your answer.

7 Write a fact sheet about alkanes and alkenes. Include how they are produced, how they are different, and how you can tell them apart.

**Summary Exercise**

**Higher Questions**

# 3. Introduction to polymers

**By the end of these two pages you should be able to:**

- describe the structure of polymers
- explain the differences and similarities between thermosetting and thermoplastic polymers.

Cracking is used to produce a mixture of smaller alkanes and alkenes from larger alkanes. These smaller hydrocarbons are more useful as fuels because they ignite more easily. But alkenes are also useful as **raw materials** for making other substances, in particular **polymers**. Polymers are more commonly known as plastics.

**A** Polymers have many different uses.

## Have you ever wondered?

How do those plastic creatures, that grow when put in water, actually work?

Under the right conditions, small alkenes can join together end to end to form large molecules. The small alkenes are called **monomers**. The large molecules are called polymers and the process that makes them is called **polymerisation**.

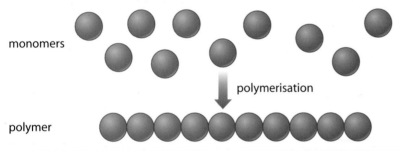

monomers

polymerisation

polymer

**B** Many small monomer molecules combine to form a large polymer molecule.

In reality, several thousand monomers may join together to make one polymer molecule. For example, ethene monomers make polyethene. This is commonly called polythene and is used to make carrier bags.

Alkenes have a double bond. The double bond in ethene allows ethene monomers to join together to form a molecule of polyethene.

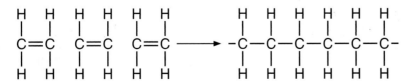

**C** Ethene monomers join to form polyethene. There is no other product apart from the polymer itself.

1 What is meant by:
  **a** a monomer
  **b** a polymer?

2 Suggest the names of the polymers formed from these monomers:
  **a** propene
  **b** styrene.

**3** This is chloroethene. Draw a diagram to show how three molecules of chloroethene join together to make a section of polychloroethene.

**4** How many products are formed when fluoroethene monomers join together?

(chloroethene structure)
H   H
|   |
C = C
|   |
Cl  H

Have you ever staggered home from the shops only to have your carrier bag stretch, tear, then spill your shopping all over the ground? If so, you are likely to have been the victim of a thermoplastic polymer! There are two main types of polymer: **thermoplastic** polymers and **thermosetting** polymers. They have very different properties, as shown in table E.

|  | **Thermoplastic** | **Thermosetting** |
|---|---|---|
| polymer | polyethene | melamine |
| flexibility | can stretch or bend | rigid – breaks when bent |
| effect of being heated | softens and melts | chars or decomposes |
| re-moulding | can be re-moulded into new shapes | cannot be re-moulded into new shapes once set |
| diagram | no cross-links between polymer molecules | cross-links between polymer molecules |

**E** Some of the typical properties of the two types of polymer.

The molecules in thermoplastic polymers are often tangled around each other and make the polymer flexible. There are weak forces of attraction between the molecules. When a thermoplastic polymer is heated up, these forces are overcome and the molecules can slide past one another. This allows the polymer to be remoulded. When it cools down, the forces of attraction form again.

When a thermosetting polymer is made, covalent bonds form between the polymer molecules. These **cross-links** are very strong and stop the molecules moving past one another. This is why the polymer is rigid and cannot be remoulded. If you heat up a thermosetting polymer, it does not melt. It just chars or burns when heated strongly.

**D** Carrier bags are made from polyethene, a thermoplastic polymer.

**5** Plastic mouth guards for hockey players soften in hot water so they can be moulded to fit the player's mouth. Which type of plastic is likely to be used? Explain your answer.

**6** Old-fashioned telephones were made from a rigid but brittle plastic called Bakelite. Which type of plastic is Bakelite likely to be? Explain why it is difficult to recycle these telephones.

**7** Melamine is a hard, heat-resistant polymer used for kitchen worktops.
   **a** Is melamine likely to be a thermosetting polymer or a thermoplastic polymer?
   **b** Explain why melamine is hard and heat-resistant.
   **c** The plastic film for wrapping sandwiches is a thermoplastic polymer. Give the important properties for this plastic film, and explain why they are useful.

**Summary Exercise**

**Higher Questions**

# 4. Formation and uses of polymers

**By the end of these two pages you should be able to:**

- explain how addition polymers are formed and draw a section of an addition polymer
- suggest uses of polymers from their properties
- explain how and why the properties of a plastic can be altered
- discuss the problems of disposing of some plastics.

Polymers like polyethene and polypropene are made from **unsaturated monomers**, such as ethene and propene. They are called **addition** polymers because the monomers add to each other to form the long polymer chains. The only product of addition polymerisation is the polymer itself. This is different from **condensation** polymers such as nylon and Kevlar, where another substance, water, is also made in the reaction.

## Have you ever wondered?

How is plastic made from oil?

**1** What is an addition polymer?

**2 a** What is the raw material for addition polymers, such as polyethene?
   **b** How is it processed to get the monomer needed?

Thousands of monomers may join together during addition polymerisation. This would be very difficult to draw, so you only have to draw a section. This is sometimes called a **repeating unit**.

**3** Here are the displayed formulae of styrene and ethene.
Draw a section of:
   **a** polyethene
   **b** polystyrene.

styrene          ethene

Polymer chains may have branches on them. This affects the strength of the polymer. For example, high-density polyethene (HDPE) has few branches, while low-density polyethene (LDPE) has many branches. HDPE is much stronger than LDPE. It stretches less than LDPE and can be used at temperatures up to 120 °C. LDPE can only be used up to about 85 °C.

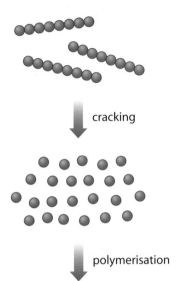

**A** Cracking produces shorter carbon chains and polymerisation produces longer ones.

**1** Look at the monomer (this is propene).

**2** Draw the monomer but use a single bond instead of a double bond.

**3** Draw a bond on each side of where the double bond would have been.

**B** How to draw a section of polypropene, starting with its monomer, propene.

**4** Would LDPE or HDPE be the best choice for a hot drinks cup? Give reasons for your answer.

## Have you ever wondered?

Is sucking plastic toys dangerous for a baby?

The properties of polymers may make them unsuitable for our needs. Scientists can alter their properties by adding other substances. **Plasticisers** allow polymer chains to slide over each other more easily. This makes the polymer softer and more flexible. For example, uPVC or unplasticised PVC is a hard polymer used for pipes and window frames. PVC containing plasticisers is soft and flexible, and is useful for floor coverings and car dashboards. Some plasticisers are now banned because they were found to be **toxic** and could leak out of the plastic.

## Have you ever wondered?

How do you make slime/super balls?

PVA (polyvinyl alcohol) glue contains water which acts as a plasticiser. If PVA is mixed with borax solution, weak cross-links form between the polymer chains and a gooey slime is made. The more borax that is added, the thicker the slime becomes.

## Have you ever wondered?

Why can't we make plastic bags that biodegrade?

Thermoplastic polymers can be recycled. But the very properties that make polymers useful can also make it difficult to dispose of them. Polymers are resistant to acids and other chemicals, but this means that they do not rot easily. Polymers must be incinerated at very high temperatures to avoid harmful fumes.

**C** Most polymers are not biodegradable and cause environmental problems when not disposed of properly.

Some polymers are degradable. They contain additives that make them break down faster than normal. Others contain starch granules and are **biodegradable**. They can be decomposed by soil bacteria and rot quickly.

5 What are plasticisers and what do they do?

6 **a** What features of polymers make it difficult to dispose of them?
   **b** Suggest some good uses for degradable polymers and some uses that they would not be suitable for.

7 How do branches, plasticisers and cross-links affect the properties of polymers? Give an example of each in your answer.

**Summary Exercise**

**Higher Questions**

# 5. It's all fat, but does it make you fat?

**By the end of these two pages you should be able to:**

- discuss some of the consequences of our dependence on oil
- explain the difference between polyunsaturated and monounsaturated vegetable oils
- explain why polyunsaturated oils are thinner than saturated ones
- describe how hydrogenated vegetable oil is made and what it is used for.

**A** The tar sands in Canada contain huge reserves of oil. But the remote location and the thickness of the oil make tar sands difficult to exploit.

Around 38% of the world's energy comes from crude oil. Unfortunately, it is a non-renewable resource. It is likely that half of the world's oil reserves have already been used up. A lot of the remaining reserves are difficult to extract. There is probably less than 40 years' supply left.

As oil begins to run out, oil companies are turning to reserves that used to be too expensive or difficult to use. Extracting this oil is more expensive, so prices rise. This makes alternative energy resources more attractive. Vegetable oils from plants such as rapeseed are already being used to make biodiesel for vehicles. They may also be used in the future as a raw material for the chemical industry.

**1** Describe two uses of oil.

**2 a** Explain why oil prices rise as oil supplies begin to run out.
**b** Describe two other things that might happen as oil runs out.

**Have you ever wondered?**

Food labels give 'total fat' and 'saturated fat' – but what's the difference?

Vegetable oils such as rapeseed oil, sunflower oil and olive oil are used for cooking, and to make margarine. If you look on the side of a tub of margarine you will see that it contains **monounsaturated** and **polyunsaturated** oils. These names refer to how many double bonds there are in the oils. Vegetable oils are made of compounds called triglycerides. Each triglyceride molecule is made from three fatty acid molecules joined to a smaller molecule called glycerol. In a monounsaturated oil each fatty acid contains one double bond. In a polyunsaturated oil each fatty acid contains more double bonds.

**3** What is a triglyceride molecule made from?

**4** What is the difference between a monounsaturated oil and a polyunsaturated oil?

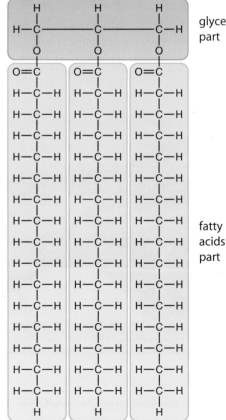

**B** Vegetable oils contain triglyceride molecules, each made from glycerol and three fatty acids.

The triglyceride molecules in saturated oils only have single bonds between their carbon atoms. They can line up close to each other, so they have strong forces of attraction between them. This makes them solids at room temperature or thick, **viscous** liquids. The double bonds in polyunsaturated oils put bends into the molecules. The molecules cannot line up closely, so the forces of attraction between them are weaker. This makes polyunsaturated oils runny liquids at room temperature.

5  **a** Fish oil is polyunsaturated. Is it likely to be viscous or runny? Explain your answer.
   **b** Explain why saturated oils are more viscous than monounsaturated oils like olive oil.

Vegetable oils are too runny to make margarine. They must be **hydrogenated** by adding hydrogen at high temperatures. This changes some of the double bonds into single bonds. The oils become more saturated. This is sometimes called hardening because their melting point increases, making them solid at room temperature. Hydrogenated oils are blended with unsaturated oils to make margarine that spreads straight from the fridge.

C Hydrogenated vegetable oils are used in the food industry as an ingredient of pastry and other foods such as cakes, biscuits and pies. Too much fat in your diet can make you overweight.

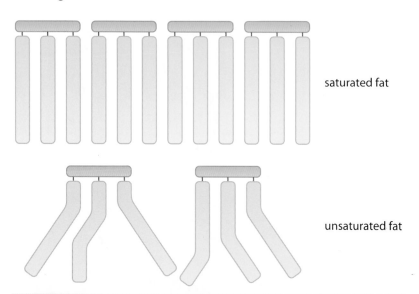

saturated fat

unsaturated fat

D The molecules in saturated fats can line up closely but those in polyunsaturated oils cannot.

6  Why are vegetable oils hydrogenated?

7  Hard fats such as lard are often used in pastry making.
   **a** Are the fats in lard likely to be saturated or unsaturated?
   **b** Lard is unsuitable for vegetarians. Explain how a runny vegetable oil could be hardened for use in pastry making.

Summary Exercise

Higher Questions

**By the end of these two pages you should be able to:**

- describe how chemists deal with toxic chemicals when making new substances
- recognise that chemists use information about known reactions to make new chemicals
- predict the product of a reaction using information about a similar reaction.

P

P

?

Hazard warning signs on bottles of chemicals are common in school laboratories and on containers of household chemicals such as bleach. Some chemicals are toxic. It is important to know which chemicals are toxic so that you can avoid contact with them.

Substances are tested to assess their **toxicity**. This includes using computer models and tests on cells grown in the laboratory. In the UK, chemicals such as new medicines, pesticides and some food ingredients must also be tested on animals. But it is illegal to test cosmetics and tobacco products on animals. A typical test is the fixed-dose procedure. A known amount of the substance is given to animals, which are then carefully monitored for any side-effects.

Most everyday substances contain artificial chemicals. These are made using chemical reactions, in a process called **synthesis**. Chemists can usually find several ways to synthesise a particular substance. For example, aspirin can be synthesised from salicylic acid in two different ways:

Method 1: salicylic acid + ethanoic anhydride $\longrightarrow$ aspirin + ethanoic acid
Method 2: salicylic acid + ethanoyl chloride $\longrightarrow$ aspirin + hydrogen chloride

In both methods, salicylic acid is a reactant and aspirin is a product. But the second reactant in each method is different. The second product in each method, called the by-product, is also different. The first method is used because ethanoic anhydride is safer than ethanoyl chloride, which is toxic.

## Have you ever wondered?

Why do chemical factories discharge waste products into the environment?

Some by-products are useful but many are not. Too much space would be needed to store them, so they are usually discharged into the environment. Hazardous by-products are treated first.

toxic

**A** Toxic chemicals can kill you if you touch them, swallow them or breathe them in. This hazard sign warns you that a substance is toxic.

**1 a** Write down two toxicity tests that do not involve animals
  **b** Write down one that does involve animals.

**B** Chemists research the different ways to synthesise new chemicals. Then chemical engineers plan how to carry out the process on a large scale for industrial use.

**C** Toxic industrial waste needs careful handling. It may be incinerated, released into the air, or discharged into rivers after treatment to make it safer.

**2** What are by-products?

**3** Why do chemical factories discharge waste products into the environment?

You have looked at different types of chemical reaction, including polymerisation and neutralisation. If you wanted to make a salt, you could use a base and an acid as reactants. If you wanted copper sulphate as your product, you would use copper oxide and sulphuric acid as your reactants. Chemists can use their knowledge of one reaction to predict the products of another similar reaction.

For example, bromoethane is the product of the reaction between ethene and hydrogen bromide. It is easy to predict that if you used propene instead of ethane, the product would be bromopropane.

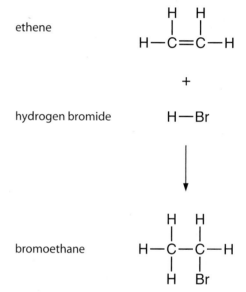

**D** Ethene reacts with hydrogen bromide to make bromoethane.

**4** Sodium hydroxide and sulphuric acid react to make sodium sulphate. What reactants do you need to make potassium sulphate?

**5** Ethanoic acid is synthesised by oxidising ethanol. Which acid is synthesised by oxidising methanol?

**6** Aminoethane is synthesised from chloroethane and ammonia. Hydrogen chloride is the by-product.
$C_2H_5Cl + NH_3 \rightarrow C_2H_5NH_2 + HCl$
**a** What reactants do you need to synthesise aminopropane, $C_3H_7NH_2$?
**b** Write the equations for the reaction.

**7 a** Give an example of how you can predict the product of a reaction if you know something about a similar reaction.
**b** Explain why you need to check whether a reactant or product is toxic.

**Summary Exercise**

**Higher Questions**

# 7. Synthesis in action

## By the end of these two pages you should be able to:

**H**
- describe the stage method for synthesising new drugs
- calculate the number of possible products from a staged synthesis experiment.

### Have you ever wondered?

How do chemists discover new drugs?

In modern drug development, thousands of new substances are synthesised and then tested to see if they have any useful effects. This includes experiments on individual biological substances, on cells grown in the laboratory, and on animals. Modern laboratories use automated machinery to carry out many of these tests very quickly. But how do we get the thousands of new substances to test in the first place?

**1** How many stages does it take to make aspirin from phenol?

**2** What sort of tests can be done on new substances in the laboratory?

One way to obtain large numbers of products is to react mixtures of similar reactants together. For example, propene reacts with bromine to form dibromopropane. Propene also reacts with chlorine to form dichloropropane. So, if you react propene with a mixture of bromine and chlorine, you get both products at once. But you also get two extra products, each containing a bromine atom and a chlorine atom. In this way, you can get four products from three reactants in a one-stage process. With more complex molecules you can get even more products.

phenol

salicylic acid

aspirin

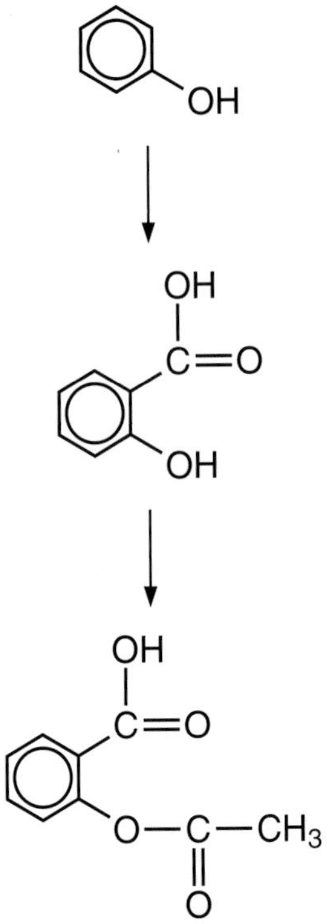

**A** Willow tree bark was used as a remedy for aches and pains. It was discovered that the active ingredient was salicylic acid. Chemists later discovered how to make aspirin from phenol, a readily available substance, in two stages.

**3** Methylpropene reacts in a similar way to propene.
  **a** How many products could you get from reacting methylpropene with a mixture of bromine and chlorine?
  **b** How many products could you get from a mixture of propene, methylpropene, bromine and chlorine?

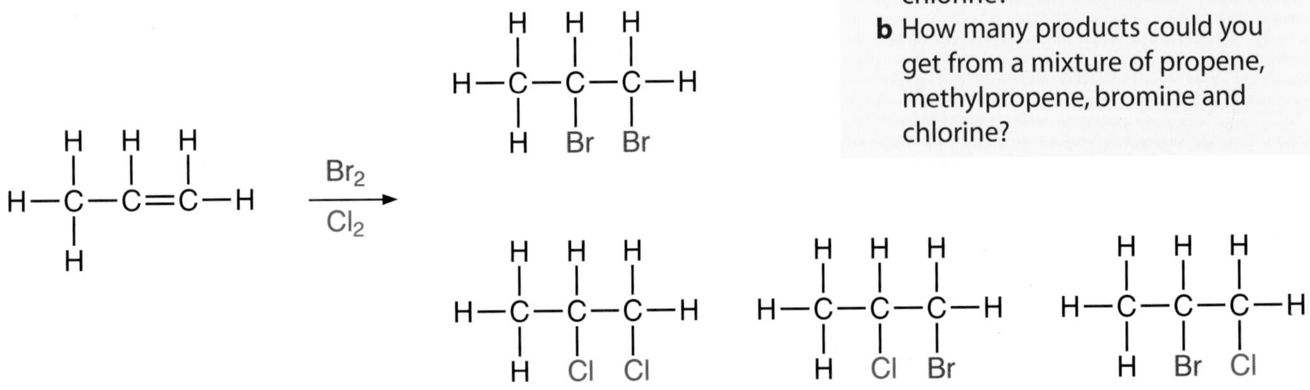

**B** You can get four products by reacting propene with a mixture of bromine and chlorine.

Very few substances pass all the laboratory and clinical tests, making it very expensive to develop new drugs. So, if lots of substances can be synthesised quickly, it helps to reduce the cost. You can make several products at once using mixtures, but you can also make many products by using more than one stage. The synthesis of aspirin from phenol happens in two stages, and the middle product (salicylic acid) also has pain-killing properties. In fact, it was also used as a pain-killer until aspirin became more popular. This was because aspirin is less irritating to the stomach.

**4** Explain how drug companies use mixtures and stages to produce many substances to test.

**H** You can calculate how many products can be made in a staged synthesis. A simple example where just one product is made at each stage is the reaction of ethene and steam to make ethanol. There is one stage and just one product.

ethene + steam $\longrightarrow$ ethanol
$C_2H_4(g) + H_2O(g) \longrightarrow C_2H_5OH(l)$

It is also possible to make ethanol from ethene in two stages. In this case, there are three products. Two of them are organic substances that might be tested for their biological effects.

Stage 1:  ethene + hydrogen chloride $\longrightarrow$ chloroethane
$\quad\quad\quad C_2H_4(g) + \quad\quad HCl(g) \quad\quad \longrightarrow \quad C_2H_5Cl(g)$
Stage 2:  chloroethane + sodium hydroxide $\longrightarrow$ ethanol + sodium chloride
$\quad\quad\quad C_2H_5Cl(g) \quad + \quad NaOH(aq) \quad \longrightarrow C_2H_5OH(aq) + \quad NaCl(aq)$

In some synthesis experiments more than one potentially useful product is made at each stage. Here is a three stage-process that results in eight products. The substances are represented by letters to make it simpler.

**5** What are the organic chemicals in the examples above?

**6** Suggest a possible biological effect of ethanol.

Stage 1    A $\xrightarrow{\;+B\;}$ AB                                    (1 product)

Stage 2    AB $\xrightarrow{\;+C\;}$ AC + BC                            (2 products)

Stage 3    AC + BC $\xrightarrow{\;+D\;}$ ACD + BCD + AD + DC + BD    (5 products)

In this example, the substances represented by A and B combine in stage 1. In stage 2, the substance represented by C can substitute for another substance, so AB can become AC or BC. In stage 3, the substance represented by D can add and substitute, giving several products.

**7** A certain synthesis happens in three stages. In stage 1, two products are formed. Each of these can form two products in stage 2, so there are four ($2 \times 2 = 4$) products from stage 2.
  **a** Each of the products from stage 2 can form three products in stage 3. How many products are made in stage 3?
  **b** How many products are made in total from all three stages, assuming that every product at each stage is different?

<!-- buttons -->
Summary Exercise          Higher Questions

# 8. Chemical calculations

**By the end of these two pages you should be able to:**

- calculate relative formula mass from relative atomic masses
- use chemical equations to calculate masses of reactants and products.

| Element | Symbol | $A_r$ |
|---|---|---|
| hydrogen | H | 1 |
| carbon | C | 12 |
| nitrogen | N | 14 |
| oxygen | O | 16 |
| sodium | Na | 23 |
| magnesium | Mg | 24 |
| aluminium | Al | 27 |
| sulphur | S | 32 |
| calcium | Ca | 40 |
| iron | Fe | 56 |

**A** The relative atomic masses for some common elements. The standard atom, carbon, has an $A_r$ of 12. An atom with a lower $A_r$ is lighter than a carbon atom. An atom with a higher $A_r$ is heavier than a carbon atom.

Atoms have very little mass. Just one gram of carbon contains around fifty thousand billion billion atoms. So, instead of talking about their mass in grams or kilograms, you can use the idea of **relative atomic mass**, $A_r$. This gives the mass of an atom compared to a standard atom: carbon.

Once you know the relative atomic mass of an atom, you can use this to find the masses of molecules and compounds. If you add together the $A_r$ values for all the atoms in the formula of the molecule or compound, you will get its **relative formula mass**, $M_r$.

For example, to work out the relative formula mass of water, $H_2O$:
1  Find the relative atomic masses of the two elements in water, hydrogen and oxygen. These are often shown in the Periodic Table or in separate tables of $A_r$ values. The $A_r$ of H is 1 and the $A_r$ of O is 16.
2  Add these together, remembering that there are two hydrogen atoms and one oxygen atom:
   $M_r$ of $H_2O$ = 1 + 1 + 16 = **18**.

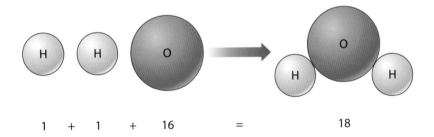

1  +  1  +  16        =        18

**B** Relative formula mass of water.

1  What is meant by relative atomic mass, $A_r$?

2  If the $M_r$ of water is 18, is a molecule of water heavier or lighter than a carbon atom?

3  Work out the relative formula masses of the following compounds:
   **a** magnesium oxide, MgO
   **b** sodium hydroxide, NaOH
   **c** carbon dioxide, $CO_2$
   **d** sodium sulphate, $Na_2SO_4$

Some formulae have brackets in them and you must take these into account when calculating the relative formula mass. For example, magnesium hydroxide is written as $Mg(OH)_2$. This tells you that there is one Mg atom, two O atoms and two H atoms.

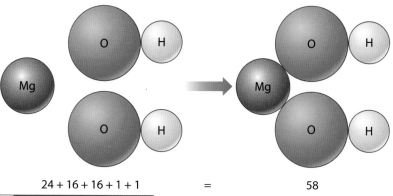

$24 + 16 + 16 + 1 + 1$ = $58$

| C | The $M_r$ of $Mg(OH)_2$ is 58. |

4 Calculate the relative formula masses of the following compounds:
   a calcium hydroxide, $Ca(OH)_2$
   b ammonium sulphate, $(NH_4)_2SO_4$
   c magnesium nitrate, $Mg(NO_3)_2$

5 Explain in your own words how you work out the relative formula mass of a substance. Include some examples in your answer.

**H** The total mass of reactants and products stays the same during chemical reactions. None of the atoms involved is lost or destroyed: they just join together in a new way. You can use relative atomic mass and relative formula mass to calculate the masses of individual reactants and products. This is very useful in industry where raw materials might be expensive, bulky or difficult to transport. Only the required amounts have to be brought onto the site, and the amount of any waste materials can be worked out in advance.

6 Why is it useful to be able to calculate the masses of reactants and products in a chemical reaction?

Hydrogen can be manufactured by reacting methane with steam:

$$CH_4(g) + H_2O(g) \rightarrow CO(g) + 3H_2(g)$$

If you start with 8 g of methane, you can find how much waste carbon monoxide will be produced.
The $M_r$ of $CH_4$ is $12 + 1 + 1 + 1 + 1 = 16$
The $M_r$ of CO is $12 + 16 = 28$

The mass of carbon monoxide $= \dfrac{\text{mass of } CH_4}{M_r \text{ of } CH_4} \times M_r \text{ of CO}$

$= \dfrac{8}{16} \times 28 \text{ g}$

$= 0.5 \times 28 \text{ g}$

$= 14 \text{ g}$

7 Look at the reaction of methane with steam above.
   a What mass of steam reacts completely with 8 g of methane?
   b What mass of hydrogen can be made from 8 g of methane?

**Summary Exercise**

**Higher Questions**

# 9. Using chemical reactions

**By the end of these two pages you should be able to:**

- explain why it is important for reactions to be as efficient as possible
- define the term 'atom economy'
- calculate the atom economy of a reaction.

The manufacture of fertilisers, cement, metals, plastics, medicines and many other substances involves chemical reactions. The amount of waste produced from manufacturing processes like these must be kept to a minimum. Efficient manufacturing means less pressure is put on natural resources. This helps with **sustainable development** – making sure that the way we do things now will not make problems for future generations.

Processes are more efficient if they have a high **atom economy**. The atom economy of a process is the proportion of reactants that are converted into useful products rather than waste products. Processes with a high atom economy produce the least waste.

**A** This power station is fuelled by waste gases from an oil refinery. Excess heat is used to make steam for use as a raw material in a nearby chemical plant. This makes the refinery and chemical plant very efficient.

**1** What is sustainable development?

**2** Why is it important that manufacturing processes are efficient?

Hydrogen is used as a fuel, and to make margarine and fertilisers. It can be produced from steam, either by reacting it with hot coal (which is mostly carbon) or with natural gas (which is mostly methane). These are the equations for the reactions:

Using coal:   carbon + steam → carbon monoxide + hydrogen
$$C(s) + H_2O(g) \rightarrow CO(g) + H_2(g)$$

Using natural gas:   methane + steam → carbon monoxide + hydrogen
$$CH_4(g) + H_2O(g) \rightarrow CO(g) + 3H_2(g)$$

Notice that both processes produce carbon monoxide as a waste product but the second one produces more hydrogen. It can be shown that the atom economy of the first process is 6.7% and the atom economy of the second process is 17.6%. The second process produces a higher proportion of useful product.

**3** Explain what is meant by the atom economy of a process.

**4** Which process for producing hydrogen from steam is likely to be the best for sustainable development: the one using coal or the one using natural gas? Mention their atom economies in your answer.

**H** The atom economy of a process is the percentage of the total mass of products that is useful. It can be calculated using this formula:

$$\text{atom economy (\%)} = \frac{\text{mass of useful products made}}{\text{total mass of all products made}} \times 100$$

The reaction between coal and steam to make hydrogen is a useful example.

Write the balanced equation: $C(s) + H_2O(g) \rightarrow CO(g) + H_2(g)$

Calculate the $M_r$ of each product:

$M_r$ of $CO = 12 + 16 = 28$
$M_r$ of $H_2 = 2 \times 1 = 2$

Add together all the relative formula masses of the products:

$= 28 + 2 = 30$

$$\text{atom economy} = \frac{\text{mass of useful products made}}{\text{total mass of all products made}} \times 100$$

$$= \frac{2}{30} \times 100 = 6.7\%$$

We are assuming here that all the reactants become products. In real industrial processes some of the reactants often remain unconverted. One example of this is the production of ammonia for fertilisers.

Carbon monoxide is a toxic gas but it can be reacted with steam to make even more hydrogen:
$CO(g) + H_2O(g) \rightarrow CO_2(g) + H_2(g)$

This also has the advantage that carbon dioxide is the waste product, rather than carbon monoxide. It dissolves easily in sodium hydroxide solution to leave pure hydrogen behind, helping to reduce the cost of purifying the product. The reaction also releases energy, which helps to improve the overall efficiency of the process.

**B** Hydrogen and nitrogen are used to manufacture ammonia, which is used to make the fertilisers needed to help crops grow well.

**5** Calculate the atom economy of the following reactions to produce hydrogen:
  **a** $CO(g) + H_2O(g) \rightarrow CO_2(g) + H_2(g)$
  **b** $CH_4(g) + 2H_2O(g) \rightarrow CO_2(g) + 4H_2(g)$

Summary Exercise

Higher Questions

# 10. Formulae and percentage yields

**By the end of these two pages you should be able to:**

P
- explain what is meant by the term empirical formula
- calculate the formulae of simple compounds from reacting masses

H
- calculate theoretical and percentage yields of reactions.

How do we know the formulae of all the different chemicals? A water molecule is made from two hydrogen atoms and an oxygen atom joined together, giving the formula $H_2O$. But you cannot tell this from looking at a glass of water. You can work it out from the masses of the different substances involved in a reaction.

If sodium is heated in air, it reacts with oxygen to form sodium oxide. The sodium oxide is made of sodium atoms and oxygen atoms. But how many are there in the formula? In a typical experiment, 0.46 g of sodium forms 0.62 g of sodium oxide. This means that it must have reacted with 0.16 g of oxygen (0.62 − 0.46 = 0.16 g). To find the formula, you also need to know the relative atomic masses of sodium and oxygen.

**A** Sodium reacts violently with oxygen to form sodium oxide.

| Step | Action | Result | |
|---|---|---|---|
| 1 | Write down the symbols of the elements involved: | Na | O |
| 2 | Write down the mass of each element involved: | 0.46 g | 0.16 g |
| 3 | Write down their $A_r$ values: | 23 | 16 |
| 4 | Work out mass / $A_r$: | $\frac{0.46}{23} = 0.02$ | $\frac{0.16}{16} = 0.01$ |
| 5 | Divide both numbers by the smallest number: | $\frac{0.02}{0.01} = 2$ | $\frac{0.01}{0.01} = 1$ |
| 6 | Write out the formula: | $Na_2$ | O |

**B** How to calculate the formula of sodium oxide. The calculated formula is $Na_2O$. This shows that there are two sodium atoms for every oxygen atom.

P

1 24 g of magnesium reacts with 16 g of oxygen to form 40 g of magnesium oxide.
The $A_r$ of Mg is 24 and the $A_r$ of O is 16.
Work out the formula of magnesium oxide, making sure you show how you did it.

2 1.2 g of carbon reacts with oxygen to form 4.4 g of a carbon oxide.
The $A_r$ of C is 12 and the $A_r$ of O is 16.
Work out the formula of the carbon oxide and name the oxide.

The formulae you get from experiments like these are called **empirical** formulae. They contain the simplest whole numbers of each element in the compound. They may be different from the true molecular formula. For example, the molecular formula of propene is $C_3H_6$, but the empirical formula is $CH_2$. In this case, to get the simplest whole numbers, each is divided by three.

**3** The molecular formula of dinitrogen tetroxide is $N_2O_4$.
 **a** What is its empirical formula?
 **b** Explain why dinitrogen tetroxide is not the same as nitrogen dioxide, $NO_2$.

**H** The atom economy of a process is not the whole story about its efficiency. You usually get less product than you expect. The amount you expect to get from your calculations is called the **expected yield** or **theoretical yield**. The **actual yield** (how much you really get) is usually less than this, because your raw materials might not be pure or the reaction may be only partially completed. This can make the manufacturing process more expensive to run.

The **percentage yield** tells you how close to the theoretical yield you have got. The higher the percentage yield, the closer you are to the theoretical yield. The balanced equation for the reaction between calcium carbonate and hydrochloric acid is:

$$CaCO_3(s) + 2HCl(aq) \rightarrow CaCl_2(aq) + H_2O(l) + CO_2(g)$$

For calcium carbonate $M_r = 100$ and for carbon dioxide $M_r = 44$, so the theoretical yield of carbon dioxide from 100 g of calcium carbonate is 44 g. But you may actually only get 33 g of carbon dioxide, so the percentage yield is:

$$\text{percentage yield} = \frac{\text{actual yield}}{\text{theoretical yield}} \times 100$$
$$= \frac{33}{44} \times 100 = 75\%$$

**4** What is the difference between the theoretical yield of a process and the actual yield?

**5** Suggest why the percentage yield is only 75% in the example above.

**6** The theoretical yield of a certain process is 25 tonnes but only 20 tonnes of product is made. What is the percentage yield?

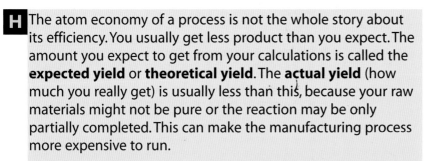

**C** Propene, $C_3H_6$, and butene, $C_4H_8$, are different compounds. They have the same empirical formula, $CH_2$.

**Summary Exercise**

**Higher Questions**

# 11. Questions

## Multiple choice questions

**1** Which hydrocarbon has the formula $C_3H_8$?
  **A** methane
  **B** ethane
  **C** propane
  **D** propene

**2** Cracking alkanes involves
  **A** producing shorter alkanes and alkenes.
  **B** producing longer alkanes and alkenes.
  **C** joining many small molecules together.
  **D** cooling and condensing vapours at different temperatures.

**3** What happens when bromine water is added to a saturated hydrocarbon and an unsaturated hydrocarbon?
  **A** There is no change with either hydrocarbon.
  **B** Both hydrocarbons change the bromine water from colourless to brown.
  **C** The saturated hydrocarbon changes the bromine water from brown to colourless.
  **D** The unsaturated hydrocarbon changes the bromine water from brown to colourless.

**4** Which of these molecules could be the monomer for polyethene?

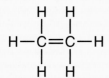

**5** Which statement about thermoplastic and thermosetting polymers is correct?
  **A** Melamine is a thermoplastic polymer and polyethene is a thermosetting polymer.
  **B** Thermoplastic polymers cannot be remoulded but thermosetting polymers can.
  **C** Thermoplastic polymers are rigid and break instead of bending but thermosetting polymers stretch and bend.
  **D** Thermoplastic polymers do not have cross-links but thermosetting polymers do.

**6** Four different polymers might be used to make disposable plastic cups to hold hot drinks. Using the information in the table, which one is likely to be the best?

| Polymer | Melting point (°C) | Price per cup (p) |
|---------|--------------------|--------------------|
| **A** | 80 | 0.5 |
| **B** | 80 | 1.0 |
| **C** | 120 | 0.5 |
| **D** | 120 | 1.0 |

**7** Which statement about oils is correct?
  **A** Saturated oils are likely to be less viscous than unsaturated oils.
  **B** Saturated oils are likely to be more viscous than unsaturated oils.
  **C** Saturated oils can be made by dehydrogenating vegetable oils.
  **D** Monounsaturated oils contain more double bonds than polyunsaturated oils.

**8** What is the relative formula mass of sodium nitrate, $NaNO_3$?
$A_r$ of Na = 23, $A_r$ of N = 14 and $A_r$ of O = 16.
  **A** 53  **B** 85  **C** 37  **D** 48

**9** In making hydrogen, $H_2$, which reaction is likely to have the highest atom economy?
  **A** $CH_4 + H_2O \rightarrow CO_2 + 3H_2$
  **B** $CO + 2H_2 \rightarrow CH_3OH$
  **C** $C + H_2O \rightarrow CO + H_2$
  **D** $CO + H_2O \rightarrow CO_2 + H_2$

**10** Using the following information, what is the empirical formula of beryllium fluoride?
$A_r$ of Be = 9 and $A_r$ of F = 19
Mass of Be in compound = 1.8 g and mass of F in compound = 3.8 g
  **A** $Be_2F$  **B** BeF  **C** $Be_2F_2$  **D** $BeF_2$

**H** **11** Which statement about the reaction between ethene and steam is correct?
  **A** The only product is ethanol, an unsaturated hydrocarbon.
  **B** Ethene is a saturated hydrocarbon.
  **C** The only product is ethanol.
  **D** The reaction is called dehydration.

**12** Ethanol reacts with propanoic acid to make ethyl propanoate, and propanol reacts with butanoic acid to make propyl butanoate. What is made when propanol reacts with propanoic acid?

  **A** propyl ethanoate
  **B** propyl propanoate
  **C** ethyl propanoate
  **D** butyl propanoate

**13** A staged synthesis involves two stages. This is what happens in the first stage:

$$AB \xrightarrow{+C} ABC$$

In the second stage, reactant D is used. It can add to the product of the first stage (ABC) and it can also replace one of A, B or C. How many products overall are made in these two stages?

  **A** 3   **B** 4   **C** 5   **D** 6

**14** Hydrogen reacts with oxygen to make water:
$$2H_2(g) + O_2(g) \longrightarrow 2H_2O(l)$$
What mass of steam can be made from 1 g of hydrogen gas?
$A_r$ of H = 1 and $A_r$ of O = 16

  **A** 2.25 g   **B** 4.5 g   **C** 9.0 g   **D** 18 g

**15** Oxygen can be made by the decomposition of hydrogen peroxide:
$$2H_2O_2(aq) \longrightarrow 2H_2O(l) + O_2(g)$$
What is the atom economy of this reaction?
$A_r$ of H = 1 and $A_r$ of O = 16

  **A** 33%   **B** 47%   **C** 64%   **D** 94%

## Short-answer questions

**1** Angela did some research on the Internet about alkanes and alkenes. This is what some of what she found:

| | Alkanes | Alkenes |
|---|---|---|
| example | $C_2H_6$ | $C_2H_4$ |
| reaction with bromine water | no reaction | reaction seen |
| notes | saturated | unsaturated |

  **a** Name the alkane and alkene in Angela's table.
  **b** The empirical formula of the alkane is $CH_3$. What is the empirical formula of the alkene?
  **c** Why are alkanes and alkenes also called hydrocarbons?
  **d** Apart from the numbers of atoms they contain, what is the difference between saturated and unsaturated hydrocarbons?

**2** Rubber for car tyres undergoes a process called vulcanisation. The rubber is reacted with sulphur, forming cross-links between the polymer chains. Short sulphur cross-links make a tough rubber with good heat resistance, while longer cross-links make a flexible rubber with poor heat resistance.

  **a** What sort of polymer is unvulcanised rubber?
  **b** What sort of polymer is vulcanised rubber?
  **c** Explain why tyre manufacturers might carefully adjust the length of the cross-links in vulcanised rubber.
  **d** Why is it difficult to recycle vulcanised rubber?

**3** Sanjit carried out an experiment to find the empirical formula of copper sulphide. He weighed a copper strip and found that it had a mass of 6.35 g. He heated the copper strip, and carefully placed it into a boiling tube of sulphur vapour in a fume cupboard. When the reaction was complete, he re-weighed the copper strip and found that it had a mass of 7.95 g.

  **a** What mass of sulphur was gained by the copper strip during the reaction?
  **b** The $A_r$ of Cu is 63.5 and the $A_r$ of S is 32. Work out the empirical formula of Sanjit's copper sulphide.
  **c** What is the relative formula mass of CuS?

**4** Aluminium can be produced by passing electricity through molten aluminium oxide:

  **a** Calculate the relative formula masses of aluminium oxide and oxygen gas.
    $A_r$ of Al = 27 and $A_r$ of O = 16
  **b** **i** What mass of aluminium could be produced from 102 tonnes of aluminium oxide?
    **ii** What mass of oxygen gas could be produced at the same time?
  **c** During the process, some of the oxygen reacts with the carbon electrodes used, forming carbon dioxide gas.
    **i** Write the balanced equation for this reaction.
    **ii** Calculate the relative formula mass of carbon dioxide ($A_r$ of C = 12).
    **iii** If all the oxygen in your answer to part **b ii** reacted with carbon, what mass of carbon dioxide would be produced?
    **iv** If the percentage yield is 10%, what mass of carbon dioxide is actually produced?

# 12. Glossary

**actual yield** The amount of product obtained from a chemical reaction in reality. This may differ from the theoretical or expected yield because the raw materials may not be pure or because the reaction may not be complete.

**\*addition** In polymer chemistry, a large molecule formed from alkene monomers added together to form chains.

**\*alkane** A hydrocarbon in which all the bonds between the carbon atoms are single bonds.

**\*alkene** A hydrocarbon in which two or more carbon atoms are joined by double bonds.

**atom economy** The proportion of reactants that are converted into useful products.

**biodegradable** Able to be broken down by soil bacteria.

**\*condensation** A type of reaction in which two molecules join together to make a larger one, with water as a by-product.

**\*covalent bond** A type of chemical bond in which a pair of electrons is shared between two atoms.

**\*cracking** A type of chemical reaction in which large alkane molecules are decomposed to form smaller alkanes and alkenes.

**cross-links** Strong covalent bonds that form between polymer molecules.

**displayed formula** A diagram of the structure of a molecule in which the elements are represented by letters and the bonds are shown by straight lines.

**\*double bond** Two covalent bonds between two atoms, involving two shared pairs of electrons.

**\*empirical** Worked out from an experiment. An empirical formula is worked out dividing the mass of each element in a compound by its relative atomic mass.

**\*expected yield** See theoretical yield.

**\*formula (pl formulae)** An abbreviation for a substance with two or more atoms. The formula contains the symbols for the different elements in the substance, with numbers to show if there are two or more atoms of a particular element present.

**fraction** A constituent part of crude oil produced by fractional distillation.

**fractional distillation** An industrial process used to separate the constituent parts of crude oil.

**hydrocarbon** An organic compound containing just hydrogen and carbon.

**\*hydrogenate** To react with hydrogen.

**molecular formula** A chemical code that shows how many of each atom there are in a molecule.

**\*monomer** A small molecule, for example an alkene, that can be joined to many other small molecules to form a much larger molecule.

**\*monounsaturated** A substance (usually a fat) that only has one double bond.

**\*percentage yield** The percentage of a theoretical yield that you actually get in a reaction.

**plasticiser** A substance added to polymers to make them softer and more flexible. Plasticisers allow polymer chains to slide over each other more easily.

**\*polymer** Large molecule made by linking together many small molecules (monomers).

**polymerisation** In chemistry the process by which small alkenes (monomers) join together to form large molecules (polymers).

**\*polyunsaturated** A substance (usually a fat) that has more than one double bond.

**raw material** A starting substance for the manufacture of a particular chemical.

**relative atomic mass** The mass of an atom compared to the mass of a carbon atom, which has a relative atomic mass of 12. Abbreviated to $A_r$.

**relative formula mass** The mass of a molecule relative to the mass of a carbon atom. Abbreviated to $M_r$.

**repeating unit** A section or monomer of a polymer which shows its structure.

**\*saturated hydrocarbon** A compound of hydrogen and carbon in which there are only single bonds. Alkanes are saturated hydrocarbons.

**state symbol** Symbol used in chemical equations to show whether a substance is solid (s), liquid (l), gas (g) or dissolved in water (aq).

**\*sustainable development** Meeting the needs of the existing population without damaging the ability of future generations to meet their own needs.

**\*synthesis** Making a substance using chemical reactions.

**\*theoretical yield** The maximum calculated amount of product that can be obtained from a particular quantity of reactants. Also called expected yield.

**\*thermoplastic** A polymer that softens or melts when heated and becomes hard again when cooled.

**\*thermosetting** A polymer that cannot be melted or remoulded again once formed.

**toxic** Poisonous. Toxic substances may cause death if they are swallowed, breathed in or come into contact with the skin.

**\*toxicity** How toxic or poisonous a substance is. Very toxic substances have a high toxicity.

**\*unsaturated hydrocarbon** A compound of hydrogen and carbon in which there is one or more double bond. Alkenes are unsaturated hydrocarbons.

**\*unsaturated monomer** A small molecule that can form a polymer because it contains a double bond.

**viscous** Sticky or thick. Liquids with high viscosity are difficult to pour.

*glossary words from the specification

# In your element

**A** This plant manufactures many chemicals that we use every day.

It is easy to take for granted all the manufactured things around us. From spectacle frames that spring back into shape after being sat on, to chlorine for keeping our drinking water safe, we are surrounded by chemicals. A detailed knowledge of their properties is needed to manufacture them, but the Periodic Table can help.

It is possible to predict the properties of elements if you know something about their atomic structure, and this is where the Periodic Table comes in. In addition, different substances often have properties in common that are easily understood by looking at the type of bonding they have. With this knowledge manufacturers can make important raw materials such as hydrogen, chlorine and sodium hydroxide just by passing electricity through salty water. We can also explain why metals behave as they do, and why some elements are more reactive than others.

Look at these statements and sort them into the following categories:

I agree, I disagree, I want to find out more

- The most useful metals are pure metals rather than mixtures.

- All atoms contain a nucleus with electrons arranged randomly around it.

- Some metals can lose electrons easily and some non-metals can gain electrons easily.

- Common salt is only useful for putting on fish and chips.

- All atoms of an element are identical.

- The chemical reactions of an element are determined by the number of electrons in its atoms.

## In this topic you will learn:

- that the number of outer electrons in an element determines its position in the Periodic Table and its reactivity
- about the process of electrolysis
- about the existence of isotopes and their relationship to relative atomic mass
- about the importance of electrons in ionic and metallic bonding.

# 1. Explaining the properties of metals

**By the end of these two pages you should be able to:**

- describe and explain the physical properties of metals
- describe and explain how alloying can change the properties of metals.

## Have you ever wondered?

What is the difference between 9 and 18 carat gold jewellery?

Metals are all around us. We rely on steel to provide the strength for buildings, bridges, ships and cars. We use copper for electricity cables, aluminium for cooking foil and gold for jewellery. Some of the useful **properties** of metals are:

- they are solid at room temperature (except for mercury, which is a liquid)
- they are malleable and ductile
- they have a high **conductivity** (they are good conductors of electricity)
- most metals are also hard.

1 Why is copper used for electricity cables?

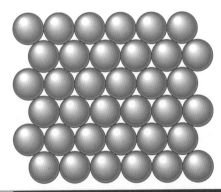

**A** Metals have many everyday uses.

The **atoms** in metals are close together and arranged in a regular pattern. There are forces of attraction, called **bonds**, between the atoms. The bonds in metals are strong, so a lot of energy is needed to break them. This is why metals are hard. When you try to dent a metal, it is difficult to push the atoms into different places.

Strong bonds also explain the high melting and boiling points of metals. To melt a metal, you need to supply enough heat energy to break some of the bonds and allow the atoms to move around each other. To produce a gas, you need to supply even more heat energy to break all of the bonds and let the atoms escape into the air.

**B** Metal atoms are arranged in a regular pattern.

**2** Caesium is the softest metal and chromium is the hardest. Which one has the strongest bonds?

**3** Gallium melts at 29.8 °C and tungsten melts at 3422 °C. Which one has the strongest bonds?

Metals are **malleable**, which means that they can be hammered or rolled into shape without shattering. Gold is the most malleable metal. Just 1 cm³ of gold will make a circle of foil five metres in diameter. Metals are also **ductile**, which means that they can be pulled into wires.

Metal atoms release some **electrons** into the structure of the metal. These charged **particles** are free to move and are the reason why metals are good conductors of electricity. As the electrons move through the metal, they carry electrical charge through it.

Most of the metals we use are not pure. Gold, for example, is too soft for most jewellery and is usually mixed with copper to make it stronger. Mixtures of metals are called **alloys**. Some alloys have been known since ancient times, such as bronze. This is an alloy of copper and tin that is much tougher than copper alone.

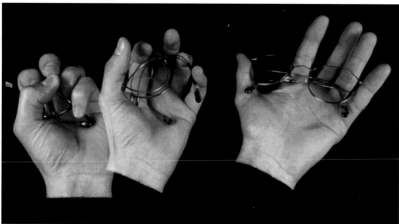

**D** Shape memory alloys spring back into shape after warming. They are useful for some medical parts and 'unbreakable' spectacle frames.

**5** An alloy of tin and copper melts at just 227 °C. Why is it useful as a solder for joining electrical parts?

Alloys are often stronger than the main metal alone. Aluminium may be used where a light metal is needed, for example in aircraft, but it is mixed with other metals such as copper and manganese to make it stronger. Smaller atoms fit into the gaps between larger atoms, disrupting the regular arrangement and making it more difficult for the layers of atoms to slide past each other.

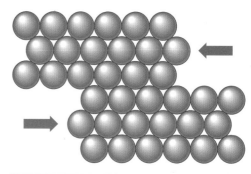

**C** When you bend a piece of metal, layers of atoms slide over each other.

**4** What feature of metals allows them to conduct electricity?

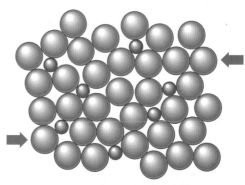

**E** Different sized metal atoms in alloys make it more difficult to push layers over each other.

**6 a** Explain why titanium is a hard metal, has a high boiling point and conducts electricity.
  **b** Iron is a soft metal. Mild steel, which contains about 0.25% carbon, is stronger. Carbon atoms are half the size of iron atoms. Suggest a reason why adding carbon makes iron stronger.

**Summary Exercise**

**Higher Questions**

# 2. Elements and their parts

**By the end of these two pages you should be able to:**

- explain the terms atomic number, mass number and relative atomic mass
- recall the relative charges and masses of protons, neutrons and electrons
- give an example of an imaginative idea that helped in the discovery of new elements or the development of the Periodic Table.

## Have you ever wondered?

Why do some scientists think life began in space, and came to Earth on a comet?

Dmitri Mendeleev (1834–1907) developed a **Periodic Table** in 1869. Unlike other scientists at the time, he realised that new elements were still being discovered and so he needed to leave gaps for them. Mendeleev also put the elements in order of increasing **relative atomic mass**. Atoms are so light that their masses are not usually shown in grams. Instead, we use the relative atomic mass, $A_r$. Carbon is chosen for the standard atom and it is given an $A_r$ of 12. The masses of all the other atoms are then compared to this atom. A hydrogen atom has an $A_r$ of 1, so it is 12 times lighter than a carbon atom.

There is a **nucleus** at the centre of each atom. This contains two types of subatomic particle, the positively charged **proton** and the electrically neutral **neutron**. Clouds of negatively charged electrons surround the nucleus.

The mass and charge of subatomic particles can be measured but the numbers are incredibly small. To make things easier, you can just show the masses and charges compared to the mass and charge of a proton.

| Particle | Relative mass | Relative charge |
|----------|---------------|-----------------|
| proton | 1 | +1 |
| neutron | 1 | 0 |
| electron | 0.0005 | −1 |

**C** The relative masses and charges of protons, neutrons and electrons.

1 Which particle in the atom has the smallest mass?

2 Where is most of the mass of atom found?

**A** The $A_r$ of magnesium is 24. One magnesium atom has the same mass as two carbon atoms.

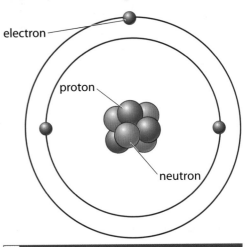

**B** Atoms consist of protons and neutrons in a nucleus surrounded by electrons.

**Elements** can be represented by **chemical symbols** such as C and Na. However, you can also use full chemical symbols like $^{12}_{6}C$ and $^{23}_{11}Na$. These have extra information to show the number of particles in the atom. The bottom number is the **atomic number**. It is the number protons in the nucleus and also the number of electrons in the atom. The top number is the **mass number**. It is the total number of protons and neutrons in the nucleus.

mass number

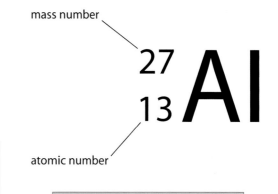

atomic number

number of neutrons = 27 – 13 = 14

**D** The number of neutrons is the mass number minus the atomic number.

> **3 a** How many protons does an atom of Na have?
> **b** How many electrons does it have?
>
> **4** Work out the number of neutrons in:
> **a** $^{12}_{6}C$
> **b** $^{23}_{11}Na$.

Mendeleev arranged the elements in order of increasing relative atomic mass in his Periodic Table. He also put elements with similar chemical properties into **groups**. However, he sometimes had to move elements around to do this. For example, iodine should be before the metal tellurium, based on relative atomic mass, but they would be in the wrong groups for their chemical properties. So Mendeleev swapped their positions to get them into the right groups. He was so sure his table was correct, he believed that tellurium's relative atomic mass was wrong.

| | Group 5 | | Group 6 | | Group 7 | |
|---|---|---|---|---|---|---|
| | N | 14 | O | 16 | F | 19 |
| | P | 31 | S | 32 | Cl | 35.5 |
| | As | 75 | Se | 79 | Br | 80 |
| | Sb | 122 | Te | 128 | I | 127 |

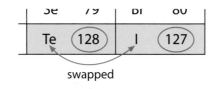

swapped

**E** Mendeleev broke his own rule to put iodine in the correct group.

In the modern Periodic Table, the elements are arranged in order of increasing atomic number. So iodine really does come after tellurium and Mendeleev was right all along.

**5** Explain why Mendeleev decided he should swap iodine and tellurium around in his table.

**6** How do we use numbers to describe atoms? Include in your answer the different particles in an atom, the arrangement of elements in the modern Periodic Table and the terms atomic number, mass number and relative atomic mass.

( Summary Exercise )

( Higher Questions )

# 3. Elements in the Periodic Table

**By the end of these two pages you should be able to:**

- explain that all atoms of any one element have the same atomic number
- explain that no two elements have the same atomic number
- describe the structure of an atom
- describe the connection between the number of outer electrons in an element and its position in the Periodic Table.

The number of protons in the nucleus of an atom is its atomic number. Because every element has a different number of protons, every element also has a different atomic number. In addition, all the atoms of each element have the same atomic number. For example, the atomic number of carbon is 6, so every carbon atom has six protons in its nucleus. If the atom had one less proton than this it would be a boron atom, and if the atom had one more proton than this it would be a nitrogen atom. This is why you cannot change one element into another element using **chemical reactions**.

## Have you ever wondered?

What makes platinum, diamond and zirconium look so different, when they're all made from the same basic ingredients?

|   | 1 | 2 | 3 | 4 | 5 | 6 | 7 | 0 |
|---|---|---|---|---|---|---|---|---|
| | 1 H 1 | | | | | | | 4 He 2 |
| | 7 Li 3 | 9 Be 4 | 11 B 5 | 12 C 6 | 14 N 7 | 16 O 8 | 19 F 9 | 20 Ne 10 |
| | 23 Na 11 | 24 Mg 12 | 27 Al 13 | 28 Si 14 | 31 P 15 | 32 S 16 | 35.5 Cl 17 | 40 Ar 18 |
| | 39 K 19 | 40 Ca 20 | | | | | | |

atomic number

**A** Each element has a unique atomic number.

The nucleus of an atom contains protons and neutrons. It is surrounded by clouds of electrons. The electrons are arranged in different **shells** around the nucleus, rather like the layers of an onion. The shells can only hold certain numbers of electrons. The first shell can contain up to two electrons and the next two can contain up to eight electrons. Other shells can contain more electrons than this.

In most atoms the outermost shell is not full. However, the atoms of Group 0 elements, the noble gases, all have full outer

1 One atom has 13 protons and another has 15 protons. What does this tell you about these two atoms?

2 Which subatomic particles are found in the nucleus?

3 What is the maximum number of electrons allowed in each of the first three shells?

shells. An **electron shell diagram** shows the arrangement of all the electrons in an atom. The particular arrangement of electrons in an atom is called its **electron configuration**.

The atoms of Group 0 elements all have full outer shells but the atoms of the other elements have incomplete outer shells. For example, a carbon atom has six electrons. Its first shell contains two electrons and is full, but the second shell (its outer shell) only contains four electrons. The electron shells always fill starting from the first shell, the innermost one.

## Have you ever wondered?

Can the Periodic Table help you learn chemistry in a lot less time?

A carbon atom has four electrons in its outer shell and carbon is in Group 4 of the Periodic Table. The number of electrons in the outer shell equals the group number. There are some exceptions. A hydrogen atom has one electron in its outer shell but hydrogen is not normally included in Group 1.

**4** Two different atoms have six electrons in their outer shell. Which group do they belong to?

**5 a** What do all the atoms of a particular element have in common?
   **b** The outer shell of atom X has three electrons and the outer shell of atom Y has five electrons. Do these atoms belong to elements in the same group or different groups? Give a reason for your answer.
   **c** What is the link between group number and the number of electrons in the outer shell?

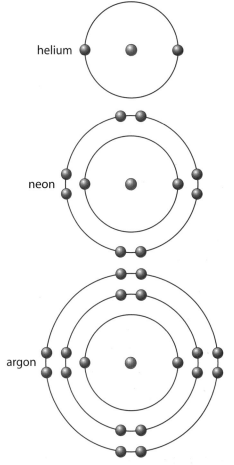

**B** Electron shell diagrams for the noble gases helium, neon and argon.

**C** Electron shell diagrams for the first twenty elements.

Summary Exercise          Higher Questions

# 4. Ions and ionic bonding

**By the end of these two pages you should be able to:**

- recall that an ion is an atom or group of atoms with a positive or negative charge
- describe how sodium ions (Na⁺) and chloride ions (Cl⁻) form
- work out which ions should form from a given atom
- explain that ionic bonds form between positive and negative ions.

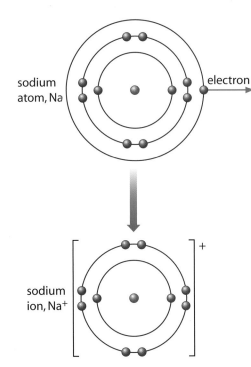

**A** The formation of a sodium ion from a sodium atom. The brackets show that the positive charge belongs to the whole ion and not just to part of it.

The atoms of most elements have incomplete outer shells of electrons. They can lose or gain electrons during chemical reactions to get full outer shells. Atoms that lose or gain electrons become charged particles called **ions**.

**1 a** What are ions?
 **b** How do ions form?

Metal atoms can lose electrons, which are negatively charged, to become positively charged ions. For example, Na atoms become Na⁺ ions. The '+' sign in the symbol tells you that the sodium ion has a single positive charge.

**2** Lithium atoms have three electrons: two in the first shell and one in the outer shell. Draw diagrams to show how a lithium ion, Li⁺, is formed from a lithium atom.

When a sodium atom becomes a sodium ion, the electron in the outer shell is lost. This is why sodium atoms, from Group 1, form Na⁺ ions with a single positive charge. Magnesium atoms, from Group 2, have two electrons in their outer shells so they form $Mg^{2+}$ ions. The '2' in front of the '+' sign shows that the ion has two positive charges.

| Group | 1 | 2 | 3 |
|---|---|---|---|
| **Charge on ion** | 1+ | 2+ | 3+ |
| **Example** | Na⁺ | $Mg^{2+}$ | $Al^{3+}$ |

**B** The link between group number and the symbol for a metal ion.

**3** Predict the symbols of the ions formed by the following metals:
 **a** Potassium, K, found in Group 1
 **b** Calcium, Ca, found in Group 2.

When an atom gains electrons, it becomes a negatively charged ion. Non-metal atoms can gain electrons to become negatively charged ions. For example, Cl atoms become $Cl^-$ ions. The '−' sign in the symbol tells you that the ion has a single negative charge. When non-metal atoms form ions, the end of the name changes to -ide, so $Cl^-$ is the chloride ion.

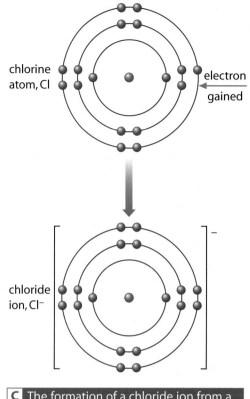

**4** Fluorine atoms have nine electrons: two in the first shell and seven in the outer shell. Draw diagrams to show how a fluoride ion, $F^-$, is formed from a fluorine atom.

Non-metal atoms form ions by gaining just enough electrons to fill their outer shells. For example, chlorine is in Group 7. Its outer shell can hold eight electrons, but contains only seven electrons. So it needs one electron to fill the outer shell, forming a $Cl^-$ ion. Oxygen is in Group 6. Its outer shell can hold eight electrons but contains only six electrons. So it needs two electrons to fill the outer shell and forms the oxide ion, $O^{2-}$.

| Group | 5 | 6 | 7 |
|---|---|---|---|
| **Charge on ion** | 3− | 2− | 1− |
| **Example** | $N^{3-}$ | $O^{2-}$ | $Cl^-$ |

**D** The number of negative charges on a non-metal ion is equal to eight minus the group number.

**C** The formation of a chloride ion from a chlorine atom.

**5** Predict the symbols of the ions formed by the following non-metals:
**a** Bromine, Br, found in Group 7
**b** Sulphur, S, found in Group 6.

Sodium and chlorine react to form sodium chloride. During the reaction, electrons are transferred from the outer shells of sodium atoms to the outer shells of chlorine atoms. $Na^+$ ions and $Cl^-$ ions are formed. They have opposite charges, so they attract each other. The force of attraction between oppositely charged ions makes a chemical bond called an **ionic bond**. Substances that contain ions, like sodium chloride, are called **ionic compounds**.

**6 a** Why do sodium atoms form $Na^+$ ions and chlorine atoms form $Cl^-$ ions?
**b** Why are there ionic bonds in sodium chloride?

Summary Exercise

Higher Questions

# 5. Ions and giant structures

**By the end of these two pages you should be able to:**

- predict the formulae of ionic compounds, given the charges on the ions
- describe and explain the physical properties of giant ionic structures.

You can work out the **formulae** of ionic compounds if you know the ions they contain. Sodium chloride contains sodium ions, $Na^+$, and chloride ions, $Cl^-$. Ionic compounds are neutral overall because they contain equal numbers of positive and negative charges. Since the $Na^+$ ion has one positive charge, and the $Cl^-$ ion has one negative charge, the formula of sodium chloride is $NaCl$. You do not need to write the + and − signs because they have cancelled each other out.

It is the same when both ions have two charges. For example, magnesium oxide contains magnesium ions, $Mg^{2+}$, and oxide ions, $O^{2-}$. So the formula of magnesium oxide is $MgO$.

**3** Calcium oxide contains $Ca^{2+}$ ions and $O^{2-}$ ions. What is its formula?

Many ionic compounds have ions with different numbers of charges. For example, sodium oxide contains $Na^+$ ions and $O^{2-}$ ions. Two $Na^+$ ions give us a total of two positive charges that cancel out the two negative charges on the $O^{2-}$ ion. The formula of sodium oxide is $Na_2O$.

**4** Aluminium oxide contains $Al^{3+}$ ions and $O^{2-}$ ions. What is its formula?

Groups of atoms can also become ions by losing or gaining electrons. These ions are sometimes called **compound ions** because they contain more than one element. For example, the hydroxide ion $OH^-$ consists of an oxygen atom joined to a hydrogen atom and an extra electron.

**A** The number of $Na^+$ ions and $Cl^-$ ions in a crystal of sodium chloride is enormous, but there are equal numbers of each.

**1** Potassium chloride contains $K^+$ ions and $Cl^-$ ions. What is its formula?

**2** Lithium bromide contains $Li^+$ ions and $Br^-$ ions. What is its formula?

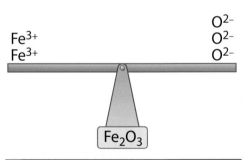

**B** It may help to imagine balancing the charges on a see-saw.

| Element ions | | Charge |
|---|---|---|
| sodium | $Na^+$ | 1+ |
| calcium | $Ca^{2+}$ | 2+ |
| magnesium | $Mg^{2+}$ | 2+ |
| aluminium | $Al^{3+}$ | 3+ |
| chloride | $Cl^-$ | 1− |
| oxide | $O^{2-}$ | 2− |

| Compound ions | | Charge |
|---|---|---|
| ammonium | $NH_4^+$ | 1+ |
| hydrogen carbonate | $HCO_3^-$ | 1− |
| hydroxide | $OH^-$ | 1− |
| nitrate | $NO_3^-$ | 1− |
| carbonate | $CO_3^{2-}$ | 2− |
| sulphate | $SO_4^{2-}$ | 2− |

**C** Some common ions.

There is one extra rule when we write formulae using these ions: if more than one compound ion is needed to balance the charges you need to put it in brackets. Sodium hydroxide contains $Na^+$ ions and $OH^-$ ions, and its formula is NaOH. Magnesium hydroxide contains $Mg^{2+}$ ions and $OH^-$ ions, and its formula is $Mg(OH)_2$. This is because we need two hydroxide ions to balance the two positive charges on the magnesium ion. The brackets show that the '2' applies to the whole compound ion.

5 Work out the formulae of the following compounds:
 a aluminium hydroxide
 b calcium nitrate
 c sodium sulphate
 d ammonium carbonate.

Ionic compounds form **giant ionic structures**. This doesn't mean that the ions are giant, just that there are billions of them joined together in a regular way.

The regular arrangement of ions, called a **lattice**, gives crystals their regular shapes. Different crystals have different shapes because their ions are arranged differently. The ions in sodium chloride pack together in a box-like arrangement, so sodium chloride crystals form cubes.

6 Describe how the ions are arranged in sodium chloride.

Ionic compounds are solid at room temperature. This is because ionic bonds (the forces of attraction between oppositely charged ions) are very strong. A lot of energy is needed to break these bonds. This gives the compounds high melting points and boiling points. Ionic compounds can conduct electricity when they are molten (in their liquid state) or when they are dissolved. This is because their ions are free to move and carry electrical charge from place to place.

7 a Magnesium oxide has a higher boiling point than sodium chloride. Which compound is likely to have the strongest ionic bonds? Explain your answer.
 b Explain why sodium chloride forms crystals with a regular shape.

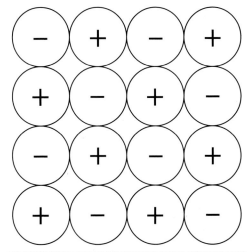

**D** Simplified diagram of the arrangement of ions in an ionic compound.

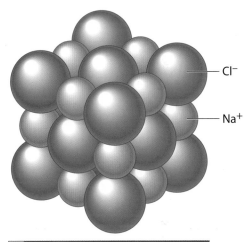

Cl⁻

Na⁺

**E** The structure of sodium chloride.

Summary Exercise

Higher Questions

# 6. Electrolysis of salts and solutions

**By the end of these two pages you should be able to:**

- recall that electrolysis is the movement of ions towards oppositely charged electrodes
- predict the products when a given salt undergoes electrolysis
- write balanced half equations for the reactions at the electrodes.

Within weeks of the display of the first battery in 1800, William Nicholson (1753–1815) had made his own and used it to pass electricity through water. He found that hydrogen and oxygen were given off: the electricity had split or **decomposed** the water into its elements. Decomposing a compound into simpler substances using electricity is called **electrolysis**, and it works because of ions.

**1** What is chemical electrolysis?

**A** Water is decomposed into hydrogen and oxygen by electrolysis.

## Have you ever wondered?

How does hair removal by electrolysis work?

For electrolysis to work, you need three things:
- an electricity supply
- two **electrodes**
- an ionic compound, either molten (in liquid form) or in **solution** (dissolved in water).

Electrodes are rods of an unreactive electrical conductor, usually graphite, copper or platinum. One electrode, the **cathode**, is negatively charged. The other electrode, the **anode**, is positively charged. As opposite charges attract, ions are attracted towards the oppositely charged electrode. Positively charged ions, like hydrogen ions and metal ions, are attracted to the negative electrode. Negatively charged ions, like oxide and other non-metal ions, are attracted to the positive electrode. The ions must be free to move, and this only happens when the substance is molten or in solution.

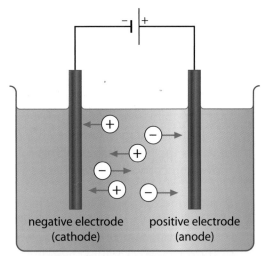

**B** Ions move towards oppositely charged electrodes during electrolysis.

**2** What is an electrode?

**3** Why are ions attracted to electrodes?

**H** Electrolysis is often demonstrated using copper chloride solution or molten lead bromide. Both compounds are **binary salts** because they are made of two elements only, a metal and a non-metal. When copper chloride solution is electrolysed, copper forms at one electrode and chlorine at the other.

> **4** What is a binary salt?
>
> **5** Where will copper form during the electrolysis of copper chloride? Explain your answer.

Aluminium and oxygen are produced by the electrolysis of molten aluminium oxide. Similarly, lead and bromine are produced by the electrolysis of molten lead bromide. Lead ions are attracted to the cathode, where they receive electrons and become lead atoms. The balanced equation for the reaction at the cathode is:

$$Pb^{2+}(aq) + 2e^- \rightarrow Pb(s)$$

Notice that the symbol for an electron is $e^-$. We need to add two electrons to change a lead ion $Pb^{2+}$ into a lead atom. This equation is a **half equation**. It shows what happens at one of the electrodes. **State symbols** are used in the equations: (s) means the substance is solid, (l) means liquid, (g) means gas, and (aq) means aqueous or dissolved in water.

Bromide ions are attracted to the anode, where they lose electrons and form bromine molecules:

$$2Br^-(aq) \rightarrow Br_2(l) + 2e^-$$

Electrolysis is used on an industrial scale to produce important **raw materials** from concentrated sodium chloride solution (salt water or brine). There are three products of this process: hydrogen, chlorine and sodium hydroxide solution.

> **6** Write balanced half equations for the reaction of $H^+$ ions at the cathode and the reaction of $Cl^-$ ions at the anode.

In the electrolysis of a molten binary salt, the hydrogen or metal in the salt is always deposited at the cathode, and the non-metal is always deposited at the anode.

> **7 a** Which ions are attracted to the cathode? Give two examples.
> **b** Which ions are attracted to the anode? Give an example.
> **c** Why does electrolysis only happen when the substance is molten or in solution?

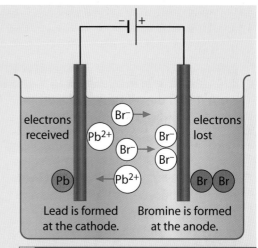

electrons received    electrons lost

Lead is formed at the cathode.    Bromine is formed at the anode.

**C** The electrolysis of molten lead bromide.

**D** Electrolysis being carried out on an industrial scale.

**Summary Exercise**

**Higher Questions**

# 7. Isotopes

**By the end of these two pages you should be able to:**

P   H
- explain the existence of isotopes
- calculate the relative atomic mass of an element from the relative masses and abundance of its isotopes.

An English chemist called John Dalton (1766–1844) did many careful experiments early in the nineteenth century. He used his results to come up with the first detailed atomic theory of matter. Two of Dalton's ideas about atoms and elements are:
- all the atoms of an element are identical
- the atoms of any one element are different from those of any other element.

All atoms of a given element contain the same number of protons, or atomic number. No two elements have the same atomic number. So, an atom with one proton can only be a hydrogen atom, and an atom with seventeen protons can only be a chlorine atom.

But Dalton was not entirely correct. All the atoms of an element contain identical numbers of protons and electrons, but we now know that the number of neutrons can vary. Atoms of an element with the same number of protons and electrons but different numbers of neutrons are called **isotopes**. The isotopes of an element have identical chemical properties because they have the same number of electrons.

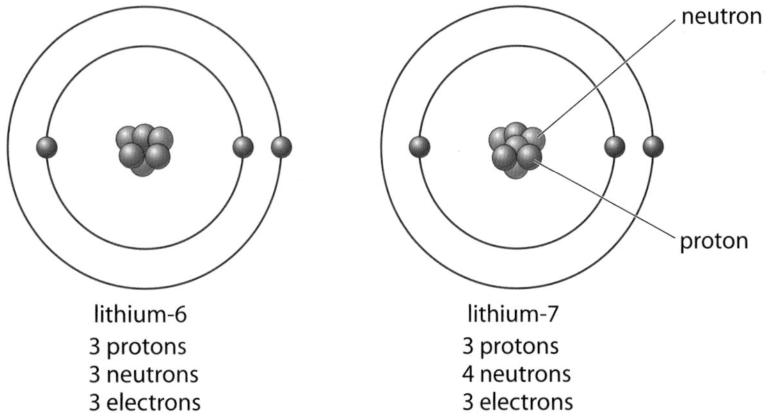

**1** In terms of their protons, why are hydrogen and chlorine different elements?

neutron

proton

| lithium-6 | lithium-7 |
|-----------|-----------|
| 3 protons | 3 protons |
| 3 neutrons | 4 neutrons |
| 3 electrons | 3 electrons |

**A** These isotopes of lithium both have three protons and electrons, but one has three neutrons and the other has four neutrons.

**2** What is an isotope?

**3** Why do the different isotopes of lithium have identical chemical properties?

You know that the atomic number of an element is the number of protons, and the mass number of an element is the number of protons and neutrons added together. So, isotopes of an element have the same atomic number because they contain the same number of protons, but their mass number is different because they contain different numbers of neutrons.

Isotopes are named after their mass number. For example, most hydrogen atoms are $_1^1H$, which is called hydrogen-1, but there are two other isotopes of hydrogen: hydrogen-2 and hydrogen-3.

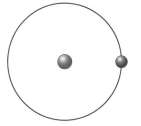 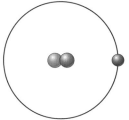 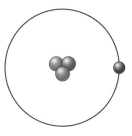

hydrogen-1

1 proton
0 neutron
1 electron

hydrogen-2

1 proton
1 neutron
1 electron

hydrogen-3

1 proton
2 neutrons
1 electron

**B** Three isotopes of hydrogen.

**C** Hydrogen-2 and hydrogen-3 are used in thermonuclear bombs.

### Have you ever wondered?

Did you know scientists can make 'heavy water', so that an ice cube sinks?

### Have you ever wondered?

How do scientists detect new elements (such as element-115) if they only last milliseconds before disintegrating?

**4** Hydrogen-2 is $_1^2H$. Write down the full chemical symbol for hydrogen-3.

**5** Suggest why hydrogen gas made from hydrogen-2 is called 'heavy hydrogen', and water made with it is called 'heavy water'.

**H** When you look at the Periodic Table, you will see that the relative atomic masses are usually shown as whole numbers. But when precise numbers are given, you can see that they are only close to being whole numbers. For example, the precise relative atomic mass of hydrogen is 1.00794 because natural hydrogen is 99.985 per cent hydrogen-1, with tiny percentages of hydrogen-2 and hydrogen-3. So, its relative atomic mass is usually shown as 1.

If chlorine only had one isotope, its relative atomic mass would be a whole number. Its relative atomic mass is 35.5 so there cannot be just one isotope of chlorine. In fact, there are two isotopes of chlorine in chlorine gas: 75 per cent is $_{17}^{35}Cl$ and 25 per cent is $_{17}^{37}Cl$. You can calculate the relative atomic mass of chlorine using these numbers.

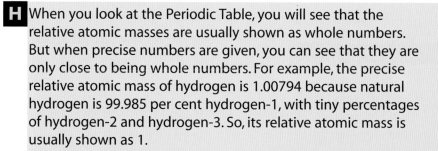

$$\text{relative atomic mass} = \frac{(75 \times 35) + (25 \times 37)}{100} = \frac{2625 + 925}{100} = \frac{3550}{100} = 35.5$$

**6** What is meant by these phrases?
  **a** relative atomic mass
  **b** mass number

**7** Bromine contains two isotopes: 50% is $_{35}^{79}Br$ and 50% is $_{35}^{81}Br$. Calculate the relative atomic mass of bromine.

**8** Explain, as fully as you can, why $_6^{12}C$ and $_6^{14}C$ are isotopes of carbon.

**Summary Exercise**

**Higher Questions**

# 8. Reactions of alkali metals

**By the end of these two pages you should be able to:**

- explain the trends in reactivity of the alkali metals by looking at the arrangements of their electrons
- **H** explain that reactions of an element depend on the arrangement of electrons in the outer shell of its atoms.

Group 1 is found on the left-hand side of the Periodic Table. All the elements in the group are metals. Like other metals, they are shiny when freshly cut, they are solid at room temperature, and they are good conductors of heat and electricity. But unlike other metals they are very **reactive**. They react rapidly and even violently with water. The reason for this reactivity lies with their electron configurations.

| 7 |
|---|
| Li |
| lithium |
| 3 |

| 23 |
|---|
| Na |
| sodium |
| 11 |

| 39 |
|---|
| K |
| potassium |
| 19 |

| 85 |
|---|
| Rb |
| rubidium |
| 37 |

| 133 |
|---|
| Cs |
| caesium |
| 55 |

| (223) |
|---|
| Fr |
| francium |
| 87 |

**A** Group 1, also called the alkali metals.

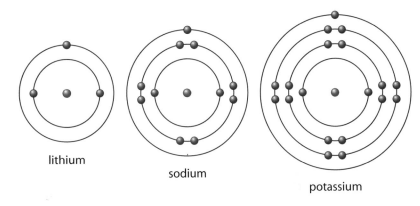

lithium

sodium

potassium

**B** Electron shell diagrams for lithium, sodium and potassium atoms.

**1** Look at the electron shell diagrams for lithium, sodium and potassium. What do they have in common?

**2** Sodium floats, so why can't it be used to make ships?

The Group 1 elements are often called the **alkali metals** because they form **alkaline** hydroxides when they react with water. The outer shells of all alkali metals have just one electron in them. This electron is transferred to another element during reactions, and the metal atom becomes a metal ion with a single positive charge.

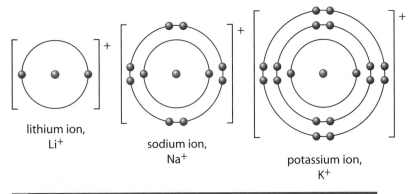

lithium ion,
Li$^+$

sodium ion,
Na$^+$

potassium ion,
K$^+$

**C** Electron shell diagrams for lithium, sodium and potassium ions.

**3** Why do all the alkali metals form ions with a single positive charge?

The alkali metals become more reactive as you go down the group. Lithium, at the top of the group, is the least reactive. Potassium, near the middle of the group, is the most reactive metal that you are likely to see because it reacts violently with water. We can explain this gradual change or **trend** in reactivity by looking at the electron shell diagrams for the alkali metals.

As you go down the group, the outer electron of each atom is further away from the nucleus because there are more filled shells between the nucleus and the outer electron. This means that the force of attraction between the positively charged nucleus and the negatively charged electron gets weaker as you go down the group. So, the outer electron is more easily lost during chemical reactions. The more easily the outer electron is lost, the more reactive the alkali metal is.

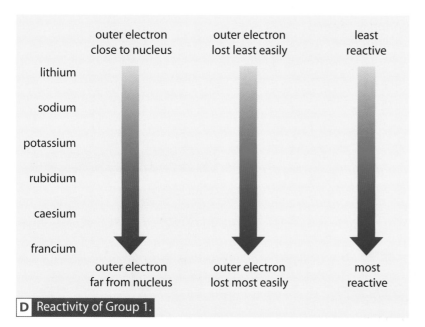

**D** Reactivity of Group 1.

**4** Which alkali metal loses its outer electron with the most difficulty?

**5** Why is francium is the most reactive alkali metal?

**H** The reactions of an element depend upon the arrangement of electrons in the outer shell of its atoms. Consider three metals from different groups in the same **period**. Sodium reacts violently with chlorine, magnesium reacts vigorously with it, and aluminium reacts slowly. You can see that the more electrons a metal atom must lose to form an ion, the less reactive the metal is.

**6 a** How many electrons will there be in the outer shells of sodium, magnesium and aluminium atoms?
  **b** Write down the symbols for the ions formed by these metals.
  **c** Which of these metals is likely to lose its outer electrons with the most difficulty? Explain your answer.

**7** Explain, mentioning electrons in your answer, why the alkali metals become more reactive going down Group 1.

Summary Exercise

Higher Questions

# 9. Reactivity of the halogens

**By the end of these two pages you should be able to:**

- explain the trends in reactivity of the halogens by looking at the arrangements of their electrons.

## Have you ever wondered?

If fluorine is so deadly, why do we add it to drinking water?

Group 7 is on the right-hand side of the Periodic Table, just to the left of the noble gases in Group 0. All the elements in the group are reactive non-metals. They are also **toxic** and must be handled with care. Chlorine, for example, was used as a poison gas in World War I. In smaller amounts chlorine is used to **sterilise** drinking water and water in swimming pools, keeping us safe from harmful microorganisms.

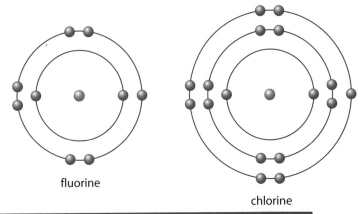

**C** Electron shell diagrams for fluorine and chlorine atoms.

The Group 7 elements are often called the **halogens**, which means 'salt formers', because they react with metals to make salts. The outer shells of all halogens need just one more electron to be complete. This electron is gained from another element during reactions, and the non-metal atom becomes a non-metal ion with a single negative charge.

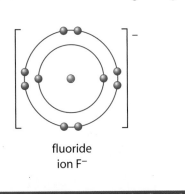
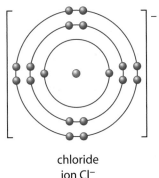

**D** Electron shell diagrams for fluoride and chloride ions.

| | |
|---|---|
| 19 | |
| F | |
| fluorine | |
| 9 | |
| 35.5 | |
| Cl | |
| chlorine | |
| 17 | |
| 80 | |
| Br | |
| bromine | |
| 35 | |
| 127 | |
| I | |
| iodine | |
| 53 | |
| (210) | |
| At | |
| astatine | |
| 85 | |

**A** Group 7, also called the halogens.

**B** Gas masks were used during World War I to protect against chlorine gas attacks.

1 Look at the electron shell diagrams for fluorine and chlorine. What do they have in common?

2 Why is chlorine used to treat drinking water?

3 Why do all the halogens form ions with a single negative charge?

The halogens become less reactive as you go down the group. Fluorine, at the top of the group, is the most reactive. It will even react with glass, so it is too dangerous to use fluorine in school. Iodine, near the bottom of the group, is much less reactive. You can explain this trend in reactivity by looking at the electron shell diagrams for the halogens.

As you go down the group, the outer shell of each atom is further away from the nucleus. This means that the force of attraction between the positively charged nucleus and negatively charged electrons becomes weaker as you go down the group. As a result, it becomes more difficult to gain the extra electron needed to complete the outer shell during chemical reactions. The more difficult it is to gain an electron, the less reactive the halogen is.

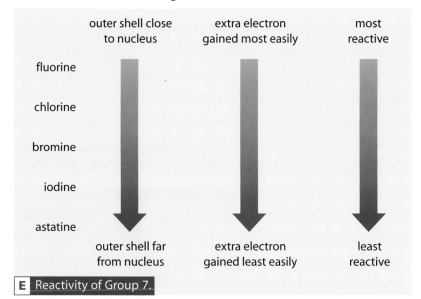

**E** Reactivity of Group 7.

The halogens react with metals to make salts. For example, aluminium reacts with bromine to make aluminium bromide:

$$\text{aluminium} + \text{bromine} \longrightarrow \text{aluminium bromide}$$
$$2Al(s) + 3Br_2(l) \longrightarrow 2AlBr_3(s)$$

The more easily the halogen can gain an electron from the metal, and the more easily the metal loses electrons, the more vigorous the reaction is.

A more reactive halogen can push out or displace a less reactive halogen from its compounds. For example, bromine is made industrially by passing chlorine gas through sea water, which contains bromine compounds such as sodium bromide. This works because chlorine can gain electrons from bromide ions, forming chloride ions and bromine:

$$Cl_2(g) + 2Br^-(aq) \longrightarrow 2Cl^-(aq) + Br_2(l)$$

**Summary Exercise**

4  Which halogen has the most difficulty gaining an outer electron?

5  Why is fluorine is the most reactive halogen?

6  Which reaction is likely to be most vigorous, the reaction between sodium and chlorine, or the reaction between sodium and iodine? Explain your answer by mentioning electrons.

7  Explain, mentioning electrons in your answer, why the halogens become less reactive going down the group.

**Higher Questions**

# 10. The noble gases

**By the end of these two pages you should be able to:**

- explain that the noble gases are unreactive because their outer shells are full
- write down the electron configurations of the first 20 elements in the Periodic Table, given the atomic numbers.

## Have you ever wondered?

Did you know the atoms in your body were born in a star?

Group 0 is on the right-hand side of the Periodic Table. All the elements in the group are very unreactive non-metal gases. Helium is less dense than air and is used to make balloons rise. Argon is used to provide an unreactive atmosphere during welding to prevent the hot molten metal from oxidising.

Electric lamps contain argon, krypton or xenon. These allow the metal filament to glow brightly without burning. The reason why the Group 0 elements are unreactive is related to their electron configurations.

| 4 |
|---|
| He |
| helium |
| 2 |

| 20 |
|---|
| Ne |
| neon |
| 10 |

| 40 |
|---|
| Ar |
| argon |
| 18 |

| 84 |
|---|
| Kr |
| krypton |
| 36 |

| 131 |
|---|
| Xe |
| xenon |
| 54 |

| (222) |
|---|
| Rn |
| radon |
| 86 |

**A** Group 0, also called the noble gases.

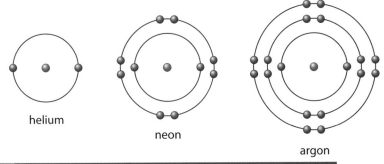

helium

neon

argon

**C** Electron shell diagrams for helium, neon and argon atoms.

**1** Look at the electron shell diagrams for helium, neon and argon. What do they have in common?

The Group 0 elements are often called the **noble gases** because they are 'too posh' to react with other elements. The outer shells of all noble gases are already complete. This means that they have no tendency to lose or gain electrons, so they do not take part in chemical reactions. It is possible to ionise the noble gases but you need high-voltage electricity, not a chemical reaction.

You have seen how you can work out the properties of elements by studying their electron configurations. This configuration is linked to an element's position in the Periodic Table. This means you can easily work out the electron configuration of any of the first 20 elements.

**B** Modern car headlights contain xenon to produce a really bright beam of light.

**2** Why are the noble gases unreactive?

| 1 | 2 | 3 | 4 | 5 | 6 | 7 | 0 |
|---|---|---|---|---|---|---|---|
| H<br>hydrogen<br>1 | | | | | | | He<br>helium<br>2 |
| Li<br>lithium<br>3 | Be<br>beryllium<br>4 | B<br>boron<br>5 | C<br>carbon<br>6 | N<br>nitrogen<br>7 | O<br>oxygen<br>8 | F<br>fluorine<br>9 | Ne<br>neon<br>10 |
| Na<br>sodium<br>11 | Mg<br>magnesium<br>12 | Al<br>aluminium<br>13 | Si<br>silicon<br>14 | P<br>phosphorus<br>15 | S<br>sulphur<br>16 | Cl<br>chlorine<br>17 | Ar<br>argon<br>18 |
| K<br>potassium<br>19 | Ca<br>calcium<br>20 | | | | | | |

**D** The symbols, names and atomic numbers of the first 20 elements.

There is a useful shorthand for electron configurations. Potassium, for example, has 19 protons and 19 electrons because its atomic number is 19. Its atoms have two electrons in the first shell, eight in the second and third shells, and one in the outer shell. You can write this as 2, 8, 8, 1 instead of drawing the diagram. You can use the Periodic Table to work out electron configurations.

- Find out which period the element is in (remember that hydrogen and helium are in period 1). This is the number of circles to draw.
- Find out which group the element is in. This is how many electrons you need to draw in the outer shell.
- Fill in the other shells with the maximum number of electrons allowed (2 then 8 then 8).
- Write out the electron configuration from the diagram.

There is another way to use the Periodic Table, this time relying on counting.

- Find the element in the Periodic Table.
- Count along each period from hydrogen until you reach the element. Each time you get to the end of a period put a comma after the number of elements you have counted.

For potassium, count two elements to helium, then eight from lithium to neon, eight from sodium to argon, and finally one to reach potassium.

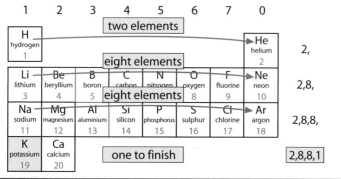

**F** Counting elements to work out the electron configuration of potassium.

potassium

**E** The electron shell diagram for potassium.

3 What is the maximum number of electrons allowed in the first and second shells?

4 a What are the atomic numbers of the following elements: helium, nitrogen, sodium, aluminium, chlorine, calcium?
  b Write electron configurations and draw electron shell diagrams for these elements.
  c Why are there no helium compounds?

**Summary Exercise**

**Higher Questions**

## Multiple choice questions

**1** Metals usually have high melting and boiling points because
  **A** they have strong bonds.
  **B** they have layers of electrons.
  **C** they are shiny and reflect the heat.
  **D** they have tiny atoms.

**2** Which of the following is true about atom $_4^{10}X$?
  **A** It has ten protons.
  **B** It has ten neutrons.
  **C** It has six neutrons.
  **D** It has six electrons.

**3** If the relative mass of a proton is 1 and its relative charge is +1, you know that
  **A** the relative mass of a neutron is almost zero.
  **B** the relative charge of an electron is –1.
  **C** the relative mass of an electron is –1.
  **D** the relative charge of a neutron is –1.

**4** An element Y has two electrons in its outer shell. This tells you that
  **A** it is in Group 2.
  **B** it is in Group 6.
  **C** it is a non-metal.
  **D** it forms ions with a 2– charge.

**5** When a metal reacts with a non-metal
  **A** the metal and non-metal lose electrons to form positive ions.
  **B** the metal and non-metal gain electrons to form negative ions.
  **C** the metal gains electrons from the non-metal.
  **D** the metal transfers electrons to the non-metal.

**6** Sodium ions are $Na^+$ and sulphate ions are $SO_4^{2-}$. What is the correct formula for sodium sulphate?
  **A** $Na^+SO_4^{2-}$
  **B** $NaSO_4$
  **C** $Na(SO_4)_2$
  **D** $Na_2SO_4$

**7** Ionic compounds such as sodium chloride conduct electricity when molten or in solution because
  **A** they contain electrons that are free to move.
  **B** they contain protons that are free to move.
  **C** they contain atoms that are free to move.
  **D** they contain ions that are free to move.

**8** Which of the following pairs of atoms are really isotopes of the same element?
  **A** $_2^4Y$ and $_2^5Y$
  **B** $_2^5Y$ and $_3^5Y$
  **C** $_4^4Y$ and $_5^5Y$
  **D** $_4^6Y$ and $_2^3Y$

**9** Which statement about trends in Groups 1 and 7 is correct?
  **A** Going down Group 1 it becomes easier to gain an electron so the elements get more reactive.
  **B** Going down Group 7 it becomes easier to gain an electron so the elements get less reactive.
  **C** Going down Group 1 it becomes easier to lose an electron so the elements get more reactive.
  **D** Going down Group 7 it becomes easier to lose an electron so the elements get less reactive.

**10** Element Z has an electron configuration of 2, 8, 5 – what does this tell you?
  **A** It is in the fifth period.
  **B** It is in Group 5.
  **C** It forms negative ions with a charge of –5.
  **D** It is a metal.

**H** **11** What products are formed during the electrolysis of molten sodium chloride?
  **A** hydrogen and chlorine
  **B** sodium and chlorine
  **C** sodium and chloride
  **D** sodium hydroxide and hydrochloric acid

**12** Which of the following is the correctly balanced half equation for a reaction at the cathode during electrolysis?
  **A** $H^+(aq) + e^- \longrightarrow H(g)$
  **B** $H(g) + e^- \longrightarrow H^-(aq)$
  **C** $2H^+(aq) \longrightarrow H_2(g) + 2e^-$
  **D** $2H^+(aq) + 2e^- \longrightarrow H_2(g)$

**13** Copper contains two isotopes, 69 per cent is copper-63 and 31 per cent is copper-65. What is the relative atomic mass of copper?
  **A** 69.0
  **B** 64.4
  **C** 64.0
  **D** 63.6

**14** Element X is in Group 6. What is the charge on its ion?

    **A** –6

    **B** –2

    **C** +2

    **D** +6

**15** Element Z is in period 3 and Group 6. Which statement about element Z is correct?

    **A** Its electron configuration must be 3, 6.

    **B** Its electron configuration must be 2, 6.

    **C** Its electron configuration must be 2, 8, 6.

    **D** It must form ions with a 3– charge.

## Short-answer questions

**1** Jayne was interested in the properties and uses of aluminium. She found this information about the metal on an Internet site recommended by her teacher:

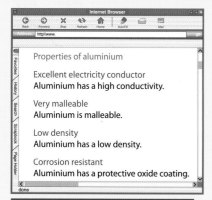

Some of Jayne's research results.

  **a** Which properties make aluminium suitable for making aircraft panels?

  **b** Which property makes aluminium suitable for making overhead electricity cables? Explain why metals have this property.

  **c** Which property makes aluminium suitable for moulding into drinks cans? Explain why metals have this property.

**2** A certain atom of element X has the following properties:

    • a nucleus containing 17 protons and 18 neutrons

    • 17 electrons surrounding the nucleus.

  **a** What is the atomic number and mass number of this atom?

  **b** What is the electron configuration of this atom?

  **c** Draw the electron shell diagram for this atom.

  **d** To which group in the Periodic Table does element X belong?

  **e** Use the Periodic Table to identify element X.

  **f** Write the full chemical symbol for the atom.

**3** Here are the electron shell diagrams for magnesium and chlorine.

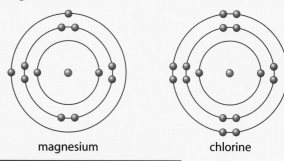

magnesium       chlorine

Magnesium and chlorine atoms.

The two elements react together vigorously to form magnesium chloride.

  **a** Draw the electron shell diagrams for a magnesium ion, $Mg^{2+}$, and a chloride ion, $Cl^-$. What do you notice?

  **b** What sort of chemical bond is present in magnesium chloride?

  **c** Why is magnesium chloride solid at room temperature?

  **d** What is the formula of magnesium chloride?

**4** The alkali metals become more reactive as you go down Group 1 but the halogens become less reactive as you go down Group 7. The noble gases of Group 0 are very unreactive.

  **a** Explain the trend in reactivity of the alkali metals.

  **b** Explain the trend in reactivity of the halogens.

  **c** Explain why the noble gases are unreactive.

**H** **5** Molten sodium chloride, NaCl, is an ionic compound that can be decomposed into its elements by electrolysis.

  **a** What two products are formed during the electrolysis of molten sodium chloride?

  **b** Write balanced half equations for the reactions at the two electrodes.

  **c** Explain why solid sodium chloride will not conduct electricity.

**6** Rubidium exists as two isotopes, $^{85}_{37}Rb$ and $^{87}_{37}Rb$.

  **a** Why are these two atoms isotopes of the same element?

  **b** In natural samples of rubidium, 72 per cent is rubidium-85 and 28 per cent is rubidium-87. Calculate the relative atomic mass of rubidium.

# 12. Glossary

**alkali metal** An element found in Group 1.

**alkaline** A substance that turns universal indicator paper blue and has a pH greater than 7.

***alloy** A mixture of metals or metals and non-metals.

***anode** A positive electrode.

***atomic number** The number of protons (positively charged particles) in the nucleus of an atom.

**atoms** A particle that is the smallest part of an element that can exist. An atom consists of protons and neutrons in a nucleus surrounded by electrons.

***binary salt** A compound of a metal and a non-metal.

**bond** An attractive force that holds atoms together in molecules and ions together in crystals.

**cathode** A negative electrode.

**chemical reaction** A chemical change in which new substances are formed but there is no change in the number of atoms of each element.

**chemical symbol** An abbreviation for an element which consists of one, two or sometimes three letters.

**compound ion** An electrically charged group of two or more different atoms. For example, the sulphate ion $SO_4^{2-}$ consists of one sulphur atom and four oxygen atoms, with two negative charges overall.

***conductivity** A property of a substance that describes its ability to allow energy (electricity or heat) to pass through it.

**decompose** To break down a compound into simpler substances.

**ductile** Can be stretched into wires.

***electrode** A rod of conductive material used in electrolysis, for example, graphite or platinum.

***electrolysis** The breakdown of an ionic compound into simpler substances using electricity.

***electron** A negatively charged particle that surrounds the nucleus in an atom.

***electron configuration** The arrangement of electrons in shells around the nucleus.

**electron shell diagram** A picture that shows the arrangement of electrons in shells around the nucleus.

**element** A substance made of only one type of atom. An element cannot be turned into another element or anything simpler using a chemical reaction.

***formulae** Abbreviations for substances with two or more atoms. The formula contains the symbols for the different elements in the substance, with numbers to show if there are two or more atoms of a particular element present.

**giant ionic structure** A repeated regular arrangement of oppositely charged ions.

**group** A column of the Periodic Table.

**half equation** Equation to show the reaction at an electrode.

**halogen** A family of reactive non-metals found in Group 7 of the Periodic Table.

***ion** An atom or group of atoms with an electrical charge. Ions can either be positively or negatively charged due to losing or gaining electrons.

**ionic bond** Force between oppositely charged ions.

**ionic compound** A substance made of oppositely charged ions.

***isotopes** Atoms of an element with the same number of protons and electrons but different numbers of neutrons.

**lattice** The arrangement of ions in a regular pattern giving crystals their regular shape.

***malleable** Can be bent or hammered into shape without breaking.

***mass number** The total number of protons and neutrons in the nucleus of an atom. Also called nucleon number.

***neutron** Electrically neutral particle found in the nucleus of most atoms.

**noble gas** An element found in Group 0.

***nucleus** In chemistry, the positively charged centre of an atom.

**particle** A tiny piece of matter, such as an atom or molecule.

**period** A row of the Periodic Table.

***Periodic Table** A chart in which all the elements are put in order of increasing atomic number, with elements that have similar chemical properties arranged in groups.

**properties** The characteristics of a substance. Chemical properties describe how the substance reacts with other substances. Physical properties include information such as colour, melting point and state.

***proton** A positively charged particle found in the nucleus of all atoms.

**raw material** A starting substance for the manufacture of a particular chemical.

**reactive** Likely to react with other substances.

***relative atomic mass** The mass of an atom compared to the mass of a carbon atom, which has a relative atomic mass of 12.

**shell** Space around a nucleus that can be occupied by electrons, usually drawn as a circle.

**solution** The mixture formed when a substance dissolves in water.

**state symbols** symbols used in chemical equations to show whether a substance is solid (s), liquid (l), gas (g) or dissolved in water, aqueous (aq).

**sterilise** To kill microorganisms such as bacteria.

**toxic** A poisonous substance. Toxic substances may cause death if they are swallowed, breathed in or come into contact with the skin.

**trend** A general direction in which something changes.

*glossary words from the specification

# Chemical structures

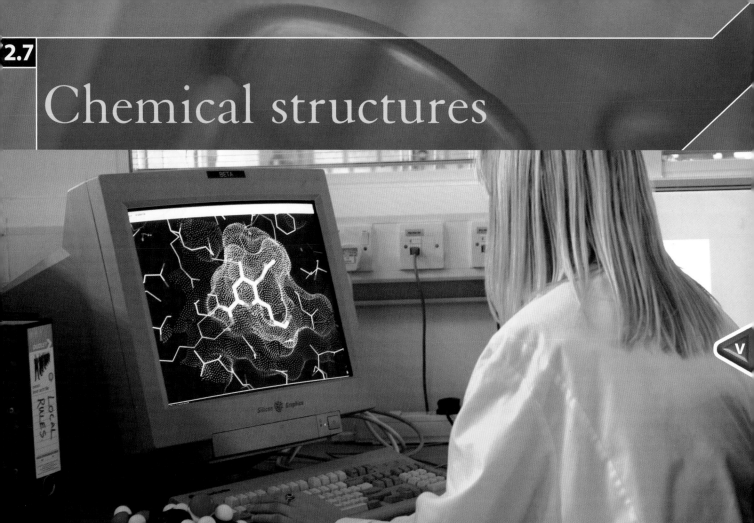

**A** Computer modelling is now an important part of the process of designing new drugs.

In the past, many scientific breakthroughs such as the discovery of new medicines were made by chance. That can still be true today but, increasingly, scientists are using their understanding of chemistry to design new drugs for specific purposes. Molecules can be modelled in 3-D on a computer screen to see how they will react. Promising new chemicals are then made in the laboratory and tested by experiment.

Before you can do this, you have to understand the ways in which atoms can join together. You have seen how metals and non-metals can form ionic compounds by the giving and taking electrons – but how can non-metals join together to form molecules on their own? In this case, it's all down to sharing!

### In this topic you will learn that:

- atoms bond to achieve a noble gas structure
- bonds result from the forces between the electrons and the nuclei of atoms
- atoms bond in different ways to form compounds
- the structure and properties of substances are dependent on the nature of the bonding.

Choose from the word pairs to finish the sentences below:

- Atoms form (molecules/particles) by swapping or sharing electrons.

- The shape of a drug molecule depends on the way (that the atoms are joined together/that the body works).

- Designing drugs means that companies (are more likely to get something that works/know that a new drug is safe to use).

- Once new drugs have been made they have to be tested by (computer simulation/experiment).

# 1. Covalent bonding

**By the end of these two pages you should be able to:**

- describe how covalent bonds can be made by atoms sharing electrons
- show the covalent bonds in some simple molecules using dot and cross diagrams.

Atoms react to get a full outer electron shell. This gives them the same electron structure as a noble gas, which makes them very stable. Water is a compound of two non-metals, hydrogen and oxygen. Non-metals need extra electrons to gain a full shell. Neither atom has any spare electrons, so they share electrons. Bonds formed like this are called **covalent bonds**.

Hydrogen atoms have just one electron in the innermost electron shell. As this is unstable each hydrogen atom joins with another to make a stable hydrogen **molecule** ($H_2$). These two atoms share a pair of electrons, one from each atom, to form a covalent bond.

**A** Oxygen shares electrons with two hydrogen atoms in water.

1 What do atoms do with some electrons when they form covalent bonds?

2 Carbon dioxide is formed from two non-metals. What type of bonds hold carbon dioxide ($CO_2$) molecules together?

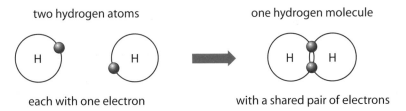

two hydrogen atoms

each with one electron

one hydrogen molecule

with a shared pair of electrons

**B** Covalent bonding in a hydrogen molecule.

In hydrogen, the single electron shell is full with just these two electrons. For shells two and three, eight electrons are needed to fill the shell. Chlorine is in Group 7 of the Periodic Table. That means it has seven electrons in its outer shell. It needs one more electron to fill that shell. In hydrogen chloride, a chlorine atom and a hydrogen atom share a pair of electrons to form a covalent bond. Both atoms now have a full outer shell and so are stable.

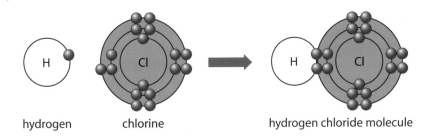

hydrogen        chlorine

hydrogen chloride molecule

**C** Covalent bonding in hydrogen chloride.

**H** We can show covalent bonds with a simple dot and cross diagram. The electron from one atom is shown as a dot, and the electron from the other atom as a cross. The dots and crosses help us to see where the electrons come from.

one shared pair – two full shells

**D** Dot and cross diagram for hydrogen chloride.

Oxygen is in Group 6, so it has six electrons in its outer shell. It needs two electrons to make a full shell. This means an oxygen atom has to join up with two hydrogen atoms to make a stable compound. The hydrogen atoms share their electrons with the oxygen atom to make a full outer shell. This produces water ($H_2O$).

Carbon is in Group 4, so it has four electrons in its outer shell. It needs four electrons to make a full shell. One way it can do this is to share four electrons with two oxygen atoms to make carbon dioxide ($CO_2$). Each oxygen atom provides a pair of electrons.

As carbon needs to make four covalent bonds to fill its outer shell, it can form very large and complex molecules. Carbon atoms can also form crystals that may contain billions of atoms all joined by covalent bonds, such as **diamond** and **graphite**.

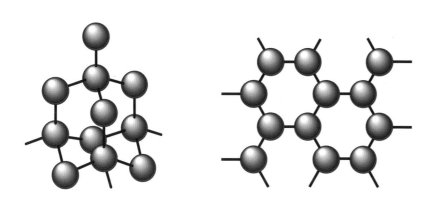

**F** Carbon atoms are held by covalent bonds in diamond and graphite.

## Have you ever wondered

Why is life on Earth based on the carbon atom?

**Summary Exercise**

water molecule

two single covalent bonds

carbon dioxide molecule

two double covalent bonds

**E** Water and carbon dioxide molecules and dot and cross diagrams.

**3** Nitrogen is in Group 5 of the Periodic Table.
   **a** How many electrons does it have in its outer shell?
   **b** How many electrons does it need to share to fill its shell?

**4** Fluorine has seven electrons in its outer electron shell, like chlorine. How many hydrogen atoms will a fluorine atom join with to form the covalent compound hydrogen fluoride?

**5** Write a paragraph to explain what a covalent bond is and why they form. Include the words: electrons, stable, full, share.

**Higher Questions**

# 2. Giant covalent structures

**By the end of these two pages you should be able to:**

- describe the giant covalent structures of graphite and diamond
- explain the similarities and differences between their physical properties.

Diamond is the hardest substance known. That is one of the reasons why diamonds make such good jewellery, as they cannot easily be scratched or damaged. Diamond-studded drills are also used to cut through rock. This is obviously very different from the 'lead' in a pencil which is so soft that it can be rubbed off onto paper. Pencil 'lead' is made from a mineral called graphite. It is soft and grey – unlike hard, clear diamond. Yet diamond and graphite have one thing in common. They are both made from carbon atoms that are joined together by covalent bonds to form **giant covalent structures**.

1 Why would it be difficult to make jewellery out of graphite?

2 **a** Are the bonds in diamond formed by giving and taking of electrons, or by the sharing of electrons?
**b** What is this type of bonding called?

A  Carbon in the form of diamond.

B  Carbon in the form of graphite.

## Have you ever wondered?

Why are diamonds so expensive when scientists can create them in a few hours?

Carbon atoms have just four electrons in their outer electron shell, so they need to share another four electrons to fill the shell. This means that each carbon atom can make four covalent bonds. In diamond, each carbon atom is joined by a single covalent bond to four other carbon atoms in a regular 3-D pattern. So within a diamond, every carbon atom is held in place by four strong covalent bonds. That's why diamonds are so hard.

But in graphite the structure is very different. Only three covalent bonds form with three other atoms forming 2-D sheets. The 'unused' electrons from the missing fourth bond join up to form an electron 'cloud' between the layers, holding them loosely together. So within each sheet the covalent bonds are strong but between the sheets there is only a weak force of attraction because of the electron cloud. If you rub a graphite crystal, the sheets of atoms can easily slide over one another. When you use a pencil, you are simply rubbing sheets of atoms off onto the paper.

**3** Why are diamonds so hard?

**4** Covalent bonds usually form to fill an electron shell. What is odd about graphite?

In both graphite and diamond, all of the carbon atoms are held in place by strong covalent bonds. It takes a lot of energy to break these bonds and free the atoms, so the melting points of both graphite and diamond are very high (above 3500 °C).

There is one other big difference between the properties of diamond and graphite. In diamond, all of the outer electrons are 'trapped' in covalent bonds, so diamond does not conduct electricity. But in graphite, electrons in the 'electron cloud' between the sheets can move about from atom to atom. Because of this, graphite can conduct electricity.

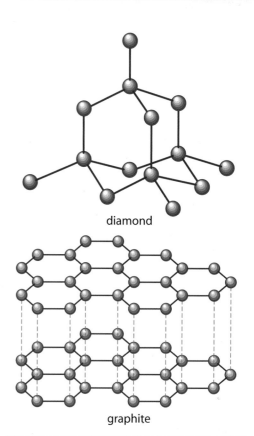

diamond

graphite

**C** Same atoms, different structure. The grey lines show the covalent bonds.

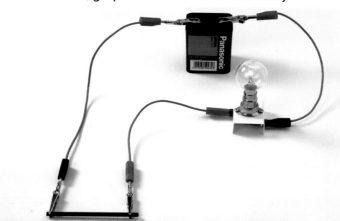

**D** Graphite conducts electricity shown by the lit bulb.

**5** Copy and complete this table using appropriate words:

|  | Diamond | Graphite |
|---|---|---|
| melting point | very high |  |
| hardness | very hard |  |
| electrical conductivity |  | conducts electricity |

Summary Exercise

Higher Questions

### By the end of these two pages you should be able to:

- recall that carbon can form other giant covalent structures such as fullerenes and nanotubes
- suggest uses for fullerenes and nanotubes, given data about their properties.

### Have you ever wondered?

Did you know there is a molecule that organises itself into the shape of a soccer ball?

Carbon can make four covalent bonds and this can lead to some very complicated molecules. You have seen the 3-D giant covalent structures of diamond and graphite, while long chains of carbon atoms form the basis of life chemistry. But carbon sheets similar to those found in graphite can also form a huge variety of molecules in the shape of balls or tubes. These are called **Buckminster fullerenes** after the American architect Buckminster Fuller who designed buildings with similar shapes. They are sometimes called **buckyballs** or **buckytubes** for the same reason! The most famous molecule has 60 carbon atoms arranged in a hollow ball the shape of a soccer ball.

A

C

Nature got there first… Both soccer balls and dome structures like those at the Eden Project mimic the $C_{60}$ buckyball molecule.

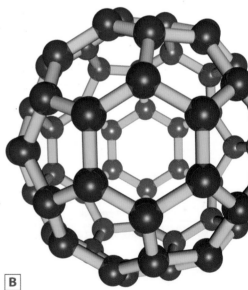

B

1 What type of bonds are there between the carbon atoms in a buckyball molecule?

2 Each carbon atom in a buckminster fullerene has only three bonds. Is that more like diamond or graphite?

Buckminster fullerenes were discovered unexpectedly in 1985. They were clearly unusual molecules with unusual properties so scientists have been trying to find uses for them. Buckyballs are hollow spheres and some scientists have found a way to trap a metal ion inside them. This changes the properties of the metal ion. Perhaps these 'caged' ions could be used to make a better catalyst to speed up reactions for industry? Buckyballs also react with chemicals called free radicals. Free radicals in the human body are thought to be the cause of ageing, and they may also cause cancer. So it is possible that buckyballs could help to keep us young, or they could be used to attack and destroy cancer.

Like graphite, the carbon atoms in Buckminster fullerenes have one electron that is not used for covalent bonding. These 'loose' electrons mean that fullerenes can conduct electricity. Much research is now going into making **carbon nanotubes** (buckytubes), which are thin tubes made from rolled up graphite sheets. These tubes are very tiny, just a few tens of nanometres across and yet they can carry high electric currents. This property has led researchers to look at how they could be used in the next generation of super-fast, super-small computer chips. Nanotubes could also be used to make improved solar cells for generating electricity.

Nanotubes have another important property. In stretch tests they are shown to be immensely strong, as each carbon atom is joined to its neighbour by a strong covalent bond. Carbon nanotubes can be up to 50 times stronger than steel wires of the same size. The problem is that at the moment scientists can only make very short tubes. If they could find a way to make long nanotubes it would revolutionise the way buildings are constructed.

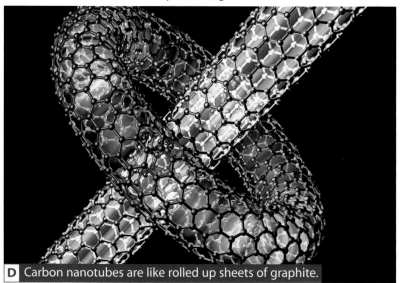
**D** Carbon nanotubes are like rolled up sheets of graphite.

3 What have scientists been able to 'trap' inside buckyballs?

4 Why are carbon nanotubes being used as 'wires' in some of the latest super-small and super-fast computer chips?

5 a Describe the structure of Buckminster fullerenes.
  b Compare this to the structure of graphite.
  c Suggest three possible uses of these molecules.

**Summary Exercise**

**Higher Questions**

# 4. Simple covalent structures

**By the end of these two pages you should be able to:**

- describe and explain some the physical properties of simple covalent molecular substances

Diamonds are giant covalent molecules so they are very hard and have high melting and boiling points. Perfume chemicals have very different properties. They have to evaporate easily into the air so that we can smell them. Perfume chemicals are also made from covalent molecules, but the molecules are very small. Small molecules (also called **simple molecular structures**) have low melting points and low boiling points.

**A** Giant covalent and small covalent molecules in use…

| Substance | Melting point (°C) |
|---|---|
| hydrogen chloride | −114 |
| water | 0 |
| graphite | 3675 |

**B** Melting points of some covalent substances.

1 The chemicals shown in the table all have covalent bonds.
   a Which form giant covalent structures and which form small covalent molecules?
   b How can you tell?

2 How do the low boiling points of the chemicals in perfumes help us to smell them?

## Have you ever wondered?

Do the essential oils that supermarkets spray into the air put you in a positive mood?

In a solid, the particles are held in place by forces of attraction. To melt the solid you have to put enough energy in to overcome these forces. In giant covalent molecules every bond is a strong covalent bond, so a large amount of energy is needed to break them. But in small molecules things are very different. The bonds within the molecule are strong covalent bonds, but the **inter-molecular force** – the force of attraction between the molecules – is weak. This means that you don't have to put so much energy in to separate the molecules, so it's easier to melt the solid.

Because of the weak inter-molecular forces, many substances made from small molecules, such as methane or ammonia, have such low boiling points that they are gases at room temperature. When the molecules are larger there is more force between them so the melting points and boiling points are higher. Some simple molecular substances are even solid at room temperature. But they form very soft solids and still melt and boil at relatively low temperatures.

## Have you ever wondered?

If particles in a solid are closer than a liquid, why doesn't ice sink?

Small covalent molecules have no overall charge and all of their electrons are held tightly in place. There are no free electrons to move between the atoms and carry a charge. Because of this, substances made from small covalent molecules do not usually conduct electricity.

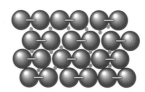
iodine crystal

crystal breaks up easily

weak force easily overcome

heat source

━ strong covalent bond within the molecule

● weak attractive force between the molecules

**C** Iodine crystals break up to give a purple gas if heated.

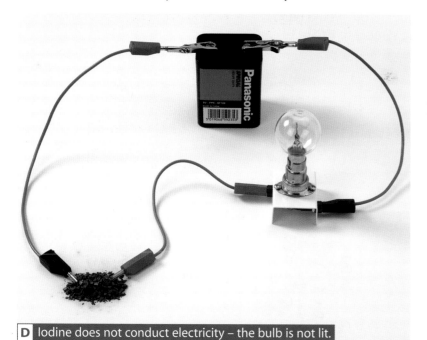

**D** Iodine does not conduct electricity – the bulb is not lit.

3  Explain what happens to the particles when you heat a solid made from small molecules.

4  Why doesn't solid carbon dioxide conduct electricity?

5  Copy and complete this table.

| Covalent structure | Melting and boiling points (high or low?) | Hardness (hard or soft?) | Electrical conductor? (yes or no) |
|---|---|---|---|
| Giant | | | |
| Small molecular | | | |

**Summary Exercise**

**Higher Questions**

# 5. Physical properties of the halogens

**H** **By the end of these two pages you should be able to:**

- describe the trend in the physical properties of the halogens (Group 7)
- explain this trend in terms of their molecular structure
- draw dot and cross diagrams of these molecules.

Group 7 of the Periodic Table contains the **halogens**. They all have seven electrons in their outer electron shell and so they need one electron to fill it. This means they can form a covalent bond with another non-metal atom by sharing a pair of electrons. The atoms of each element form small molecules in which two identical atoms are joined by a covalent bond. You can show this using dot and cross diagrams, which only show the outer electron shell. The diagram shows this for iodine, but would be the same for any halogen – just change the symbol to F, Cl or Br.

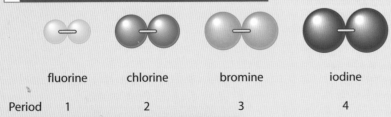

fluorine (F$_2$)    chlorine (Cl$_2$)    bromine (Br$_2$)    iodine (I$_2$)

**A** The halogens are a group of non-metals that have coloured gases.

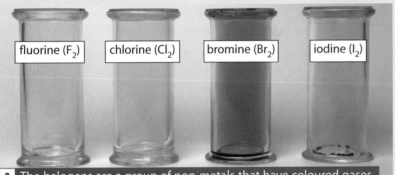

Single covalent bond formed by one shared pair of electrons.

**C** Two iodine atoms form one iodine molecule.

| Gp7 | | |
|---|---|---|
| | 9 | |
| | **F** | |
| | 19 | |
| | 17 | |
| | **Cl** | |
| | 35.5 | |
| | 35 | |
| | **Br** | |
| | 80 | |
| | 53 | |
| | **I** | |
| | 127 | |

**B** The halogens in the Periodic Table.

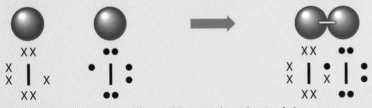

fluorine    chlorine    bromine    iodine

Period    1      2      3      4

**D** The relative sizes of halogen molecules.

The halogens all form coloured gases but only two, fluorine and chlorine, are gases at room temperature. Bromine is a dark brown liquid that gives off a brown vapour. Iodine is a purple-grey solid which forms a purple vapour if heated gently.

**1** What is the relationship between the period of a halogen and the size of its atom?

**2** Astatine is a rare, radioactive halogen found below iodine in Group 7. Draw a dot and cross diagram to show how the covalent At$_2$ molecule might form.

The physical properties of the halogens also change steadily as you move down the group. As the atoms get larger, the melting and boiling points get higher. This is because the force of attraction between the molecules increases as the size of the molecule increases. As the molecules are not charged, halogens do not conduct electricity.

| Halogen | Symbol | Atomic number | Mass number | Period (number of shells) | Melting point (°C) | Boiling point (°C) |
|---------|--------|---------------|-------------|---------------------------|--------------------|--------------------|
| fluorine | F | 9 | 19 | 2 | −220 | −188 |
| chlorine | Cl | 17 | 35.5 | 3 | −101 | −34 |
| bromine | Br | 35 | 80 | 4 | −7 | 59 |
| iodine | I | 53 | 127 | 5 | 114 | 184 |

**E** Physical properties of the halogens.

chlorine gas

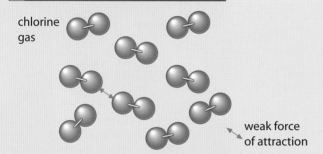

weak force of attraction

Chlorine molecules are small so the force between them is very weak. Even at room temperature the chlorine molecules have enough energy to break free from one another, so chlorine is a gas.

liquid bromine

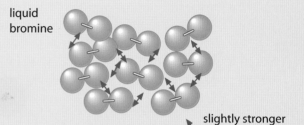

slightly stronger force of attraction

Bromine molecules are a little larger, so the force between them is a little greater. At room temperature there is enough vibration energy to melt the bromine, but not enough to boil it. So bromine is a liquid.

solid iodine

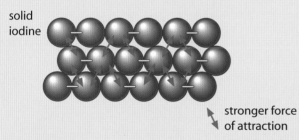

stronger force of attraction

Iodine molecules are larger still so the force of attraction between them is greater. At room temperature iodine is a solid – but still a very soft one that easily vaporises!

**F**

**G** Soft iodine crystals turn to purple iodine vapour very easily.

**3** Explain why fluorine is a gas at room temperature.

**4** Look at table E. How can you tell that bromine is a liquid at room temperature?

**5** Draw a scatter graph of the melting point of the halogens (y-axis) plotted against the number of electron shells (x-axis). Draw a line of best fit and describe the relationship shown.

**Summary Exercise**

**Higher Questions**

# 6. Giant metallic structures

**By the end of these two pages you should be able to:**

- recall that metals have giant structures of ions held in place by a 'cloud' of loose electrons
- explain that metals conduct electricity because these electrons can move freely.

If you arrange many marbles onto a tray they will stack up to form a pyramid – but you can't make any other shapes unless you start to stick them together with glue. The atoms in a metal object stack up in this way to form giant structures, but there are forces between the atoms that stick them together.

Most metals are found in Groups 1, 2 and 3, and in the transition block of the Periodic Table. That means they all have one, two or three electrons in their outermost electron shell. When metals react with non-metals, they lose these electrons to form positive ions with full outer electron shells. This makes them stable.

When metal atoms are stacked in a giant structure, the loose outer electrons can move freely from atom to atom. So although solid metal is made of closely packed atoms, it can also be thought of as a collection of positive ions trapped in a 'cloud' of negative electrons. It is the force of attraction between this 'cloud' of negative electrons and the positive ions that holds the ions together.

When you hit a metal, the layers of atoms slide over each other. The 'cloud' of electrons holds the ions together and so the metal bends instead of breaking.

**A** Lego™ models are made from small blocks. That's also true of all solids, even metals – it's just that the atomic 'blocks' are far too small to see.

1 Why do solid metal objects keep their shape?

2 What holds the metal ions together in the metal structure?

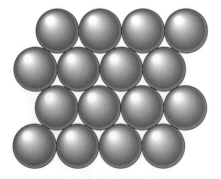

metal atoms stacked in a giant structure

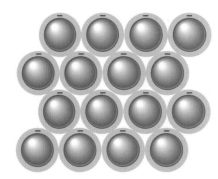

inner ions and outer loose electrons

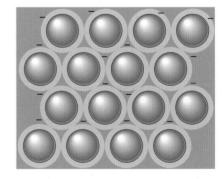

inner ions trapped in a cloud of electrons

**B** Three ways of looking at the structure of a metal.

The electrons in the 'cloud' between the ions of a metal are free to move randomly about the structure. But if you put an electrical potential across the metal, the negative electrons will all start to move in the same direction, towards the positive side. An electric current will flow. That is why metals have high **conductivity**.

Adding atoms of different metals to the structure often makes metals stronger. The different atoms lock the structure together, stopping the atoms from slipping over one another easily. But these different atoms will also get in the way of the flow of electrons, increasing the electrical resistance. So metals used for electrical cables have to be as pure as possible. Copper has to be 99.9% pure before it can be used for wiring.

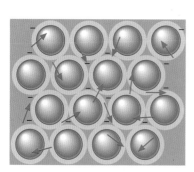
Electrons move randomly.

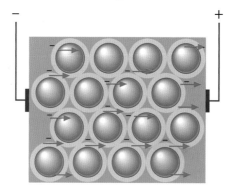
Electrons move in the same direction.

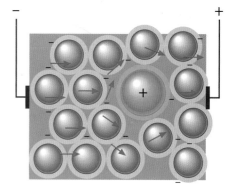
Impurities disrupt the flow.

**C** How metals conduct electricity.

As a metal gets hot, its atoms vibrate more. The vibrations can disrupt the flow of electrons, so cold metal is a better conductor than hot metal. Metal coils cooled to −270 °C in liquid helium can become superconductors that carry enormous currents. Superconductors are used to make powerful electromagnets for medical scanners.

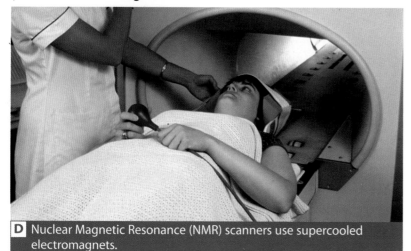
**D** Nuclear Magnetic Resonance (NMR) scanners use supercooled electromagnets.

**3** Why do electrons move towards the positive terminal?

**4** Why must electrical cables be made from pure copper?

**5** Describe the giant structure within a metal. Explain how the metal keeps its shape and why it conducts electricity.

P

**Summary Exercise**

**Higher Questions**

# 7. Scientific discoveries by chance

**By the end of these two pages you should be able to:**

- recognise how important chance discoveries are to science.

Scientists work in a very controlled way. They gather evidence and think carefully about a problem. Then they plan experiments to test out their ideas. They try very hard to make the tests fair by controlling other variables that might affect the result. It is a very logical process.

Coming up with a new idea is a creative act. You need inspiration – and sometimes just a bit of good luck. Many scientific discoveries have come about by chance when something unexpected has happened.

- Alexander Fleming carelessly let some mould infect some dishes of bacteria he was growing – and accidentally discovered the antibiotic penicillin.
- Wilhelm Roentgen accidentally discovered X-rays when he noticed that a fluorescent screen in his lab started to glow when he experimented with beams of electrons.
- Henri Becquerel discovered radioactivity when he noticed that a photographic plate had been exposed when kept near some uranium ore, even though it was wrapped in light-proof paper.

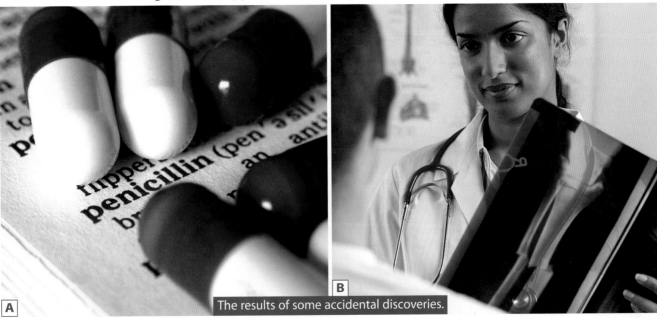

A  B  The results of some accidental discoveries.

Of course, nothing would have come of any of these ideas if the scientist had not noticed that something unusual had happened. Careful, logical thought was needed before the idea became a scientific theory that could be tested by experiment. Even so, good luck often plays an important role in scientific breakthroughs.

1 Which part of science is often not logical?

2 Why should we be thankful that Fleming was a 'careless' scientist?

The discovery of buckyballs and the other fullerenes is another example of scientific discovery by chance. It also shows how new ideas can often be generated when scientists in different areas of study work together and share their ideas.

C Harold Kroto is a British scientist. He was interested in how long-chain carbon molecules – the molecules of life – could form. He wanted to test his idea that this might happen in stars at high energy levels.

D Richard Smalley is an American scientist. He used a high-powered laser to vaporise chemicals in a vacuum. He was then able to analyse the molecules that were being produced.

Harold Kroto and Richard Smalley started their joint experiments in 1985. They fired lasers at graphite and analysed the gas that came off, hoping to find long carbon-chain molecules like those found in living materials. They soon found that they were indeed making lots of large carbon molecules – but not at all like those they expected! In particular, they found they were getting some stable molecules with 60 carbon atoms. But instead of long chains, these molecules were hollow balls. They had accidentally discovered buckyballs!

Of course, it took a lot of careful, detailed work before they fully understood the significance of their chance discovery. But this was such a breakthrough that the scientists were awarded the Nobel Prize for chemistry in 1996.

3 Kroto and Smalley expected to find carbon-chain molecules with many different numbers of carbon atoms. What was unexpected about Kroto and Smalley's discovery?

4 a Give three examples where chance has played an important role in a major scientific discovery.
  b Suggest a reason why no scientist had ever tried to discover buckyballs before Kroto and Smalley.

Summary Exercise

Higher Questions

# 8. Molecular models

**By the end of these two pages you should be able to:**

- recognise the different models that are used to represent molecules
- explain why different models are used for different purposes.

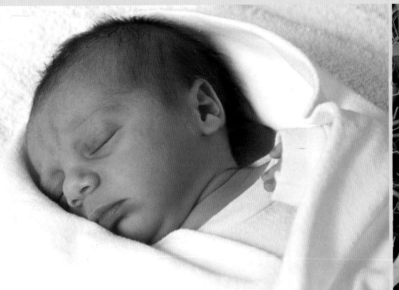
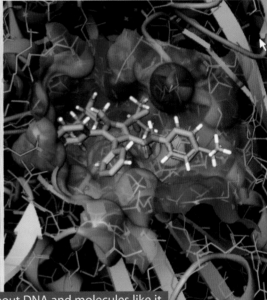

**A** To understand more about this baby we need to understand more about DNA and molecules like it.

Scientists have discovered many things about atoms and molecules. We know:

- that atoms are built from electrons orbiting a nucleus
- how atoms combine to form ionic or covalent compounds
- why these chemicals have such different properties in bulk.

We are even beginning to unravel the very mysteries of life, from the complex molecules of DNA up to a living organism.

All these objects and processes can be described in words and mathematical equations, but we are used to dealing with images. Images are easier to understand. We cannot see pictures of atoms and (most) molecules because they are so small that it is impossible to see or photograph them, even with a powerful microscope.

So we can use models to help us. A model is a representation of something. Different models can show different features of atoms and molecules. You can use the model that is best suited to the job you have in mind.

You can use the simplest model that gives the information you need. But there is also a limitation with the 2-D models shown in diagram B: they do not show us the actual shape of the molecules.

1 Why is it not possible to see atoms and molecules?

2 Why do we use models to show the features of atoms and molecules, instead of just describing them in words or mathematical equations?

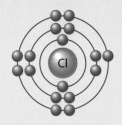

Cl — Cl

$Cl_2$

Electrons in their shells around a chlorine atom.

The outer electrons only are shown in this stylised dot and cross diagram of a chlorine molecule.

A single covalent bond can be shown as a simple bar.

The chemical formula represents the two atoms in the chlorine molecule.

**B** Different ways of showing atoms and bonding.

Three-dimensional models are used to show the molecular shape more clearly. You can make simple molecular models with balls and springs – or fantastically complex models like the one of DNA. These models are good if you are focusing on the covalent bonds, but in real molecules the atoms pack closely together like a cluster of bubbles. These 'close-packed' models give a better idea of the shape of complex molecules.

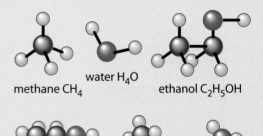

methane $CH_4$     water $H_4O$     ethanol $C_2H_5OH$

A          B          C

**C** Ball and stick and 3-D models.

**D** Physical models give you a better idea of what complex molecules actually look like.

**E** Three different representations of carbon dioxide.

Computer models can take this much further by using animations to show how molecules look from all directions as they move about. This can help to show the shape of complex molecules even more clearly, and so help scientists to understand how they react. Drug companies use powerful computer programs to map out the shapes of the chemicals they are investigating. This helps them to research new drugs.

**3** Match the 3-D models A, B and C to the ball and stick models for water ($H_2O$), methane ($CH_4$) and ethanol ($C_2H_5OH$) shown in figure C.

**4** Why do drug companies use powerful software to show the shapes of their drug molecules?

**5** Describe the difference between a real molecule and a model of it.

**6 a** For each of the following, use a suitable model to show:
  **i** the electron structure of carbon and hydrogen
  **ii** how the covalent bond forms by sharing electron pairs in a methane molecule ($CH_4$)
  **iii** how the particles are arranged in methane gas
  **iv** the shape of a methane molecule.
  **b** Give one advantage and one disadvantage of each of the models you have used.

Summary Exercise

Higher Questions

# 9. Homeopathic medicine

**By the end of these two pages you should be able to:**

- describe the difference between homeopathic and conventional medicine
- explain why most scientists find it difficult to accept homeopathic ideas.

A

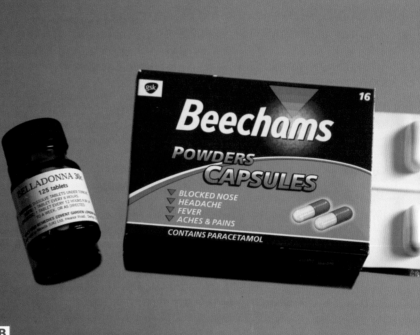

B

What's better, the conventional or 'alternative' approach?

When you are ill you might take medicine prescribed by your GP, such as antibiotics for an ear infection. This is called conventional medicine, and it is based on a scientific approach. This means that it relies on a theory that follows certain rules:

- it is based on observation
- it can be tested to see if the theory is valid
- it is supported by scientific evidence
- it can make predictions.

In this case the theory might be 'antibiotics kill the bacteria that give us infections'. Scientists observed that bacteria could be affected by certain substances that we now know as antibiotics. They then tested the theory by growing the bacteria in the lab and adding these substances to see what happened. When this worked, they gave the substances to lots of people with infections. The bacteria were killed in a significant number of cases, so the theory was accepted. Doctors can reliably predict that if they give antibiotics to a patient with an ear infection, it will make the patient better.

1 How do you know if a theory is scientific?

2 Why might a scientific approach be important in medicine?

Some people prefer to use alternative medicines, such as **homeopathic** remedies. Homeopathy is not based on scientific theory, but on the idea that 'like cures like'. Some natural substances cause the body to develop symptoms very similar to particular illnesses. The homeopath attempts to cure an illness with a substance that causes some of the same symptoms. For example, the plant belladonna can cause high fever, so a homeopath might use it to treat a fever like you get with an ear infection. Many people use homeopathic treatments and believe that they are helpful to them.

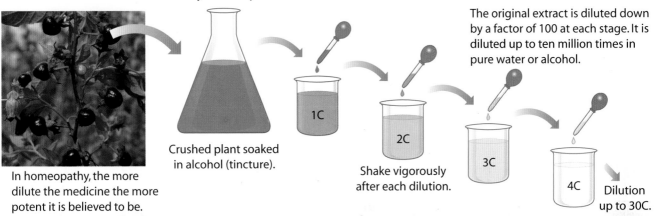

In homeopathy, the more dilute the medicine the more potent it is believed to be.

Crushed plant soaked in alcohol (tincture).

Shake vigorously after each dilution.

The original extract is diluted down by a factor of 100 at each stage. It is diluted up to ten million times in pure water or alcohol.

Dilution up to 30C.

**C** Homeopathic remedies are extremely dilute. They are mixed with so much water that often not even one single molecule of the active ingredient remains. This makes the medicine safe to use even if made from a deadly poison – but how then can it cure an illness?

## Have you ever wondered?

Why do people think crystals have mysterious healing qualities?

## Have you ever wondered?

If homeopathy works, why don't scientists believe it?

Scientists find it difficult to accept the homeopathic approach. The principle that diluting a substance makes it more potent contradicts accepted scientific theory of how medicine works. This principle is not based on reliable observation and it cannot be tested, as there is no clear explanation of how it might work. There is little scientific evidence to support it, and it cannot be used to predict measurable effects on people.

However, some evidence suggests that homeopathic medicine can help people feel better. In medical trials, people given the homeopathic pills often do better than people who get nothing. There is still much argument and debate.

## Have you ever wondered?

People have been wearing copper and magnetic bracelets for 2000 years, but do they work?

**Summary Exercise**

3 Describe the 'like cures like' approach used in homeopathic medicine.

4 Why are homeopathic medicines safe to use?

5 Many people who take homeopathic pills say they get better. Why doesn't this prove that the pills work?

6 Why do scientists have difficulty accepting homeopathic ideas?

7 You and your mother both develop a stomach ache. Your mother goes to her GP and you go to a homeopath.
  a Describe the treatment your mother might receive from the GP.
  b Compare it to the treatment you might receive from the homeopath.
  c Explain the differences.

**Higher Questions**

# 10. Chemical based therapies

**H**

**P**

**By the end of these two pages you should be able to:**
- use information to assess the effectiveness of a new drug.

A From discovery...

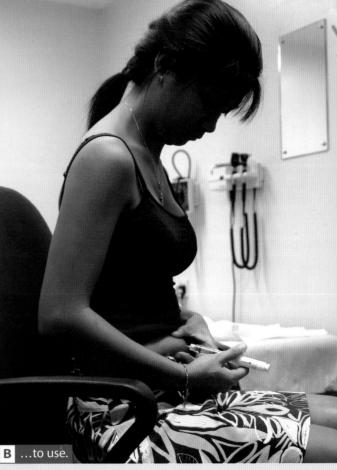

B ...to use.

New drugs have to go through rigorous testing before they can be used on people. Scientists have to make sure that the drug is effective in treating the illness or disease. They also have to check that it is not dangerous and has no major side effects. The first part of the testing will involve:

- Computer analysis and simulations of how the drug might interact with body chemicals. This will pick up many of the obvious potential problems.
- Testing on tissue cultures grown in the laboratory. This will show the effect of the drug on individual cells.
- Testing on animals – usually rats or mice. This is controversial, but most scientists think that it is still necessary, as drugs that don't affect individual cells might affect organs like the kidneys or the liver. Rats and mice are genetically similar to us but obviously not exactly the same. So there is no guarantee that drugs that are fine for rats will be fine for humans.

1 Why do most scientists think that animal testing for new drugs is essential?

2 Give a reason why successful animal testing is not a guarantee of drug safety.

Once a new drug passes its laboratory tests, it then has to be tested on people. The drug has to pass three phases of testing on humans.

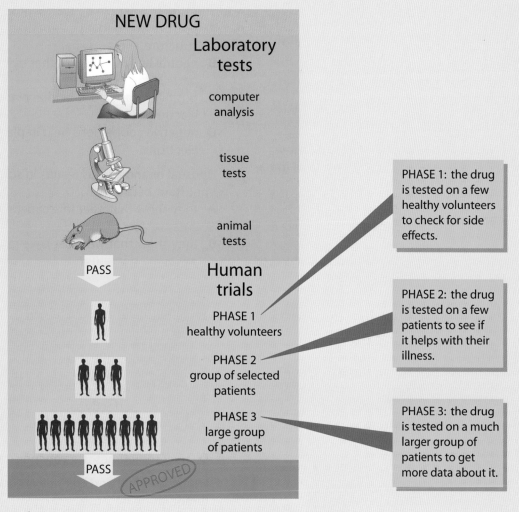

PHASE 1: the drug is tested on a few healthy volunteers to check for side effects.

PHASE 2: the drug is tested on a few patients to see if it helps with their illness.

PHASE 3: the drug is tested on a much larger group of patients to get more data about it.

There are always two groups of patients in the tests. One group is given the drug, the other group is given something that looks like the drug but has no active ingredients. This is called a **placebo**. The patients – and often the scientists as well – do not know if they are getting the real drug or the placebo. There may also be a third group that gets no treatment at all.

If the drug works, then the patients who get the drug should do better than those who do not. But patients who take the placebo often improve as well – they get better because they *believe* that they are taking a drug that will help them. There must be a large difference between the group given the drug and the group given the placebo for the drug to pass the test. When the new drug has successfully passed all three tests can it be licensed for use by the Medical and Healthcare Regulatory Agency (MHRA).

3 List the test stages that a new drug has to pass before it gets a license for use on humans.

4 a What is a placebo?
  b Why is it given to some patients in a drug trial?

5 In a trial for a new hayfever drug, 10 sufferers were given drug X. Three said it cured their hayfever and five said they felt a little better.
  a Does this trial prove that drug X works?
  b What else would you need to know to tell if drug X was any good?

Summary Exercise

Higher Questions

## Multiple choice questions

**1** Sulphur dioxide must be a covalent compound because
   **A** all dioxide compounds are covalent.
   **B** all sulphur compounds are covalent.
   **C** sulphur is a metal and oxygen is a non-metal.
   **D** sulphur and oxygen are both non-metals.

**2** Sulphur is in Group 6 of the Periodic Table. How many covalent bonds will it need to make to get a share of a full shell of electrons?
   **A** 1   **B** 2   **C** 3   **D** 4

**3** Which of the following crystals does NOT have a giant covalent structure?
   **A** diamond            **B** salt (sodium chloride)
   **C** silica (silicon dioxide)   **D** graphite

**4** Why does graphite conduct electricity?
   **A** Each carbon atom has three instead of four possible covalent bonds, so one electron is free to move.
   **B** Each carbon atom has five instead of four covalent bonds, so there are extra electrons.
   **C** All of the electrons in carbon atoms are only weakly held in place and so can move about.
   **D** Carbon atoms repel electrons when a battery is connected to them.

**5** Fullerenes were named after Buckminster Fuller because he:
   **A** discovered them.
   **B** paid for the research that led to their discovery.
   **C** designed buildings that had a similar structure.
   **D** founded the university where they were discovered.

**6** Which one of the following compounds has small covalent molecules?
   **A** methane   **B** salt   **C** diamond   **D** steel

**7** Substances with small covalent molecules have low melting points because
   **A** the bonds within and between the molecules are very strong.
   **B** the bonds within and between the molecules are very weak.
   **C** the bonds within the molecules are strong but the forces of attraction between the molecules are weak.
   **D** the bonds within the molecules are weak but the forces of attraction between the molecules are strong.

**8** The structure within a piece of pure copper is
   **A** positive and negative ions arranged in a giant structure.
   **B** neutral atoms held together by weak inter-particle forces.
   **C** positive copper ions held in place by a 'cloud' of electrons.
   **D** negative copper ions held in place by a 'cloud' of electrons.

**9** Unusual or anomalous results in science are important because
   **A** they show that scientific experiments are creative acts.
   **B** they show that we must have made a mistake in our measurements.
   **C** they show that we must have been observing and measuring carefully.
   **D** they sometimes lead on to new discoveries or scientific breakthroughs.

**10** Many scientists find it difficult to accept the idea of homeopathic medicines because
   **A** they are only made from natural materials.
   **B** they are perfectly safe to use.
   **C** nobody can give a testable explanation of how they might work.
   **D** they sometimes use very poisonous plants.

**H** **11** Iodine is a solid and chlorine is a gas at room temperature because
   **A** iodine has bigger molecules than chlorine, so the forces between them are larger.
   **B** iodine has smaller molecules than chlorine, so the forces between them are larger.
   **C** iodine has bigger molecules than chlorine, so the forces between them are smaller.
   **D** iodine has smaller molecules than chlorine, so the forces between them are smaller.

**12** Oxygen has eight electrons arranged in two shells and is in Group 6 of the Periodic Table. It forms $O_2$ molecules joined with covalent bonds. Which of these dot and cross diagrams best represents the $O_2$ molecule?

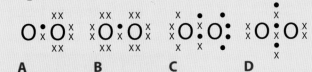

   **A**        **B**        **C**        **D**

**13** Which of the following models could represent water, $H_2O$?

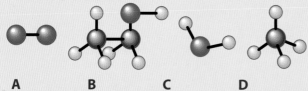

    A          B          C          D

**14** Which of the following dot and cross diagrams could represent water, $H_2O$?

    A          B          C          D

**15** In drug trials, patients taking the placebo often show improvements in their condition because
  **A** the sugar used in the placebo pill has medicinal qualities.
  **B** the researches must have muddled up their results.
  **C** the patients didn't have the medical problem in the first place.
  **D** if they patients believe they have been given a drug to make them better, then their body can sometimes react as if they really had been given the drug.

## Short-answer questions

**1** Nitrogen is in Group 5 of the Periodic Table.
  **a** How many electrons does nitrogen have in its outer electron shell?
  **b** How many extra electrons does it need to fill this shell?
  **c** If a nitrogen shares electrons with another non-metal atom, how many covalent bonds can it form?

**2** Carbon atoms can form giant covalent structures such as diamond, graphite and fullerenes.
  **a** Why are the melting points of graphite and diamond almost the same?
  **b** Why is diamond so hard, but graphite so soft?
  **c** How many other carbon atoms is each carbon atom joined to by strong covalent bonds in diamond?
  **d** How many other carbon atoms is each carbon atom joined to by strong covalent bonds in graphite?
  **e** Why can graphite conduct electricity?
  **f** Carbon nanotubes conduct electricity. Is their structure more like diamond or graphite?

  **g** A single nanotube grown into a very thin wire has a much greater strength than steel. Why is it so strong?

**3** Metals have a giant structure with positive ions trapped in a 'cloud' of electrons. Knowing this structure, why is it that metals:
  **a** conduct electricity
  **b** have high melting points
  **c** are strong
  **d** can be squashed or stretched by large forces, after which they keep their new shape?

**4 a** Nitrogen in the air is in the form of $N_2$ molecules, which have a triple covalent bond. Draw a dot and cross diagram to show an $N_2$ molecule. **H**
  **b** Why is nitrogen a gas at room temperature?
  **c** Nitrogen forms the gas ammonia ($NH_3$) with hydrogen. Draw a dot and cross diagram for an ammonia molecule.

**5** Read the following passage and answer the questions below.

The herb Valerian contains a chemical called valerianic acid ($C_4H_9COOH$) which has a tranquillising effect. You can buy 500 mg valerian tablets in a health food shops that contain up about 0.5 mg of the valerianic acid. You can also buy homeopathic Valerian tablets of 6C potency. This means the original preparation has been diluted down a million million times. Homeopaths think that the more you dilute the medicine, the more you 'acitivate' it and the more 'potent' it becomes.

  **a** Why do drug companies look at herbal remedies such as valerian seriously?
  **b** As the effect of valerian is thought to be due to the chemical reactions of valerianic acid in the body, why is the size of the dose important? (How could you make the effect of the drug greater or smaller?)
  **c** If a drug company made valerianic acid in the laboratory, what procedures would they go through before it could be licensed to go on sale?
  **d** Homeopaths think that their products get more 'potent' the more they are diluted. Does this agree with the scientific view based on chemistry?
  **e** Suggest another reason why scientists have difficulty accepting homeopathic ideas.
  **f** Suggest a possible explanation for the fact that many people claim that homeopathic remedies work for them.

# 12. Glossary

**\*Buckminster fullerenes** A form of carbon in which graphite-like sheets of carbon atoms form balls or tubes.

**buckyballs** Hollow, ball-shaped Buckminster fullerenes.

**buckytubes** Hollow, tube-shaped Buckminster fullerenes. Also called carbon nanotubes.

**\*carbon nanotube** A type of Buckminster fullerene in which the sheet structures of carbon atoms are rolled into very thin tubes. Also called buckytubes.

**\*conductivity** A property of a substance that describes its ability to allow energy (electricity or heat) to pass through it.

**\*covalent bond** A chemical bond that forms when two atoms share a pair of electrons.

**\*diamond** A very hard, natural form of carbon which has a 3-D giant covalent structure in which every atom is joined to four neighbours.

**\*giant covalent structure** A structure built from billions of atoms in which every atoms is joined to its neighbours by strong covalent bonds.

**\*graphite** A very soft, natural form of carbon which has a sheet-like giant covalent structure in which every atom is joined to just three neighbours.

**\*halogen** A family of reactive non-metals found in Group 7 of the Periodic Table.

**\*homeopathic** A form of 'alternative' medicine based on the 'like cures like' principle using very dilute forms of natural materials.

**\*inter-molecular force** The force of attraction between molecules.

**molecule** Two or more atoms joined together by covalent bonds.

**placebo** A harmless substance given to one group of patients during a drugs trial to allow a comparison with the drug.

**\*simple molecular structure** Atoms joined together by covalent bonds to form individual molecules which may be as small as two atoms.

\*glossary words from the specification

# How fast? How furious?

**A** Carefully controlled chemical reactions are needed to turn nitrogen in the air into fertilisers that give us bigger crops.

Chemical reactions range from the very slow – like the weathering of granite to sand and clay that takes thousands of years – to the very fast – like the explosion that destroyed the Buncefield fuel depot in December 2005, which took just a split second.

Industry relies on chemical reactions to make its materials so it needs to be able to control how fast those reactions take place. If they are too slow, the process will be uneconomical. If they are too fast, it could be very dangerous.

To be able to control reaction speed, you need to understand the different factors at work. For a reaction to happen, particles have to collide with enough energy to break up existing arrangements of atoms and allow new combinations to form. You need to find out more about the factors that control this.

## In this topic you will learn that:

- different chemical reactions occur at different rates and these rates can be changed
- some reactions give out energy while others take in energy
- chemical reactions involve breaking bonds and forming bonds
- some reactions are reversible.

For each of the following statements, suggest the key factor at work and its effect.

- Food cooks faster when fried in oil than when it is boiled in water.
- Bleach is diluted before being used on clothes, but is used undiluted in the toilet.
- Fine caster sugar tastes sweeter than granulated sugar when sprinkled on strawberries.
- Food cooks faster in an oven if you turn up the temperature.
- Diced carrots cook faster than whole carrots.

# 1. What are chemical reactions?

**H** **By the end of these two pages you should be able to:**

- recall that reactions occur when particles collide with enough energy to break their existing chemical bonds
- explain why many reactions need a 'push' to get them started.

Hydrogen is a flammable gas which burns in oxygen to give water.

**A** Hydrogen is a dangerously flammable gas – but a bubble of hydrogen mixed with oxygen does not explode on its own.

In a mixture of hydrogen and oxygen gases, the atoms within the molecules are held together by strong covalent bonds. These bonds have to be broken so that the molecules separate into atoms before new bonds – and so new compounds – can form.

1 Look at the number of hydrogen and oxygen atoms on each side of the equation. Is the equation balanced?

2 Which bond must be broken in this reaction and which bonds must form?

| hydrogen | + | oxygen | → | water | | plus energy |
| $2H_2$ | + | $O_2$ | → | $2H_2O$ | | (plus energy) |

**B**

## Have you ever wondered?

Why do some chemicals explode when you mix them?

## Have you ever wondered?

### How do you make rocket fuel?

In a hydrogen and oxygen gas mixture at room temperature, molecules are moving at high speed and are colliding all the time. However, the collisions do not have enough energy to break the bonds. For this to happen, they need more energy – they need to move at even higher speeds. One way to do this is to raise the temperature. That's what you are doing when you put a flame – or even a spark – to the gas mixture. This gives some molecules enough energy to collide with such force that the bonds are broken. The newly released atoms then recombine to give water molecules, giving out some energy as they do this. Overall, this is an **exothermic reaction** once the reaction has started, it generates enough energy of its own to keep the reaction going.

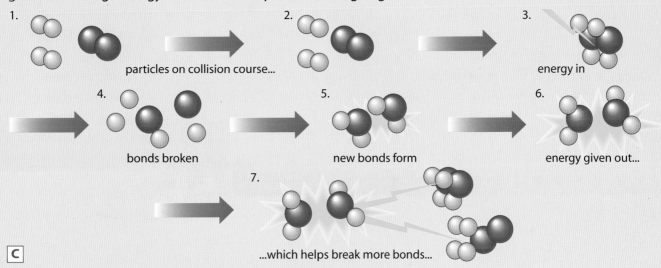

1.
2.
particles on collision course...
3.
energy in

4.
bonds broken
5.
new bonds form
6.
energy given out...

7.
...which helps break more bonds...

C

Many reactions need extra energy to break some bonds and start the reaction. But once the reaction starts, it will continue on its own. The hotter the mixture gets the faster the particles will move and the more often they will collide. That is why increasing the temperature usually increases the **rate of reaction**.

In the Hindenberg disaster an accident tore the balloon and released the hydrogen. A spark from scraping metal set it on fire as it mixed with the air. If you mix hydrogen and oxygen in a bubble, the molecules are all mixed up, ready to react. A spark or flame here will trigger a rapid chain reaction giving out a lot of energy. You get an explosion and a very loud bang! It's the same with natural gas. Mix it with air slowly and it burns steadily. If you let a lot of it leak into the air, you have a dangerous mixture ready to explode.

3  Why don't hydrogen and oxygen explode as soon as they are mixed?

4  Why is the build-up of gas after a gas leak dangerous, but it is perfectly safe to turn on and light the gas in an oven?

5  Describe one way to increase the rate of a chemical reaction.

6  The methane molecules in natural gas react with the oxygen molecules in air in a similar way to hydrogen. Describe what is happening to the molecules, step by step, from turning on the gas tap to lighting the burner.

**Summary Exercise**

**Higher Questions**

# 2. Energy in reactions

**By the end of these two pages you should be able to:**

- explain that exothermic reactions give out energy
- explain that endothermic reactions take in energy
- recall that breaking bonds is endothermic but making bonds is exothermic.

## Have you ever wondered?

How do the hot and cold packs that athletes use to treat injury work?

It is important to go through a warm-up routine before exercise to help avoid injury. But what if you want quick, localised heat to one particular muscle or joint? Many people use a chemical 'hot pack' to apply instant, controlled heat energy.

Many chemical reactions give out heat – they are exothermic reactions. Burning any fuel in oxygen gives a very strong exothermic reaction, but that would be difficult to control safely. Sports hot packs need to give off energy in a controlled way to avoid the risk of a burn.

Some heat packs use a perforated bag containing a damp mixture of iron filings with salt and charcoal. You know that iron left in water will slowly rust if oxygen is present. The reaction is exothermic and is speeded up by the salt and charcoal. The pack is in sealed bag which keeps out the oxygen. When you open the bag and squeeze it to let oxygen from the air in, the reaction starts and it soon starts to warm up.

iron + oxygen ➤ iron oxide (plus energy)

**A** Sportspeople use hot packs to relax healthy muscles and cold packs to relieve injuries.

1 How can you tell that burning natural gas in air is an exothermic reaction?

2 What type of chemical reaction goes on inside some sports hot packs?

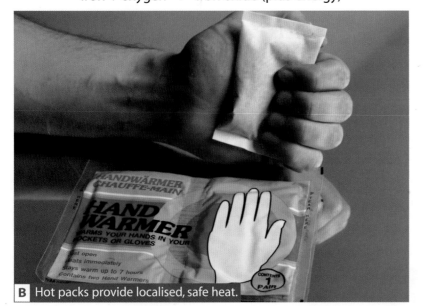

**B** Hot packs provide localised, safe heat.

3 What stops the iron heat pack from getting hot before it is needed?

Other reactions need energy to make them work – these are **endothermic reactions**. The energy breaks the bonds between the particles. Many chemical reactions are endothermic, but that means you have to put energy in to make them work. Some cold packs rely on an unusual endothermic reaction which takes the energy it needs from the surroundings and so lowers the temperature. When ammonium nitrate dissolves in water, it breaks into ions. Breaking bonds like this needs energy, so it is an endothermic process.

## warm

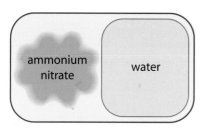

The water is kept separate in a thin plastic bag.

squeeze and burst inner bag

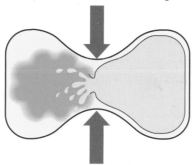

## cold

The mixture cools as the ammonium nitrate dissolves.

**C** Squeeze the cold pack to start the endothermic reaction.

Chemical reactions are both endothermic and exothermic. You have to break old bonds (endothermic) before you can make new bonds (exothermic). But:

- in an exothermic reaction you get more energy out when the new bonds form than you had to put in to break the old bonds
- in an endothermic reaction you have to put more energy in to break the old bonds than you get back when the new bonds form.

**4** What is unusual about the cold pack reaction for an endothermic process?

**5** Exothermic is made from the word roots 'exo' meaning outside, and 'thermic' meaning heat. What do you think the 'endo' part of endothermic means?

**6** Hydrogen reacts with oxygen to give water *plus energy*.
  **a** Explain the energy changes that happen as bonds are broken and reformed in this reaction.
  **b** Explain why this reaction is exothermic overall.

Summary Exercise

Higher Questions

**By the end of these two pages you should be able to:**

P

H
- describe the effects of temperature, surface area and concentration on the rate of a reaction
- explain these effects in terms of the way in which particles collide.

When you cook food, useful chemical reactions take place that start to break down the food, which can help you digest it. When food goes bad, other chemical reactions start to break the food down. Temperature affects the speed of the reaction. The hotter your oven is, the faster the food cooks. The colder you keep your food, the longer it takes to go bad.

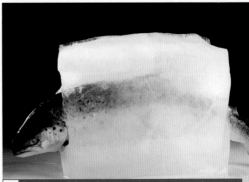

**A** Freezing food slows the chemical reactions that make it go bad.

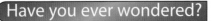

## Have you ever wondered?

? 

Why do chips cook much faster than roast potatoes?

For a chemical reaction to occur, you need enough energy to break the old bonds and to give new and different bonds a chance to form. One way to increase the speed – or rate – of the reaction is to raise the **temperature**. In many reactions, the rate doubles with every 10–15 °C rise.

P

You can also increase the speed of a reaction by:
- increasing the **concentration** – this gives more of the reacting chemical, so the reaction will be faster. For many simple reactions the rate doubles if you double the concentration.
- increasing the **surface area** – solids can only react on their surface, so the bigger the surface area, the faster the reaction. Smaller pieces give a bigger surface area overall, so react faster.

1 Water boils at 100 °C, and cooking oil will heat up to 200 °C. Why does deep-fried food cook faster than boiled food?

2 Chlorine is put into swimming pools to kill bacteria. Why isn't a high concentration used?

**B** The smaller pieces of limestone react with acid much faster than the larger pieces because the total surface area is bigger.

**H** So why do these changes affect the rate of reaction? According to **collision theory** it's all to do with the particles – how often they collide and whether they have enough energy to break bonds when they do.

The higher the temperature, the faster the particles move. This means that they are more likely to collide with enough energy to break some bonds and start the reaction.

Concentration is a measure of how many particles there are in a given volume. The greater the concentration, the more chance there is of the particles colliding and so reacting.

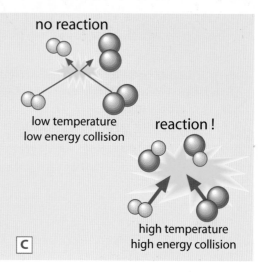

no reaction

low temperature
low energy collision

reaction !

**C** high temperature
high energy collision

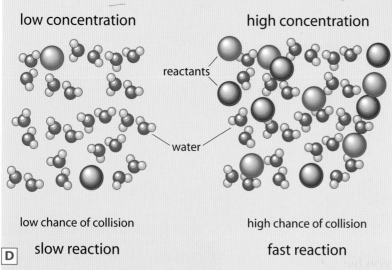

low concentration          high concentration

reactants

water

low chance of collision          high chance of collision

**D** slow reaction          fast reaction

When a large piece is broken up, there is a bigger surface area exposed to the reacting particles. If you halve the size of the pieces of solid, you double the surface area and so can double the rate of reaction. Powders have tiny particles so they have a huge surface area and reactions are very fast.

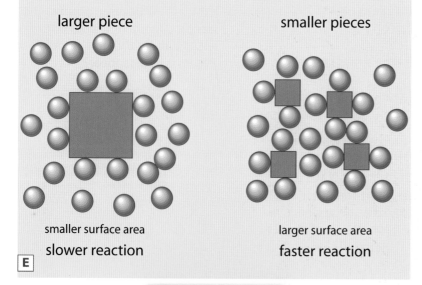

larger piece          smaller pieces

smaller surface area          larger surface area

slower reaction          faster reaction

**E**

3 In Wales it is cool and wet; in Borneo it is hot and wet. Where do you think a piece of iron will rust faster, Wales or Borneo? Explain your answer.

4 Why does chewing your food up into tiny pieces rather than swallowing it whole help you to digest it?

5 Solid zinc reacts with sulphuric acid giving off hydrogen gas. Describe and explain what would happen to the rate of reaction if you:
   a heated it up
   b used stronger (more concentrated) acid
   c used larger pieces of zinc.

Summary Exercise

Higher Questions

H

**By the end of these two pages you should be able to:**

- describe experiments to investigate the effects of temperature, concentration and surface area on the rate of a reaction
- interpret the results of these experiments.

You have already seen how to increase the rate of a chemical reaction. But in science it is important to carry out experiments to test out your ideas. A good reaction to investigate is sodium thiosulphate and acid. This slowly produces a **precipitate** of yellow sulphur.

sodium thiosulphate + hydrochloric acid ⟶ sodium chloride + sulphur dioxide + water + sulphur

This reaction typically takes about a minute. If you put the reactants in a beaker over a piece of paper with a cross marked on it, the cross will gradually disappear. You can time how long it takes for this to happen. You can then find the rate of reaction by performing the calculation:

$$\frac{1}{\text{time taken}}$$

start     going...     going...     go

This measures what proportion of the experiment was completed per second, so the longer it takes for the cross to vanish, the slower the rate of reaction, and vice versa.

**A** In the thiosulphate reaction, the precipitate of yellow sulphur gradually makes the mixture opaque so that the cross disappears.

You can use this reaction to investigate the effect of temperature on the rate of reaction. To do this you must keep all other variables constant. This means making sure that for each test you use the *same*:

- concentration and volume of thiosulphate
- concentration and volume of acid
- cross under the beaker, so it looks the same – and same person watching it
- size beaker so that you are looking down through the same depth of liquid.

1 How do you know when to stop timing the reaction in this experiment?

2 If the rate of reaction doubles in a second experiment, what does this tell you about the time it took for the cross to disappear?

You can heat the acid to different temperatures in a water bath, and use a thermometer to measure the temperature of the mixture. Then you can measure the length of time it takes to complete the reaction at each temperature. Start the timer as you mix the chemicals and stop it when the cross disappears. Record your results in a table and draw graphs of time against temperature or rate against temperature. You might find a spreadsheet helpful. Harry's results are shown in table B.

| Experiment number | Temperature (°C) | Time (s) | Rate (1/s) |
|---|---|---|---|
| 1 | 22 | 320 | 0.003125 |
| 2 | 34 | 155 | 0.006452 |
| 3 | 46 | 75 | 0.013333 |
| 4 | 58 | 38 | 0.026316 |
| 5 | 70 | 20 | 0.05 |
| 6 | 82 | 9 | 0.111111 |

**B**

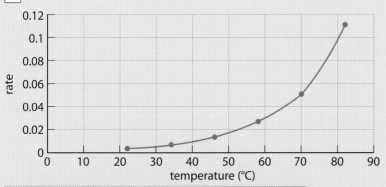

**C** Results from Harry's temperature–rate experiment.

You can perform a similar experiment using different acid concentrations. In this case you would need to:
- keep the temperature constant
- keep the volume of acid constant.

Record your results and plot graphs of time or rate, this time against the concentration. Shakir's results looked like this.

| Experiment number | Concentration (M) | Time (s) | Rate (1/s) |
|---|---|---|---|
| 1 | 2 | 75 | 0.013333 |
| 2 | 1 | 155 | 0.006452 |
| 3 | 0.5 | 320 | 0.003125 |
| 4 | 0.25 | 650 | 0.001538 |
| 5 | 0.125 | 1350 | 0.000741 |

**D**

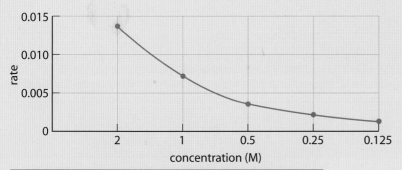

**E** Results from Shakir's concentration–rate experiment.

**Summary Exercise**

3 Use Harry's results to plot a scatter graph of the time taken (y-axis) against temperature (x-axis). Draw a curve of best fit. How does this graph compare to the rate–temperature graph shown?

4 From Harry's rate–temperature graph, roughly how many degrees did the temperature have to rise to double the rate of this reaction?

5 Look at Shakir's results. What happens to the time it takes for the cross to disappear if you double the concentration of the acid?

6 Carefully describe how you could use the thiosulphate reaction to test for the effects of temperature and concentration on the rate of the reaction.

**Higher Questions**

# 5. Catalysts and reaction rates

**By the end of these two pages you should be able to:**

- describe the effect of surface area on the rate of reaction
- describe the effect of a catalyst on the rate of reaction
- interpret the results of experiments involving catalysts
- use the state symbols (s), (l), (g) and (aq) in equations.

The exhaust gas from car engines contains polluting nitrogen oxide and carbon monoxide. These gases slowly react to form harmless carbon dioxide and nitrogen, but the reaction is too slow. Fortunately there is a way to speed up the reaction. If you pass the exhaust gas through a **catalytic converter**, over a fine mesh coated with a metal such as platinum, the reaction occurs before the gases escape.

carbon monoxide + nitrogen oxide ➤ carbon dioxide + nitrogen

$$2CO \quad + \quad 2NO \quad \longrightarrow \quad 2CO_2 \quad + \quad N_2$$

The platinum is not involved directly in the reaction. It helps to increase the rate of the reaction without being 'used up'. Substances that do this in a reaction are called **catalysts**.

A      B
Catalysts like the one above have many uses - including helping to reduce pollution, and manufacturing important chemicals.

1 Cars in Europe and the USA have catalytic converters fitted by law. Suggest a reason for this.

2 What does a catalyst do in a chemical reaction?

You can see a catalyst at work by mixing manganese dioxide with hydrogen peroxide Adding manganese dioxide clearly speeds up the breakdown of hydrogen peroxide into water and oxygen, but if you filter, dry and reweigh the black powder, you will find you have exactly the same amount you started with.

hydrogen peroxide $\xrightarrow{\text{manganese dioxide catalyst}}$ water + oxygen

$$2H_2O_2(l) \xrightarrow{\hspace{3cm}} 2H_2O(l) + O_2(g)$$

The state symbols show that hydrogen peroxide in the form of a liquid (l) produces liquid water (l) and oxygen gas (g). (The other state symbols are (s) for solid and (aq) for solution in water.)

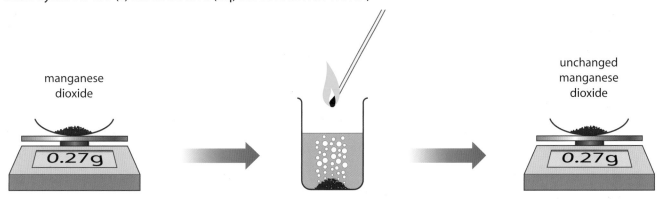

manganese dioxide

0.27g

unchanged manganese dioxide

0.27g

**C** The catalytic breakdown of hydrogen peroxide can easily be investigated in the laboratory.

To react, particles need enough energy to break their existing bonds. This is called the **activation energy** for the reaction. Catalysts work by lowering the activation energy, making it easier for the reaction to take place.

Catalysts need to be finely divided because reactions occur on the surface only. For a given catalyst, the smaller the pieces, the larger the surface area and so the faster the reaction.

**3** In the reaction shown above, how could you tell that the manganese dioxide is not simply reacting with the hydrogen peroxide to give oxygen?

**4** In industry catalysts are used to make reactions run at lower temperatures as this saves energy costs and so saves money. The table shows the temperature needed to run one particular reaction successfully using different catalysts. Which catalyst should be used, and why?

| Catalyst | Working temperature |
|---|---|
| iron oxide | 760°C |
| nickel oxide | 630°C |
| vanadium oxide | 475°C |

**5** A company needs to speed up one of its chemical reactions and is thinking of doing this by raising the temperature. Explain how they might be able to do this using a catalyst instead. Make sure you include a description of how a catalyst works and explain the importance of having the catalyst in a finely divided form. How would this save the company money?

Summary Exercise

Higher Questions

### By the end of these two pages you should be able to:

- describe how data from experiments about rates of reaction can be captured by data-logging
- explain how this data can be manipulated and displayed using spreadsheet software.

How do you monitor a volcano, to see if it is going to erupt? You could make the strenuous climb into the crater regularly to take readings of the gas temperature in the vents, or the vibrations from the lava chamber. Or you could put some sensors in the crater and have the data transmitted to the safety and comfort of your own laboratory every few minutes. Which would you prefer?

Data-logging relies on having a suitable **sensor** that can send electrical signals to your computer. These signals have to be **calibrated** – matched against a scale so that they can be read in the correct units of measurement (such as °C for temperature, or newtons for force). The data-logging software stores this information so that you can display it in tables or graphs or analyse it in other ways.

**A** Data-logging makes life easier – and safer – for scientists.

Data-logging allows you to take readings in distant, difficult or dangerous places, such as a volcanic crater or the core of a nuclear reactor. Readings can also be taken much faster – perhaps hundreds of readings per second. You can also take readings over a very long period of time.

**1** What form of energy does a temperature sensor measure? What does it turn this energy into, to transmit it to a computer?

**2** Give two examples of extreme conditions where data-logging could be used.

Data-logging can also be usefully used in the laboratory, for example in experiments on rates of reaction. In the thiosulphate and acid experiment on page 184, you have to make a judgement as to when you can no longer see the cross. This can lead to errors, as you might not do this in exactly the same way every time. Using data-logging equipment can reduce these kinds of errors.

Mix the reactants and
start the computer.

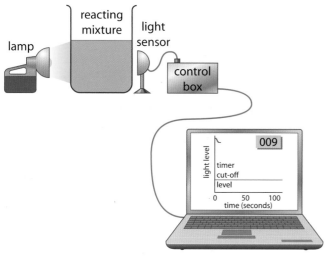

The computer software
stops the timer when
the preset level is reached.

The light level reaching
the sensor drops as
the precipitate forms.

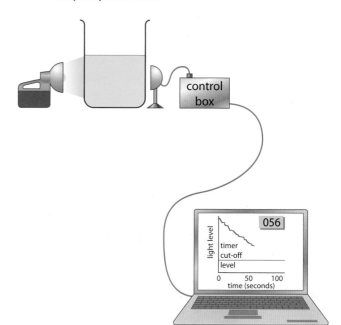

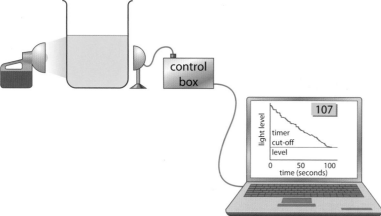

**B** Using data-logging in the thiosulphate and acid experiment.

As the reaction progresses, the light level picked up by the sensor falls. You can calibrate this so that the timer stops at exactly the same light levels every time. This cuts out the risk of human error when stopping the timer, and so it makes the experiment much more reliable.

The computer program can also export your data to a spreadsheet, which makes it easier to do calculations. To convert the time taken to a rate of reaction, you need to divide 1 by the time value. This can be done easily on a spreadsheet by using the formula '=1/(time value)'. You can then use this to plot a scatter graph of your results.

3 Suggest a reason why the data-logged version of this experiment might be more accurate than the disappearing cross version.

4 If the light source used was a torch, why would you need to make sure that you had fresh batteries at the start of the experiment? (*Hint*: what might happen to the light level long before the battery failed completely?)

5 Look at diagram B.
   a Describe how you could set up a data-logging experiment to time the thiosulphate and acid reaction. Which sensor would you use?
   b How would the computer 'know' when to stop the timer?
   c How could you convert the time taken to a rate of reaction using a spreadsheet?

Summary Exercise

Higher Questions

# 7. Enzymes – the biological catalysts

**By the end of these two pages you should be able to:**

- recall that enzymes are biological catalysts
- explain why we need enzymes to speed up the chemical reactions that keep us alive.

**A** Catalysts are used in the body…

**B** … and for things we do.

Industry relies on catalysts to speed up chemical reactions and make them more efficient. Life depends on chemical reactions and catalysts are essential to this process too. In industry, transition metals or their oxides are used as catalysts. In living organisms, the catalysts are made from protein. These biological catalysts are called **enzymes**.

Enzymes have been put to good use in other ways for centuries. The chemical reactions that make wine from grape juice or yogurt from milk rely on enzymes in the yeast or bacteria. Now, the enzymes are often taken out of the microbes and used on their own. Enzymes that naturally break down fats and oils are used in biological washing powders to help get rid of greasy stains. Other enzymes are used to pre-digest baby foods, or to break down corn starch and turn it into sugar syrup.

## Have you ever wondered?

Are there actual flesh eating bacteria?

All living things are rely on enzymes. Without them the complex processes that release energy from food could not take place fast enough. One group of enzymes controls the aerobic respiration reaction between glucose and oxygen that releases the energy you need for life. If your body cannot get enough oxygen during a burst of activity, other enzymes control the breakdown of glucose to lactic acid, in anaerobic respiration.

1 Some body enzymes speed up the chemical reactions that give us the energy we need. How does that help the athlete?

2 How do enzymes help to get your clothes clean?

Another biological process that uses enzymes is photosynthesis. The enzymes help convert light energy far more efficiently than any manufactured solar cells.

Enzymes have a wide range of functions. One group of enzymes helps break down food into small molecules during digestion. Another group helps to build up these small molecules into larger molecules for growth and repair. Others help to regulate blood sugar levels. In short, all of the chemical reactions in your body rely in some way on the action of enzymes. If the enzymes stop working efficiently, you will become ill and eventually die. As enzymes are made from protein they are damaged if overheated. Their optimum working temperature is 37 °C, which is why your body keeps itself at that temperature. If you have a fever and your temperature rises just one or two degrees, enzymes lose their effectiveness, so you will feel ill.

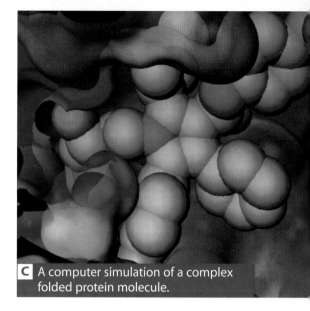

**C** A computer simulation of a complex folded protein molecule.

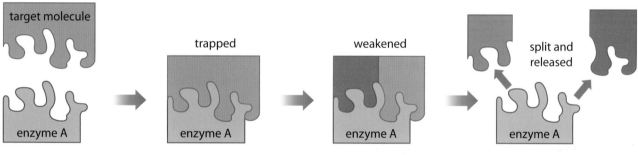

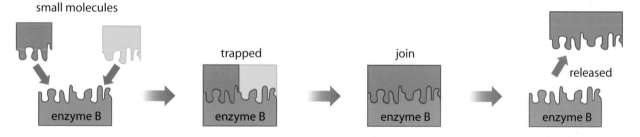

**D** Enzymes can help to break down or build up complex molecules.

Enzymes work in a different way from metal catalysts. Protein molecules are long and complicated and fold up into strange shapes. Particular molecules can fit snugly against an enzyme, like the pieces of a jigsaw puzzle. This affects the bonds within the molecule and can help break it apart. With other enzymes, two small molecules fit together, like a jigsaw. Once in position, the two molecules can then react and join together to form a new molecule before being released.

3 List three examples of the way enzymes are used in your body.

4 Why is our body temperature kept at 37 °C?

5 **a** Draw simple diagrams to show how an enzyme works when it breaks up a large molecule.
  **b** Annotate your diagrams to explain in words what is happening.

**Summary Exercise**

**Higher Questions**

# 8. Reversible reactions

**By the end of these two pages you should be able to:**

- recall that some chemical reactions are reversible and that these will often reach equilibrium
- **H** explain how this equilibrium position may be changed by changing the temperature, pressure or concentration.

## Have you ever wondered?

Can chemical reactions be undone?

You will have learnt that one way to tell the difference between a physical change and a chemical change is that physical changes are **reversible**, chemical changes are not. For example, melting wax is a physical change as it sets back to a solid when cooled, but burning wax is a chemical change as you cannot get the wax back.

physical change: solid wax ⇌ liquid wax
chemical change: wax + oxygen → carbon dioxide + water

But there are some chemical reactions that you can reverse, such as the chemical test for water. Blue copper sulphate crystals have water molecules locked up in them, chemically bonded to the copper ions. It is this combination of copper ions bonded to water molecules that gives the blue colour. If you heat these crystals, the water is driven off and you are left with a white powder – anhydrous copper sulphate (anhydrous means 'without water'). If you add water to this white powder, the bonds between the copper ion and the water are re-made and the blue colour reappears. The reaction is reversible!

blue copper sulphate ⇌ white anhydrous copper sulphate + water

It is easy to push this reaction in one direction or the other – towards the white or the blue copper sulphate. In one direction, the reaction is endothermic, so energy has to be put in. In the other direction, the reaction is exothermic, so energy is produced.

But some reactions are more awkward and tend to stop in the middle. They reach an **equilibrium** (balance) position. Dinitrogen tetroxide ($N_2O_4$) is a pale yellow gas that breaks up into two molecules of dark brown nitrogen dioxide ($NO_2$) in a reversible reaction. At room temperature, this reaction stops about halfway so you get both molecules at the same time. The mixture has a light brown colour.

**A** Most chemical reactions cannot be reversed…

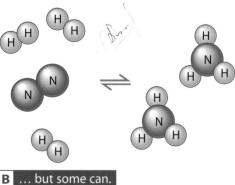

**B** … but some can.

1 Which of reactions is easily reversible? Striking a match or testing for water?

2 How can you turn:
   **a** white anhydrous copper sulphate to blue copper sulphate
   **b** blue copper sulphate to white anhydrous copper sulphate?

pale
yellow ⇌ dark
brown

...paler in cold water
(more $N_2O_4$)

light brown in warm water
(mixture of $NO_2$ and $N_2O_4$)

...darker in hot water
(more $NO_2$)

$$N_2O_4 \rightleftharpoons 2NO_2$$
pale yellow     dark brown

**C** This reaction is reversible and controlled by temperature.

**3** Energy has to be put in to split up the larger molecule on the left. Is this part of the reaction exothermic or endothermic?

**4** What is happening when this reaction reaches equilibrium?

**H** In the reaction shown in diagram C, the point at which it stops is controlled by the temperature. If you heat it up, the balance point moves to the right so you get more $NO_2$ molecules and the mixture gets darker. If you cool it down, the balance point moves to the left so you get more $N_2O_4$ molecules and the mixture gets lighter.

In different reactions, it is concentration that controls the stopping point. Bromine water is a light brown liquid made by dissolving bromine ($Br_2$) in water ($H_2O$). This ionises in a reversible reaction.

$$Br_2 + H_2O \rightleftharpoons 2H^+ + Br^- + OBr^-$$
(brown)           (all ions colourless)

**D** Reaction of bromine dissolving in water.

If you add acid, the concentration of hydrogen ions goes up. This pushes the balance point to the left and turns the mixture a darker brown. If you add alkali, the concentration of hydrogen ions goes down. This pushes the balance point to the right and the colour is lost.

In other reactions such as the production of ammonia, pressure can affect the balance point.

**5** Nitrogen dioxide ($NO_2$) gives the brown colour to city smog. Why do you think this is so much worse on hot days than on cold days?

**6** Explain how you could use bromine water as a very simple acid–alkali indicator.

Summary Exercise

Higher Questions

**H** **By the end of these two pages you should be able to:**

**P**

- explain how nitrogen and hydrogen react to form ammonia in a reversible reaction that reaches dynamic equilibrium
- explain how the Haber process shifts the balance point and makes the reaction more efficient by controlling the temperature and pressure.

**V**

**A**

**B**

Both of these involve reactions where nitrogen is combined with something else.

**?**

## Have you ever wondered?

How did the production of ammonia allow twice the world's population to be fed?

**P**

One hundred years ago crop production needed to be increased to feed the growing global population. Plants need nitrogen but unfortunately they cannot take it straight from the air. So scientists tried to find a way to turn nitrogen into ammonia to make **fertilisers**. Nitrogen and hydrogen have a reversible reaction, which is too slow at low temperatures and stops at just a few per cent of ammonia at high temperatures.

$$\text{nitrogen} + \text{hydrogen} \rightleftharpoons \text{ammonia}$$
$$N_2(g) + 3H_2(g) \rightleftharpoons 2NH_3(g)$$

When reversible reactions reach equilibrium like this, it means that the forward and backward reactions are going at the same rate. As fast as some ammonia molecules are forming, as many others are breaking up. This is why it is called **dynamic equilibrium**. To increase the amount of ammonia formed, the forward reaction needs to be speeded up to move the balance point.

1 There's plenty of nitrogen in the air, so why do we need fertilisers?

2 Why wasn't it easy to make ammonia from the nitrogen in the air?

Fritz Haber set out to solve the problem. He realised that the forward reaction was exothermic and the backward reaction was endothermic. Raising the temperature speeded up the reaction overall but meant that ammonia molecules broke up faster than they formed and the equilibrium point moved to the left – the wrong way! He needed to find a way of speeding up the reaction without raising the temperature. He did this by using an iron catalyst.

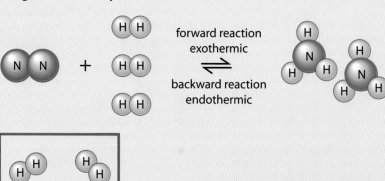

**C** Fritz Haber, a German chemist.

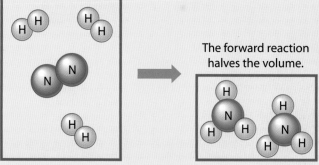

The forward reaction halves the volume.

**D** How temperature and pressure affect the balance point in the Haber process.

Next he looked at the effect of **pressure**. Here the forward reaction makes four molecules change to two. The volume of a gas depends on the number of molecules, so the forward reaction that made ammonia would reduce the volume of the gases by half. By increasing the pressure, he could encourage the formation of ammonia as this would have a smaller volume. This did make more ammonia, but still only 20 or 30% which was not enough to run the process commercially. He needed another breakthrough.

His final, winning idea can from a study of the boiling points of the gases.

Haber realised that if he reacted the gases and then cooled them, he could make the ammonia that had formed condense to a liquid and remove it. Because the ammonia was being removed, the backwards reaction could no longer occur. By recycling the unreacted gases he eventually got complete conversion to ammonia. This final breakthrough completed the **Haber process**.

| Gas | Boiling point (°C) |
|---|---|
| ammonia | −33 |
| nitrogen | −196 |
| hydrogen | −253 |

**3** What is meant by dynamic equilibrium?

**4** A modern Haber process plant runs at 450 °C and 200 atmospheres pressure.
  **a** Why is the temperature high, even though it lowers the percentage of ammonia produced?
  **b** Would the temperature have to be higher or lower if there was no catalyst?
  **c** Why is the pressure so high?

**5** Explain the three stages Haber used to solve the problem of making ammonia from nitrogen and hydrogen.

**Summary Exercise**

**Higher Questions**

# 10. Fertilisers – artificial or organic?

**By the end of these two pages you should be able to:**

- discuss the arguments for and against using artificial fertilisers in farming compared to organic methods.

**A**   **B**

Industrial fertilisers produce large crops, but organic methods have other advantages.

Artificial ammonia-based fertilisers have been around for over 100 hundred years and have increased crop yields. But organic methods are coming back into favour as people look at the wider environmental issues.

Ammonia-based fertilisers have many advantages. Ammonium nitrate ($NH_4NO_3$) has 35% useful nitrogen by mass. It can be crystallised, put in sacks and transported easily. It dissolves in water and can be sprayed onto crops. Plants can absorb it and use it directly.

In comparison, **organic** methods are slower and less effective. Organic material such as manure, compost, bone or blood and fishmeal are collected and dug into the soil. Microbes then break the organic material down. This gradually releases nitrogen compounds for plants to use. Traditionally fields were left unused for one year every four to let the soil recover. These methods are very labour-intensive and so are more expensive.

Recently people have raised concerns about artificial ammonia-based fertilisers.

- Ammonium nitrate fertiliser can wash out from fields into lakes and rivers. This causes algae to grow out of control and leads to eutrophication, which kills other wildlife. If it gets into the water supply even in small amounts it can damage the health of babies.

1 Why do artificial fertilisers show faster results than manure or compost?

2 Why do many gardeners keep a compost heap of dead plant material in their garden?

- A few crop varieties that respond well to fertiliser have taken over, and local variation has been lost. The fertilisers are also often used with pesticides to kill weeds and insects which reduces biodiversity.
- People in developing countries have to buy fertiliser from big companies. Often they cannot afford to buy them.

C An organic farm.

A growing number of people now want to use organic methods of fertilising the soil instead of the artificial fertilisers. They say that this is:
- better for the environment, as it encourages biodiversity
- better for the soil as the organic material improves its structure and helps it to hold moisture
- better for the food, as it does not contain any artificial chemicals, so it is healthier
- better for people in less developed countries as they can manage their own farms locally and do not become dependent on outside supplies or aid
- cheaper as they do not need to spend as much money on chemical fertilisers.

But there are drawbacks, of course. Organic farmers have to work a lot harder to fertilise their crops, which take longer to produce and have a lower yield, so are more expensive. The fruit and vegetables themselves may not look so perfect. Some people say that is balanced by better flavour.

There are advantages and disadvantages for both ammonia-based fertilisers and organic methods. Neither method for fertilising crops is perfect – it is still a matter for debate.

3 List two advantages of using artificial fertilisers.

4 List two disadvantages of using artificial fertilisers.

5 Write a short piece setting out argument either for or against using organic methods to fertilise crops.

Summary Exercise

Higher Questions

197

# 11. Questions

## Multiple choice questions

**1** Before a chemical reaction can occur, particles have to
  **A** be activated by a catalyst.
  **B** be heated to at least 100°C.
  **C** collide with enough energy to form new bonds.
  **D** collide with enough energy to break existing bonds.

**2** Which of the following is an endothermic reaction?
  **A** burning oil
  **B** neutralising an acid with an alkali
  **C** breaking up calcium carbonate by heating it
  **D** displacing copper from copper sulphate with iron

**3** During a chemical reaction, some bonds are broken and some are formed. Which of the following is true?
  **A** Breaking bonds is exothermic, making bonds is endothermic.
  **B** Breaking bonds is endothermic, making bonds is exothermic.
  **C** Making and breaking bonds are both exothermic.
  **D** Making and breaking bonds are both endothermic.

**4** In a timed reaction, 2.5 g of limestone dissolved completely in acid in 50 seconds. The rate of this reaction is:
  **A** 125 g/s   **B** 5 g/s   **C** 0.5 g/s   **D** 0.05 g/s

**5** In the sodium thiosulphate and acid reaction the cross disappeared in experiment A after 2 minutes, and after 1 minute in experiment B. Only one variable was changed. Which of the following is the most likely change?
  **A** The temperature for B was 12°C lower than for A.
  **B** The temperature for B was 12°C higher than for A.
  **C** The temperature for B was 82°C lower than for A.
  **D** The temperature for B was 82°C higher than for A.

**6** In a reaction between hydrochloric acid and magnesium ribbon, for experiment A, 60 cm³ of hydrogen gas was produced in one minute. For experiment B, 30 cm³ of hydrogen gas was produced in one minute. Only one variable was changed. Which of the following is the most likely change?
  **A** The acid was twice as concentrated in A as it was in B.
  **B** The acid was five times as concentrated in A as it was in B.
  **C** The acid was half as concentrated in A as it was in B.
  **D** The magnesium ribbon was cut into tiny pieces for B.

**7** If a 1 cm cube is broken up into 1 mm cubes, its surface area will have
  **A** gone down by a factor of 10.
  **B** stayed the same.
  **C** gone up by a factor of 10.
  **D** gone up by a factor of 100.

**8** A catalyst has to be in very small pieces
  **A** because catalysts are very expensive.
  **B** so that they can dissolve faster.
  **C** to give the largest possible surface area.
  **D** so that they can get hot faster.

**9** Catalysts work because they
  **A** are so reactive.
  **B** make the reactants stronger.
  **C** remove the products of the reaction.
  **D** make it easier to break the existing bonds.

**10** Using data-logging techniques to get reaction times for the sodium thiosulphate and acid reaction is more accurate that the disappearing cross method because
  **A** once calibrated, the computer will stop the timer at exactly the same point in the reaction.
  **B** once the experiment has been run a few times, the computer can predict when to stop the timer.
  **C** the sensors come with very accurate settings from the factory.
  **D** the sensor can tell when all the sulphur has been precipitated.

**11** In the 'water test' reaction:
  copper sulphate $\rightleftharpoons$ anhydrous copper sulphate + water
heating drives the reaction from left to right because the forward reaction is
  **A** a displacement reaction.
  **B** a neutralisation reaction.
  **C** an exothermic reaction.
  **D** an endothermic reaction.

**12** In bromine water
  $Br_2 + H_2O \rightleftharpoons 2H^+ + Br^- + OBr^-$
Alkali turns bromine water colourless because
  **A** it encourages the back reaction.
  **B** it reacts with all the water.
  **C** it reacts with the $H^+$ ions and so stops the back reaction.
  **D** it is a reversible reaction.

**13** In the Haber reaction:

$$2N_2 + 3H_2 \rightleftharpoons 2NH_3$$

if all the nitrogen and hydrogen molecules formed ammonia molecules the volume would
  **A** double.
  **B** stay the same.
  **C** go down to two-thirds.
  **D** halve.

**14** A century ago people were keen to find a way to make ammonia from the nitrogen in air because
  **A** the industrial revolution had raised the nitrogen levels in the air and people were worried.
  **B** ammonia was used to make smelling salts which could be used when people fainted.
  **C** ammonia could be used to make fertiliser to make crops grow better.
  **D** ammonia was a very important household cleaner.

**15** Organic food means
  **A** any food made from living things.
  **B** food grown using ammonia-based fertilisers.
  **C** food grown using 'natural' compost and manure.
  **D** food made from the cultivation of 'friendly' bacteria.

## Short-answer questions

**1** Methane ($CH_4$) burns in air with an exothermic reaction.
  **a** Which gas in air is involved in this reaction?
  **b** What are the two products of this reaction?
  **c** Explain the term exothermic.
  **d** Why doesn't a reaction occur as soon as the methane and air mix?
  **e** How does a spark or flame get the reaction started?
  **f** Why does the reaction continue once started?

**2** Marble chips (calcium carbonate) dissolve in hydrochloric acid to give calcium chloride, carbon dioxide and water.
$$CaCO_3(s) + 2HCl(aq) \rightarrow CaCl_2(aq) + H_2O(l) + CO_2(g)$$
  **a** Explain the terms (s), (l), (g) and (aq).
  **b** What would happen to the mass reading if you ran this reaction in an open beaker on a balance? Explain your answer.
  **c** Petra dissolved 1 g of marble chips in excess acid on a balance and took readings every 20 seconds. Draw a scatter graph with a best fit curve from her data below.

| Time (s) | Mass loss (g) |
|----------|---------------|
| 0 | 0 |
| 20 | 0.2 |
| 40 | 0.36 |
| 60 | 0.42 |
| 80 | 0.44 |
| 100 | 0.44 |
| 120 | 0.44 |

  **d** Why does the mass loss stop changing at 0.44 g?
  **e** Petra decided to repeat the experiment using acid that is twice as concentrated, keeping all other factors the same. Draw a sketch graph (on your graph from c) to show your prediction for her new results. Comment on your sketch graph, explaining your reasoning.
  **f** Petra then decided to repeat her first experiment using one 1 g lump of marble instead of smaller chips. Draw another sketch graph (on your graph from c) to show your prediction for this new experiment. Comment on your sketch graph, explaining your reasoning.

**3** In the Haber process, hydrogen and nitrogen combine to form ammonia. This table shows how the equilibrium for this reaction shifts as you change the temperature and pressure. **H**

| Pressure (atmospheres) | Ammonia (%) | | |
|---|---|---|---|
| | 350°C | 450°C | 550°C |
| 0 | 0 | 0 | 0 |
| 100 | 33 | 15 | 7 |
| 200 | 52 | 27 | 14 |
| 300 | 65 | 36 | 19 |
| 400 | 70 | 42 | 22 |

  **a** Draw a scatter graph for this data, plotting all three series on the same graph. Draw in three separate curves of best fit for these.
  **b** Describe the pattern shown by these three lines. How does the percentage of ammonia produced at equilibrium vary with temperature and pressure?
  **c** From your graph, what percentage of ammonia would you get:
    **i** at 550°C and 350 atmospheres pressure
    **ii** at 400°C and 200 atmospheres pressure?
  **d** The percentage of ammonia goes up as the pressure increases. Suggest a reason why very much higher pressures are not used in industry to get more ammonia.

**D**

**P**

# 12. Glossary

**activation energy** The minimum energy that is needed to break the existing chemical bonds when two particles collide.

**calibrated** Set against a known scale.

**\*catalyst** A substance which speeds up a chemical reaction without being used up.

**catalytic converter** A device fitted to vehicle exhausts which uses a catalyst to convert dangerous exhaust gases into less harmful gases.

**\*collision theory** The theory of chemical reactions that describes how particles must collide with enough energy to react.

**\*concentration** The amount of a substance in a given volume of solution.

**\*dynamic equilibrium** The equilibrium point in a reversible reaction where the rates of the forward and backward reactions are the same, so the proportions of different substances remain constant.

**\*endothermic reaction** A reaction that takes in energy.

**\*enzyme** A biological catalyst.

**equilibrium** A balance point.

**\*exothermic reaction** A reaction that gives out energy.

**\*fertiliser** Something which provides the essential minerals that plants need to grow (particularly nitrogen compounds).

**\*Haber process** The industrial process used to convert hydrogen and nitrogen into ammonia.

**\*organic** To do with living processes.

**precipitate** A solid which forms from a liquid, often when two solutions are mixed.

**\*pressure** The force exerted per unit area (e.g. $N/m^2$).

**\*rate of reaction** The speed at which a chemical reaction progresses; calculated as 1/(the time taken for the reaction to take place) or 1/(the time taken for a given amount of product to form).

**reaction (chemical)** A process through which chemicals change in some way to make new chemicals.

**\*reversible** A chemical reaction that can be made to work in either direction.

**sensor** A device which detect one form of energy and turns it into electricity.

**\*surface area** The surface of a solid that is available for chemical reactions.

**\*temperature** A measure of how 'hot' or 'cold' something is, usually measured in degrees Celsius (°C).

\*glossary words from the specification

# As fast as you can!

**A** Testing what happens is a crash is an important part of car safety design.

Most of the things we know about motion were discovered by Isaac Newton (1642–1727) in the 1600s. It may seem that there is no point in learning about things that are so old, but we have used these ideas to send probes into deep space, build supersonic aircraft, jump out of aeroplanes safely and design realistic computer games.

It may not always seem like physics is happening when you look at these things. But you will see that you can describe and predict every single part of motion with only a few simple rules.

Many of these same laws about motion are used when testing the safety of cars. The cars and the crash test dummies inside them are fitted with sensors and filmed during various tests. This allows scientists to measure the forces and velocities involved. From this information, and using knowledge of the laws of motion, designers can analyse what happens and use the results to help design new, safer cars.

---

**In this topic you will learn that:**

- the motion of moving objects can be measured
- forces can affect the motion of an object
- the speed of falling objects usually changes as they fall
- vehicles and theme-park rides have safety features to protect passengers from injury.

---

Sort these statements into three categories:

true, not true, not sure.

- Speed and velocity are two words for the same thing.

- If there are forces on an object it must be moving.

- The faster you drive the longer it takes to stop.

- Air bags are the only part of a car designed to protect you from injury in a crash.

- If you drop something from a high building it will keep accelerating until it hits the ground.

# 1. Speed and velocity

**By the end of these two pages you should be able to:**

- explain the difference between speed and velocity
- recall the equation to calculate velocity
- describe the shapes of velocity–time graphs for different moving objects.

The **speed** of an object tells you how quickly it will travel a certain distance. You can calculate speed by dividing the distance travelled by the time it takes. **Velocity** tells you more about the motion of an object. Speed tells you how fast something is moving, but velocity tells you how fast it is going and the direction it is travelling. Velocity is measured in metres per second (m/s).

Some things that you measure like temperature and mass only have a size (sometimes called **magnitude**). Quantities like velocity and force are different because they have a size and a direction. Anything that has a size and a direction is called a **vector**. If objects are travelling forwards their velocities can be shown with a positive value. If they are travelling backwards, their velocities can be shown with a negative value.

Calculating velocity is very similar to calculating speed. You need to know how far something has travelled and how long it took. Displacement is similar to distance but is a vector like velocity. It tells you the distance travelled in a particular direction. This means that it can be positive or negative, like velocity.

$$\text{velocity (m/s)} = \frac{\text{displacement (m)}}{\text{time (s)}}$$

**A** The birds may travel at the same speed, but as they travel in different directions they have different velocities.

1 What is the difference between speed and velocity?

2 Velocity is a vector. What does the word vector mean?

3 What units is velocity measured in?

For example, a car travelling on the motorway at the UK maximum speed limit (70 miles per hour, or 112.7 km/h) travels 313 metres every 10 seconds. How would you calculate its velocity in metres per second?

Answer: velocity (m/s) = distance (m)/time (s)
      = 313 m/10 s
      = 31.3 m/s.

As the car is travelling forwards, you could write this as +31.3 m/s. If it were travelling backwards at the same speed then you could write this as –31.3 m/s.

**4** What is the equation used to calculate the velocity of an object?

**5** The velocity of an object is –25 m/s.
   **a** How far will it go in 5 seconds?
   **b** If its velocity is +25 m/s what would be different about its motion?

**6** What is the velocity of a sprinter who runs +200 m in 25 seconds?

The velocity equation can tell you how far something is moving and the direction it is travelling in. But a graph of velocity against time can show much more about its movement. These graphs can have lines above and below the time axis. Lines above the time axis usually show forward motion and so lines below the axis show backwards motion.

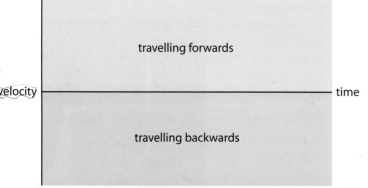

**B** Lines above the time axis usually mean forwards motion and lines below usually mean backwards motion.

If the line is horizontal then this means that the object is travelling at a constant velocity. The higher the line on the graph, the higher the velocity. If the object is travelling backwards, the lower the line, the faster it is travelling.

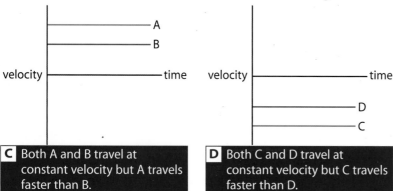

**C** Both A and B travel at constant velocity but A travels faster than B.

**D** Both C and D travel at constant velocity but C travels faster than D.

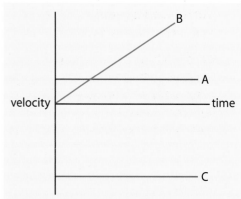

**7** Look at the lines on the graph above. State which line or lines show:
   **a** an object travelling at constant velocity
   **b** the object travelling fastest
   **c** objects travelling in opposite directions.

**8** Sketch two velocity–time graphs and explain their shapes. The first one should show a race between a slug and a fox and the second one should show the fox running home.

**Summary Exercise**

**Higher Questions**

# 2. Acceleration

**By the end of these two pages you should be able to:**

- explain what acceleration is and how it is calculated
- describe how to use a velocity–time graph to find the acceleration of an object.

**A** The acceleration in a dragster …

**B** … is much greater than any normal car.

Very few things that are moving stay at a constant velocity. They are always speeding up or slowing down. This change in velocity is called **acceleration**. Acceleration is a vector, like velocity, so it can be positive (speeding up) or negative (slowing down). Remember that vectors have direction as well as size. This means that acceleration also refers to changing direction, not just changing speed.

To work out the acceleration of something, you need to know:
- the velocity it started at (in metres per second) – this is written as *u*
- the velocity it ends up at (in metres per second) – this is written as *v*
- the time it took to change velocity (in seconds) – this is written as *t*.

The equation is:

$$\text{acceleration (m/s}^2) = \frac{\text{change in velocity (m/s)}}{\text{time (s)}}$$

This can also be written as: $a = (v - u)/t$

For example, a cheetah can start from rest and reach 26 m/s in 2 seconds. How can you find its acceleration?
Answer: $a = (v - u)/t$
$= (26 \text{ m/s} - 0 \text{ m/s})/2 \text{ s}$
$= +13 \text{ m/s}^2.$

1 What units is acceleration measured in?

2 What do the symbols *u* and *v* represent?

3 Write down the equation used to calculate acceleration in words and in symbols.

**C** Acceleration of +4 m/s² means that every second the velocity goes up by 4 m/s.

| Time (s) | Velocity (m/s) |
|----------|----------------|
| 0 | 0 |
| 1 | 4 |
| 2 | 8 |
| 3 | 12 |
| 4 | 16 |

Velocity–time graphs can also tell you about the acceleration of an object. If the line slopes upwards this means that the object's velocity is increasing (accelerating). The steeper the line, the greater the acceleration. If the line slopes downwards the object is slowing down. This is called **deceleration**.

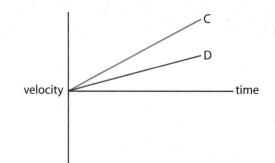

**D** Both C and D are accelerating but C is accelerating more than D.

## Have you ever wondered?

Did you realise how much you know of the laws of physics if you skate, snowboard or play flight simulators?

You can calculate the acceleration of an object using a velocity–time graph. First, look at the velocity axis and read the starting velocity ($u$) and final velocity ($v$). Then find the time ($t$) between these two values. From this, calculate the **gradient** (or slope) of the line. This gradient is the acceleration.

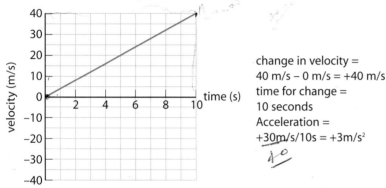

change in velocity =
40 m/s – 0 m/s = +40 m/s
time for change =
10 seconds
Acceleration =
+30m/s/10s = +3m/s²

**E** The gradient of a velocity–time graph gives the acceleration.

When using velocity–time graphs to calculate acceleration:
- make sure that you read both the initial *and* final velocities from the graph
- remember that acceleration can be negative if the velocity decreases – you must include the minus sign.

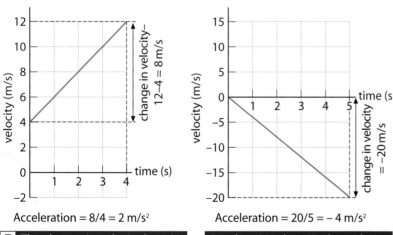

Acceleration = 8/4 = 2 m/s²

Acceleration = 20/5 = – 4 m/s²

**F** The change in velocity here is 8 m/s (not 12 m/s).

Acceleration doesn't always have to be positive.

4 An object accelerates at +3 m/s². If it starts at 0 m/s what is its velocity after 5 seconds?

5 If the line on a velocity–time graph slopes downwards, what does this tell you about the movement of the object?

6 It is possible for a stationary dragster to accelerate at +50 m/s². What will its velocity be after 0.5 seconds?

7 A sprinter travelling at 10 m/s takes 2 seconds to come to a stop. What is his deceleration?

8 Calculate the acceleration of the object from the graph.

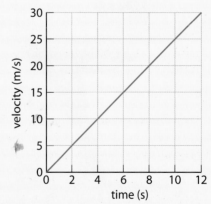

9 The Space Shuttle can accelerate initially at almost +30 m/s². Write a page from a NASA guidebook that explains what this means and how velocity–time graphs can show the motion of any object.

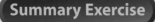

Summary Exercise

Higher Questions

# 3. Force and acceleration

**By the end of these two pages you should be able to:**

- draw a free-body diagram and explain what it shows
- recognise what a resultant force is and how it will make an object accelerate
- recall that force, mass and acceleration are all related
- recognise the equation force = mass × acceleration ($F = ma$).

If you kick a ball it will move. It accelerates from stationary. You also know that the harder you kick it the faster it will move away. You can work out how fast something will accelerate if you know how big it is and how hard it is pushed. Many of these ideas were described by Isaac Newton in the 1600s.

Most objects have more than one force acting on them. It is important to look at all of the forces acting before you try and work out what will happen. A **free-body diagram** shows all the forces acting on an object and the size and direction of those forces. It is highly simplified, so nothing else is included.

**A** Not everything you push will move.

ice pushing up

weight pulling down

**B**
You can't see the forces acting on the ice skater … but you can on a free-body diagram of her. **C**

All the forces acting on an object added together are called the **resultant force**. If the forces cancel each other out, the resultant force is zero. If the resultant force is not zero then the object will accelerate in the direction of the resultant force. The greater the resultant force, the greater the acceleration of the object. If the force is doubled, the acceleration will also be doubled.

1 How is a free-body diagram different from a normal diagram of an object and the forces acting on it?

2 Who discovered many of the laws about moving objects?

**3** What is the name for the total force that acts on an object?

**4** If this force is not zero, what will happen to the object?

**5** Draw a free-body diagram of a book weighing 4 N sitting still on a table.

**D** The thrust is much greater than the weight so the rocket accelerates upwards.

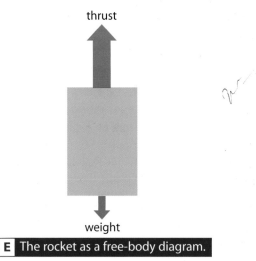

**E** The rocket as a free-body diagram.

The acceleration of an object when a resultant force is acting on it depends on the size of the force and the mass of the object. If the same force is applied to two objects of different mass, the one with the smaller mass will have the larger acceleration. To get two objects of different mass to accelerate at the same rate, you need to apply a larger force to the one with the greater mass.

One of Newton's laws describes the relationship between force, mass and acceleration:

$$\text{force (N)} = \text{mass (kg)} \times \text{acceleration (m/s}^2)$$

this is sometimes written as $F = ma$.

force causing an acceleration

force = 50 N
mass = 10 kg
acceleration = 5 m/s²

force = 50 N
mass = 10 000 kg
acceleration = 0.005 m/s²

**F** The mass of the lorry is 1000 times bigger than the mass of the bicycle. With the same force, the acceleration of the bicycle will be 1000 times bigger than the acceleration of the lorry.

**6** Write down the equation that connects force, mass and acceleration.

**7** A car and an articulated lorry are accelerating at the same rate. Which engine is providing the greater force? Explain your answer.

**8** Imagine that you are Isaac Newton, having just discovered how force, mass and acceleration are related. Write a letter (less than 150 words) to the editor of a newspaper explaining your 'new' ideas.

**Summary Exercise**

**Higher Questions**

# 4. Mass and acceleration

**By the end of these two pages you should be able to:**

- calculate the resultant force for any scenario
- recall the equation that connects force, mass and acceleration ($F = ma$).

Isaac Newton was able to look at the forces on an object and calculate exactly what would happen to it. If you look at the size and direction of all forces then you can add them together to work out the resultant force. This can tell you how the object will behave.

1 A piece of cheese sits on a plate. Its weight of 12 N is matched by the table pushing 12 N upwards. What is the resultant force?

2 When you calculate the resultant force what two things do you need to consider?

If there are more than two forces acting on the object, you can still calculate the resultant force. Add all the forces up in each direction and then find the difference. For example, if you drop a stone into the sea, its **weight** provides a downwards force, but there are also forces acting upwards as shown in diagram B.

**A** There are lots of forces on the pole vaulter, but the resultant force is upwards, so she accelerates upwards.

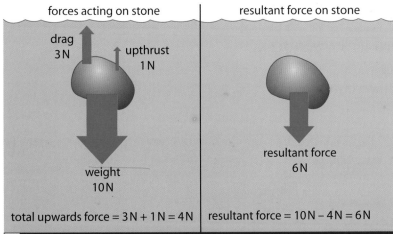

forces acting on stone

drag 3 N

upthrust 1 N

weight 10 N

resultant force on stone

resultant force 6 N

total upwards force = 3 N + 1 N = 4 N   |   resultant force = 10 N – 4 N = 6 N

**B** The resultant force is downwards, so the stone will accelerate downwards.

3 The engine of a motorbike provides a forward force of 3500 N. Air resistance (1000 N) and friction (500 N) provide forces in the opposite direction.
   a What is the resultant force on the motorbike?
   b What will happen to the motion of the motorbike?

If you know the mass and acceleration of an object, you can use Newton's equation that relates force, mass and acceleration ($F = ma$) to calculate the force.

For example, a car (mass 2000 kg) can accelerate at 7 m/s². What is the force of the engine?

Answer: $F = ma$
      $= 2000 \text{ kg} \times 7 \text{ m/s}^2$
      $= 14\,000 \text{ N}.$

**C** Cars with larger masses need higher forces to make them stop.

## Have you ever wondered?

Could you manage the acceleration to be a good Formula 1 driver?

Acceleration doesn't always cause a change in speed. The velocity of an object will change even if it only changes direction. As a bobsleigh goes round a sharp banked curve it may travel at a constant speed, but it is actually accelerating. This is because the force from the wall is causing it to change direction. This means it is changing its velocity as well.

The bigger the mass of an object the greater the force needed to make it accelerate. A four-man bobsleigh has a greater mass than a two-man one. This means that a greater force from the wall is needed to make the bobsleigh accelerate or it will fly off the track.

**D** The velocity of this bobsleigh changes as it goes round the banked track.

**Summary Exercise**

4 Can something accelerate if its speed stays constant? Explain your answer.

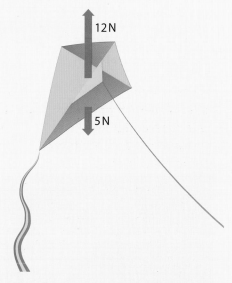

5 The diagram shows the forces on a kite of mass 0.5 kg.
   a What is the resultant force on the kite?
   b What is the acceleration of the kite?
   c If the tail (mass 0.1 kg) fell off what would the new acceleration be?

6 The total mass of the cars allowed on a rollercoaster has been increased. Write a letter to the manager saying why you think this might be dangerous. Include ideas about force, mass and acceleration and how they can be calculated.

**Higher Questions**

# 5. Falling through the air

**By the end of these two pages you should be able to:**

- explain what can happen to an object if the resultant force is zero
- describe the forces acting on falling objects
- **H** • define terminal velocity.

If the resultant force on an object is zero you might think that this means that the object will stay still. If an object is already moving and the resultant force becomes zero it will carry on moving at a constant speed in a straight line.

When you start pedalling on a bicycle, you need an initial force to start moving. Once you reach a constant speed, you don't have to pedal so hard. Your pedalling is simply keeping up with the friction and air resistance that is trying to slow you down. The forces cancel each other out, so the resultant force is zero.

It is very rare that something will carry on moving in a straight line at constant speed forever. This does happen in space, where there is no air resistance. Once space probes are launched they only need their thrusters to change direction. They will carry on moving for ever or until they hit something.

1 If the resultant force on an object is zero, what two things can happen to it?

2 Why do deep space probes not need to use their thrusters much?

3 If a bird is flying round in a circle, can the resultant force on it be zero? Explain your answer.

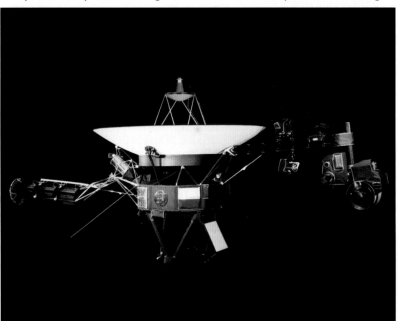

**A** There are no forces on this probe but it can still move through space.

Whenever an object moves through a liquid or gas, it experiences a **resistance** force that acts in the opposite direction to its movement. The size of the force depends upon the liquid or gas the object is moving through, and the speed at which it moves. As the object gets faster, the resistance force increases.

**B** No turning back, the resultant force is downwards and big!

Do the experiences of bungee jumping, parachuting and free-fall all feel the same?

When an object starts falling, the only force acting downwards is weight, which will always stay constant. This makes it accelerate downwards. As an object starts to fall, it gets faster, making the resistance force bigger. As long as the weight is larger than this force, the object will continue to accelerate.

**4** A child drops a coin into a wishing well. What is the direction of the resistance force from the water as the coin falls?

**5** What two things will affect the size of the resistance force from a gas or liquid?

**6** Give one example where the resistance force is large and one where this force is small.

**H** The velocity of a falling object will increase until the upward force of the resistance is the same as the weight. This will make the resultant force zero, so the object will travel at a constant velocity. This is called the **terminal velocity**.

People have survived a fall from 20 000 feet – how?

| Initially there is no air resistance. | As speed increases, so does air resistance. | Eventually weight and air resistance are the same. |
|---|---|---|
|  |  |  |
| Large resultant force downwards, the skydiver accelerates. | Smaller resultant force downwards, the skydiver still accelerates. | Resultant force is zero, terminal velocity reached. |

**C** Eventually a skydiver reaches a terminal velocity.

**7** As a skydiver falls through the air, what happens to the force caused by
**a** his weight
**b** air resistance?

**8** What is the name for the maximum speed any falling object can reach?

**9** Draw a diagram of a diver diving off a high cliff into the sea, including the labels and force arrows. Write a description of what is happening to the diver, including the words weight, resistance and acceleration in your answer.

**Summary Exercise**

**Higher Questions**

# 6. How much motion?

**H** **By the end of these two pages you should be able to:**

- define the word momentum
- calculate the momentum of an object.

When an object is moving it has more than just velocity. It also has lots of energy. To explain its motion fully we use a term called **momentum**. The momentum of an object depends on:

- its velocity
- its mass.

**A** Big things moving fast have lots of momentum.

Objects that are have a large mass and a high velocity will have a very large momentum. Small objects can have a large momentum but they must be travelling very fast.

**1** What two things does the momentum of an object depend upon?

**2** If a mouse and a cat are travelling at the same velocity, which has the greater momentum? Explain your answer.

## Have you ever wondered?

How does a jetski work?

Understanding momentum is very important when cars are crash-tested in safety trials. The mass of the car and how fast it travels in normal situations is known. So the momentum of the car can be calculated. This information helps designers work out how the momentum can be absorbed safely in an accident, without harming the drivers and passengers.

**B** Most of the momentum in a crash will be absorbed safely between the bumper and the driver.

The momentum of an object is measured in kilogram metres per second (kg m/s). To calculate the momentum of an object, use the equation:

momentum (kg m/s) = mass(kg) × velocity (m/s).

For example, to calculate the momentum of a horse of mass 300 kg galloping at 12 m/s:

momentum = mass × velocity
= 300 kg × 12 m/s
= 3600 kg m/s.

**C** Removing momentum quickly can cause massive damage.

If you want to stop an object then you need to remove its momentum. If you calculate the object's momentum, you can find out the force that will be needed to stop it in a **collision**. Sometimes this force can be very large and can damage whatever it is you are trying to slow down. You can reduce the force needed to slow something down, but this means that you must apply the force for a longer time. This idea is used in car safety design.

6 The fastest a tennis ball (mass 0.05 kg) has ever been hit is 73 m/s. What was its momentum?

7 An apple tree in Isaac Newton's garden has a mass of 30 kg and falls over with a momentum of 45 kg m/s. What velocity does it fall at?

8 What is the mass of a golden eagle that flies with a velocity of 70 m/s and a momentum of 245 kg m/s?

9 Write a brief description of what momentum is and how it can be calculated. Include two examples of things with a large momentum, and two examples of things with a small momentum.

3 What are the units of momentum?

4 What is the momentum of a 64 kg sprint runner travelling at 9.6 m/s?

5 A small dog has a mass of 5 kg but its momentum is zero. How is this possible?

**P**

**V**

**P**

**Summary Exercise**

**Higher Questions**

# 7. Thinking, braking, stopping

**By the end of these two pages you should be able to:**

- describe and use the terms thinking distance, braking distance and stopping distance
- describe what different factors can affect each of these
- explain why driving fast can be dangerous.

## Have you ever wondered?

How closely can you drive behind another moving car?

The distance a car travels from when the driver sees something to when the vehicle stops is called the **stopping distance**. It is made up of two parts: the thinking distance and the braking distance:

stopping distance = thinking distance + braking distance.

The thinking distance is the distance the car travels between when the driver sees or hears something and the moment the driver actually responds by applying the brakes.

The braking distance is the distance the car travels between when the driver applies the brakes and the vehicle stops.

**A** Driving at a reasonable speed and being alert means stopping quickly.

1 What is the stopping distance?

2 What two things are added together to make the stopping distance?

3 What is stopping distance measured in?

Thinking distance depends on the speed the car is travelling and the **reaction time** of the driver. The human brain responds quickly but not instantly. It can take from 0.2 seconds to over 1 second to react to something.

The main factor that will affect the thinking distance is the speed the car is travelling. Whatever the speed of the car, the driver will take the same time to respond. But the faster the car is travelling, the further it will go in that time. Doubling the speed will double the thinking distance.

Braking distance mainly depends on the speed of the vehicle, the slope of the road and the amount of friction between the road and the tyres. Again, speed is the most important of these factors. Doubling the speed more than doubles the braking distance. At 20 miles per hour (8.9 m/s) the braking distance is 6 m. But at 40 miles per hour (17.8 m/s) the car will travel 24 m before coming to a stop.

## Typical stopping distances

**20 mph**
6 metres  6 metres        = 12 metres or 3 car lengths

**30 mph**
9 metres   14 metres      = 23 metres or 6 car lengths

**40 mph**
12 metres   24 metres     = 36 metres or 9 car lengths

**50 mph**
15 metres    38 metres    = 53 metres or 13 car lengths

**60 mph**
18 metres     55 metres   = 73 metres or 18 car lengths

**70 mph**
21 metres      75 metres  = 96 metres or 24 car lengths

▶ Thinking distance

▶ Braking distance    average car length = 4 metres

**B** Typical thinking, braking and stopping distances.

Many factors can affect a driver's thinking distance and braking distance.

| Thinking distance | Braking distance |
|---|---|
| Speed of travel | Speed of travel |
| Effects of drugs and stimulants | Conditions of tyres |
| Alcohol (reaction time is affected even under the legal limit) | Conditions of brakes |
| Age and health of the driver | Road conditions (e.g. rain, ice, gravel or grit, oil spills) |
| Distractions (e.g. mobile phones, in-car navigation systems, adjusting the stereo, large roadside billboards) | The mass of the car (the heavier the car is, the longer it will take to stop) |
| Tiredness | Aerodynamics (the more aerodynamic a car is the longer it will take to stop!) |

**C** Using a mobile phone while driving delays your reaction time. It is also illegal.

**4** What factor affects both the thinking and stopping distance?

**5** Use the table of stopping distances to estimate the thinking, braking and stopping distances for a car travelling at 55 mph.

**6** Write a short road safety leaflet about stopping distances. Include information about the factors that affect how far a car travels before it stops.

Summary Exercise

Higher Questions

# 8. Dangerous driving

**By the end of these two pages you should be able to:**

P
H

- define action and reaction forces
- assess some of the technologies used to increase vehicle safety, including crumple zones and air bags
- explain how vehicles and theme-park rides are designed to absorb momentum.

Whenever two objects touch there are always two forces involved. If a car crashes into a bollard, the car applies a force to the bollard called the **action** force. The bollard also exerts a force back onto the car known as the **reaction** force, which is what does the damage. The forces are always equal in size and opposite in direction. These ideas are used in car safety testing to predict what might happen and to improve car design.

P

**1** Are the action and reaction forces always equal in size?

**2** What is always different about the action and reaction forces?

?

## Have you ever wondered?

Which make of car saves most lives in a crash?

All car manufacturers test their cars to make sure they are as safe as possible. The tests include front, side and pedestrian impact tests. Dummies are used in place of the driver and passengers, and the cars are crashed in various ways. Sensors on the dummies measure the forces acting on them and this data can help predict what might happen in a real accident.

P

Crumple zones and air bags are two very successful car design features that reduce injuries if a car is involved in an accident.

V

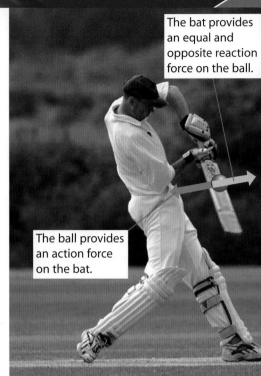

The bat provides an equal and opposite reaction force on the ball.

The ball provides an action force on the bat.

**A** The ball applies a force on the bat but the bat applies the same force back.

**3** Name three types of impact tests carried out on new cars.

**4** How are the forces involved in the crash test measured?

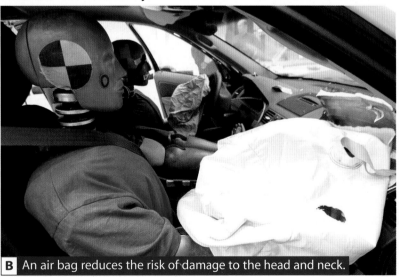

**B** An air bag reduces the risk of damage to the head and neck.

An air bag inflates automatically on impact. It cushions the head of the driver or passenger. This causes much less injury than if they were to hit the hard surface of the steering wheel or dashboard.

Crumple zones in cars work in a similar way to air bags. Parts of the front and sides of the car are designed to crumple on impact. This reduces the forces on the people in the car. However, even for a small impact, the car can look very badly damaged.

**C** Crumple zones reduce the risk of injury by absorbing momentum.

**H** Whenever anything stops, its momentum is removed. This can require very large forces. Both air bags and crumple zones work by increasing the time it takes for the car or passenger to come to a halt, reducing the forces involved and risk of injury.

Exactly the same idea is used when fast moving roller coasters come to a halt at the end of the ride. They are slowed down gradually so that you do not feel a strong jolt.

5 What are vehicles designed to absorb during a collision?

6 Why do roller coasters not come to a sudden halt at the end of the ride?

7 Write down at least four features in a car that are designed to improve safety.

8 Write a promotional leaflet for a new car, advertising its safety features. Include some data and try to make it as persuasive as possible.

**Summary Exercise**

**Higher Questions**

# 9. It's all too dangerous

**By the end of these two pages you should be able to:**

- explain the term 'risk'
- describe how numbers can be used to describe risk in different ways
- recognise some of the factors that affect how willing we are to take risks.

## Have you ever wondered?

What is the chance of you being injured in a high-speed outdoor activity?

When you talk about **risks**, you are saying how likely it is that a specific negative event might happen. Often you will look at risks as being either acceptable or unacceptable. This depends on how likely it is to happen, as well as the consequences of the risk. Acceptable risks, such as getting a minor injury playing football, do not stop us from doing something. Unacceptable risks, such as the possible accidents caused by drinking and driving, usually do stop us.

1 What is meant by risk?

2 Can a risk predict whether something will definitely happen?

"You're not driving anymore..."

Enjoy the football but remember, just the one could be too much.

**A** **B** Playing football is seen as having acceptable risks of injury. Drink driving has risks that we see as unacceptable.

Risk can be written down in many ways but two of the most common ones are:

- as a percentage – a 3% risk means that the likelihood that something will happen is three times in 100. 100% means it is certain to happen
- as a ratio – a 1 in 6 risk means that there is one chance in six that something will happen. Sometimes this is written as a fraction, e.g. 1/6.

It is useful to be able to convert between a ratio and a percentage especially as you may want to compare risks.

How could you decide which is the greater risk: 15% or 1 in 8? First, convert 1 in 8 into a percentage, and then compare them: (1/8) × 100% = 12.5%.
As 15% is larger than 12.5%, it is more likely to happen, and so is a bigger risk.

# 20% of all users get injured

## One eighth of all users suffer damage

# 1 in 5 at risk

**C** If we listened to all the warnings we'd probably never do anything.

The way you feel about something can have a big effect on whether you think it is an acceptable risk. If a risk becomes familiar, you will probably underestimate it. So if you are used to crossing a road near your house, you may feel the risk is much lower than it really is. If you don't feel that you have a choice about being exposed to risk, you will probably overestimate it. So a leak from a chemical factory may seem more dangerous than smoking, as you have no control over it.

**D** Falling off your bicycle is much more likely than being involved in a plane crash but the consequences are far less severe.

**Summary Exercise**

3 Convert the following risks into percentages.
   a 1 in 25
   b 1/5

4 The chances of injury doing sport A is 2%, for sport B it is 1 in 12 and for sport C it is ¼. In which sport is an injury:
   a most likely
   b least likely?

5 Do you think reading about bad events in the news helps you to understand risks better? Explain your answer.

6 Give three things that might affect whether we think something is risky or not.

7 Write a short newspaper style article with the headline 'Risk: how dangerous is it really?' Include an explanation of what risk is, how it can be expressed, and how people view risks.

**Higher Questions**

# 10. The fastest, most dangerous things

**By the end of these two pages you should be able to:**

- use tables and graphs to represent the same risk in different ways
- explain how spreadsheets can be used to represent the motion of objects
- describe how this software can be used to create models to help analyse risk.

As well as percentages and fractions, you can also use graphs and charts to represent risk. Using graphs rather than numbers can make it easier to get a picture of the risk involved. This can help you make a decision about whether to do something or not.

**1** Other than percentages and fractions, what other ways can be used to represent risk?

**2** What is an advantage of showing risk in this way?

Using graphs can be very useful but, as with all data, you need to be careful with what you are looking at. The data for travel safety looks very different depending on whether it shows deaths per hour travelled or per kilometre travelled as shown here.

Computers can help us to get an even better understanding of risk. Data can be put into spreadsheet software and used to create a model of what might happen. The more information is collected, the better the model will be at predicting what might happen. There are two key types of information that can be collected for modelling risk:
- data based on scientific knowledge, such as the physics of motion
- data about past events.

Car manufacturers use computers to create models of what might happen to a car and its passengers in an accident. During testing, sensors can accurately measure the position and speed of any vehicle. This data can then be put into spreadsheets to analyse the motion. From this, it is possible to calculate information such as force, acceleration and energy. This data is then used to help predict the risk of damage from a crash.

**3** What two types of information can be collected to help model risk?

**4** What type of software program can be used to analyse motion?

**5** What information about moving objects can these programs calculate?

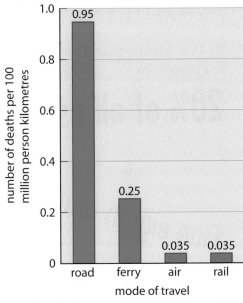

**A** Here you can clearly see that road travel has the highest risk.

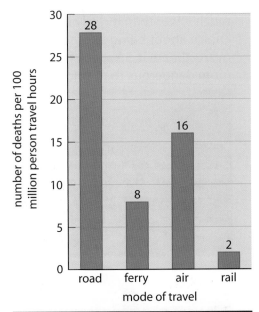

**B** Looking at the same data in a different way can give a different picture. Compare this with diagram A.

To create a model that can predict the risk of injury in the future it is useful to know about previous accidents. Once you have all the data, it is much easier to see patterns and predict the risk of injury in a range of circumstances.

V

**C** Data-capture equipment can record forces acting in collisions. This data can then be used to model risk.

Computer-based models are a useful tool to help us look at risk, but they do have limitations:
- they are only as good as the data that is used
- they are unable to consider every factor, particularly human behaviour
- they can get very complicated.

6 What is the advantage of collecting all the accident data into one place?

7 Describe some of the limitations of using computer models to identify risk.

8 Write a short information leaflet with the title 'Graphs, spreadsheets and risk'. Include information on how graphs can be used to represent risk and how spreadsheets can be used to help assess risks.

P

**Summary Exercise**

**Higher Questions**

# 11. Questions

## Multiple choice questions

**1** Which of the following is the correct equation for working out velocity?
  **A** velocity = distance/time
  **B** velocity = displacement/time
  **C** velocity = displacement × time
  **D** velocity = distance × time

**2** Which one of the following statements about speed and velocity is true?
  **A** Velocity is the speed in a particular direction.
  **B** Speed is the velocity in a particular direction.
  **C** Velocities can only be positive.
  **D** Speeds can be positive and negative.

**3** On a velocity–time graph there is a straight horizontal line. What does this tell you about the motion of the object?
  **A** It is not moving at all.
  **B** It is travelling at constant velocity.
  **C** It is accelerating.
  **D** It is decelerating.

**4** Which of the following is the correct equation for working out acceleration?
  **A** $a = (v - u)/t$
  **B** $a = (v - u) + t$
  **C** $a = (v + u)/t$
  **D** $a = (v - u) × t$

**5** What units is acceleration measured in?
  **A** metres per second
  **B** metres squared per second
  **C** metres squared per second squared
  **D** metres per second squared

**6** The gradient of a velocity–time graph shows
  **A** the speed.
  **B** the acceleration.
  **C** the displacement.
  **D** the force.

**7** If the resultant force on an object is zero, which of the following things cannot be true?
  **A** The object is travelling backwards at a constant speed.
  **B** The object is accelerating in a forwards direction.
  **C** The object is travelling forwards at a constant speed.
  **D** The object is stationary.

**8** A cyclist pedals with a force of 45 N forwards. There is a resistive force of 30 N in the opposite direction. What is the size of the resultant force?
  **A** 75 N
  **B** 15 N
  **C** 1.5 N
  **D** 1350 N

**9** Which is the correct definition of the thinking distance?
  **A** The time it takes between seeing something and reacting.
  **B** The distance the car travels between seeing something and reacting.
  **C** The distance the car travels between pressing the brakes and stopping.
  **D** The time between seeing something and the car stopping.

**10** Which of the following is the equation that relates force, mass and acceleration?
  **A** $F = ma$
  **B** $a = m/F$
  **C** $F = m + a$
  **D** $a = Fm$

**H** **11** An object is falling through a liquid. Which of the following statements about its velocity is true?
  **A** It keeps increasing as long as it falls.
  **B** It keeps increasing but eventually reaches a maximum value called the terminal velocity.
  **C** It goes up to the terminal velocity and then increases at a slower rate.
  **D** It increases, reaches a maximum and then starts decreasing.

**12** What is the momentum of a 2 kg roof tile falling at 6.4 m/s?
  **A** 12.8 kg/m/s
  **B** 3.2 kg m/s
  **C** 3.2 kg/m/s
  **D** 12.8 kg m/s

**13** Which of the following statements about car crumple zones is true?
  **A** They reduce the total momentum of the car before the collision.
  **B** They increase the time of a collision.
  **C** They speed up the removal of momentum from the head.
  **D** They reduce the force felt on impact.

**14** Which of the following statements about the resistance force on a falling object is true?

   **A** The resistance force always increases.

   **B** The resistance force acts in the opposite direction of motion.

   **C** The resistance force is usually greater than the weight.

   **D** The resistance force gets smaller as the speed increases.

**15** Why are the brakes used to stop a roller coaster at the end of the ride applied slowly?

   **A** So that there is a jolt at the end.

   **B** To remove the momentum quickly.

   **C** To remove the momentum slowly.

   **D** To provide a greater resistance force.

## Short-answer questions

**1** The following graphs show the motion of two objects. For each one describe their motion.

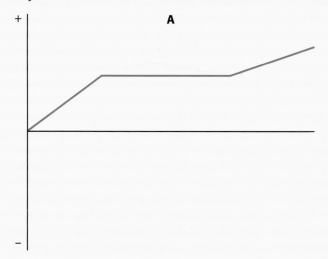

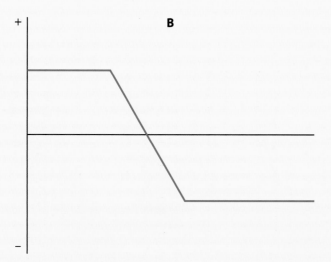

**2** There are two different key equations that involve acceleration, for each of them, write down the equation that relates them, including the units they are measured in.

**3** Describe what the term vector means, using at least one example.

**4** When a dragster starts its run, its fuel tanks are full.

   **a** What happens to the mass of the dragster during the race?

   **b** If the maximum thrust from the engines is constant, what happens to the maximum possible acceleration of the dragster?

   **c** If a dragster goes from 0 m/s to 120 m/s in 5 seconds, what is it acceleration?

   **d** If it were able to continue accelerating at that rate, how much longer would it take to reach the speed of sound (340 m/s)?

**H** **5** Steve, Duncan and Gary are talking about momentum. Steve says that a bird can have more momentum than a car. Duncan says it is possible although very unlikely. Gary says that it is never possible.

   **a** Who is correct? Explain your answer.

   **b** Write a full definition of momentum, explaining what it is and how it can be calculated with the appropriate equation.

   **c** The fastest bird (a peregrine falcon) can travel at 80 m/s. If it had a mass of 1.1 kg, what would its momentum be?

# 12. Glossary

*acceleration  A measure of how quickly the velocity of an object is changing. It can be positive (speeding up) or negative (slowing down).

*action  In physics, one of a pair of forces. The reaction force acts in the opposite direction.

*collision  When two or more objects come into contact with each other.

deceleration  Another term for negative acceleration.

free-body diagram  A simplified diagram of an object showing all the forces acting upon it and the size and direction of those forces.

*gradient  A measurement of the steepness of the slope of a graph. The steeper the graph, the higher the gradient.

*magnitude  A measure of how big something is.

*momentum  A quantity describing the movement of an object. Calculated by multiplying the mass by the velocity.

*reaction  In physics, one of a pair of forces. This acts in the opposite direction to the action force.

reaction time  The time between when you see or hear something and when you react.

*resistance  In physics, a force that acts in the opposite direction of motion. Friction is an example of a resistance force.

*resultant force  The total force that results from two or more forces acting on a single object. It is found by adding the forces together, taking into account their direction.

risk  How likely something unfortunate is to happen.

*speed  A measure of the distance an object travels in a given time. Usually measured in metres per second (m/s).

*stopping distance  The distance a car travels between when the driver sees something and when the car stops. Found by adding thinking distance and braking distance.

*terminal velocity  A constant, maximum velocity reached by falling objects. This happens when the weight downwards is equal to the air resistance upwards.

*vector  A quantity that has a size and a direction. Force and velocity are examples of vectors. Speed, mass and volume are not vectors.

*velocity  The speed of an object in a particular direction. Usually measured in metres per second (m/s).

*weight  The force pulling an object downwards. It depends upon the mass of the object and the strength of gravity.

*glossary words from the specification

# Roller coasters and relativity

**A** Most of the fun and thrills in life come from physics.

Riding on <u>roller coasters</u> in a theme park can be a thrilling experience. Every year newer and faster roller coasters are built all around the world, but the principles that make them work are the same as they were in the 1840s, when the first looping coasters were built.

These principles are based on forces, motion and energy. At the start of the ride the roller coaster is given lots of energy. Energy cannot be destroyed, so the roller coaster keeps almost all of it as it travels around the track. This is how they work without any engines. Understanding these principles has helped scientists, engineers and designers to develop many applications – from clocks to spaceships.

### In this topic you will learn that:

- physics explains how theme park rides work
- for an object to move in a circular path a force must act on it
- energy can be converted from one form to another but it cannot be made or destroyed
- new scientific theories are not always derived through experimental methods.

Draw a diagram of a roller coaster track containing loops and hills. Add notes to your diagram as well as underneath to try and explain what you know about:

- the different types of energy that the roller coaster might have
- where it might get this energy from and where it might go
- what happens to the energy that the roller coaster has during the ride and at the end when it stops
- what might happen if it has too much or too little energy.

# 1. Work it out

**By the end of these two pages you should be able to:**

- explain and use the term 'work'
- calculate the work done when you know the force and distance.

Work is all about **energy transfer** – moving energy from one place to another. Energy comes in many different forms, such as in a car battery, a moving football or even a biscuit. You can move energy around, but you cannot create it or destroy it. Whenever you lift or move anything, energy is being transferred from one form to another, but it always has to go somewhere. This is called the law of **conservation of energy**.

The energy transferred when you move something is called the **work done**. It depends on the size of the force and the **distance** the object travels. The harder you push something and the further you push it, the more effort you need to put in. Work done is measured in joules (J).

1 What is the meaning of work done?

2 Explain the meaning of conservation of energy.

3 What two things affect the amount of work done?

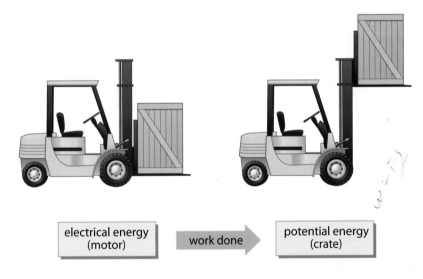

electrical energy (motor) → work done → potential energy (crate)

**A** The electrical energy from the motor provides the work needed for lifting.

You can calculate the amount of work done in any situation with the following equation:

work done (J) = force (N) × distance moved in the direction of the force (m)

The distance moved in the direction of the force is known as **displacement**. This is written as s. So the equation is often written as:

$W = Fs$

**B** If you know the force needed to lift the car and how far it is lifted, you can calculate the work Superman does. Much easier than lifting it yourself!

For example, a fork-lift truck uses a force of 700 N to lift a pile of pallets up 4 m. The work done is:

work done (J) = force (N) × displacement (m)
$$= 700 \text{ N} \times 4 \text{ m}$$
$$= 2800 \text{ J}$$

**C** The motors and winches in a roller coaster need to do a lot of work against the force of gravity to lift the cars to the top.

The work done often involves lifting something up against the force of gravity. The force needed to lift something can be assumed to be the same as its weight. So it requires a force of 35 N to lift an object that has a weight of 35 N. If you only know the **mass** of an object, you can convert it to weight. You may remember that on the surface of the Earth a 1 kg mass has a weight of 10 N. This is a very useful conversion to know.

Imagine that a vet lifts a monkey with a mass of 4 kg onto a table 1.2 m off the ground. How much work is involved?

First find the weight of the monkey:

weight (N) = mass (kg) × 10 (N/kg)
$$= 4 \text{ kg} \times 10 \text{ (N/kg)}$$
$$= 40 \text{ N}$$

Then calculate the work done:

work done (J) = force (N) × distance (m)
$$= 40 \text{ N} \times 1.2 \text{ m}$$
$$= 48 \text{ J}$$

**Summary Exercise**

**4** Write down the equation used to calculate the work done.

**5 a** What is the work done by an eagle that catches a fish, using a force of 8 N to lift it up 40 m?
  **b** If the fish was lifted up three times as high, what would the work done be?

**6** What is the work done when a 200 kg piano is lifted up to a second floor window, 7.5 metres off the ground?

**7** Think of an example when you have lifted something heavy.
  **a** Describe what you did, using the terms 'work done' and 'gravity'.
  **b** Where was the energy transferred?
  **c** Explain how you would calculate the work done.
  **d** Estimate some values and calculate the work done, showing your work.

**Higher Questions**

P

V

P

# 2. Power

**By the end of these two pages you should be able to:**

- explain the meaning of the term 'power'
- recall and use the correct equation to calculate power.

In the days before tractors and combine harvesters, horses were the main source of heavy labour in most people's day to day lives. The more horses you had, the more work you could do and the quicker you could get things done. Horsepower as a unit of measurement is still sometimes used to describe engines today, although things are measured a bit more precisely now.

Horsepower is not a measure of work; it is a measure of **power**. This tells you how quickly energy transfer is taking place. Power is now measured in watts (W). One horsepower is roughly equal to 750 W.

1  What does the term power mean?

2  Name two different units of power.

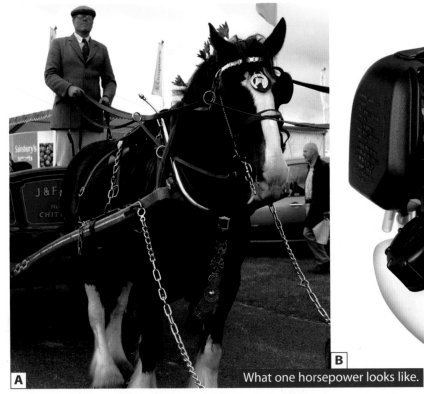

A

B

What one horsepower looks like.

Energy comes in many different forms. A machine is any device that converts energy from one form to another, which makes our lives easier. Every day you use lamps that convert electrical energy into light. If you want to compare the power of different machines, it is not enough just to know how much energy they use. You also need to know how quickly they get the job done. So you need to find out:

- the amount of energy transferred, in joules
- the time for this transfer, in seconds.

The quicker energy is transferred, the greater its power. The word power is often used to describe electrical circuits, but it can be applied to any situation in which energy is being transferred from one form to another.

**B** Powerful means doing lots of work and doing it quickly.

You can work out the power using the following equation:

$$\text{power (W)} = \frac{\text{work done (J)}}{\text{time taken (s)}}$$

This is often written as:

$$P = \frac{W}{t}$$

An electric guitar amplifier produces 8000 joules of sound energy in 20 seconds. You can use the equation to work out its power:

$$\text{power (W)} = \frac{\text{work done (J)}}{\text{time taken (s)}}$$
$$= \frac{8000\ \text{J}}{20\ \text{s}} = 400\ \text{W}$$

One watt means that one joule is converted every second. One kilowatt means that 1000 joules are converted every second. Energy-saving light bulbs have a low power rating. This tells you that every second they use less energy than traditional ones, saving energy and money.

**C** Powerful speakers use thousands of joules every second.

3 What is the definition of a machine?

4 What two things do you need to measure to calculate the power of something?

5 If an old crane lifts 20 N a distance of 100 m in 20 s and a new one does the job in 10 s, which has the greater power? Explain your answer.

6 Convert the following into watts.
   a 3 kW
   b 10 kW
   c 0.5 kW

7 What is the power of an electric cable car that uses 3500 joules every second?

8 a Write your own definitions of energy transfer and power. Include the equation in your answer.
   b Give two examples of power, and explain where the energy is transferred.

**Summary Exercise**

**Higher Questions**

# 3. Kinetic energy

**By the end of these two pages you should be able to:**

- define kinetic energy
- recognise what factors affect the kinetic energy of an object
- use the equation for calculating the kinetic energy of a moving object.

Is it more painful to be hit by a basketball or a cricket or tennis ball? Of course, it all depends upon how fast they are going. Any object that is moving has **kinetic energy**. If you want to stop it then you need to transfer its energy somewhere else. If it is transferred to you, it might hurt! The energy of any moving object has to go somewhere when it stops – this is why vehicle accidents can have such devastating consequences.

To find out the kinetic energy of any moving object there are two things that you need to know:

- its mass
- its velocity.

If either of these increases, then so does the kinetic energy.

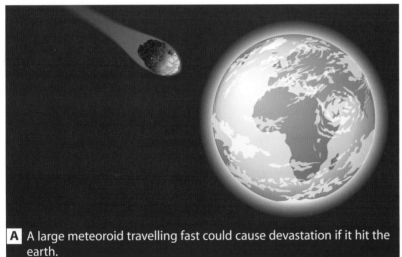

**A** A large meteoroid travelling fast could cause devastation if it hit the earth.

1 If you stop a moving object, what happens to its energy?

2 What two things need to be measured to find kinetic energy?

Like all forms of energy, kinetic energy is measured in joules. The kinetic energy of any moving object can be calculated with the following equation:

kinetic energy (J) = $\frac{1}{2}$ × mass (kg) × (velocity (m/s))$^2$

This is sometimes written as

KE = $\frac{1}{2}mv^2$

You can work out the kinetic energy of an arrow of mass 0.2 kg fired at 70 m/s using the equation above:

kinetic energy (J) = $\frac{1}{2}$ × mass (kg) × (velocity (m/s))$^2$
$= \frac{1}{2}$ × 0.2 kg × (70 m/s)$^2$ = 490 J

Only the velocity is squared, and not the mass. This tells you that changing the velocity will make a much bigger difference to kinetic energy than changing the mass. If a lot of energy is involved, it may be measured in kilojoules (1 kJ = 1000 J).

You can see how the mass and the velocity affect the kinetic energy of an object by doubling each one in turn. Take the arrow from the above example. If it was twice as heavy, the new kinetic energy would be:

KE = $\frac{1}{2}$ × 0.4 kg × (70 m/s)$^2$ = 980 J

If it was moving twice as fast, the new kinetic energy would be:

KE = $\frac{1}{2}$ × 0.2 kg × (140 m/s)$^2$ = 1960 J

So, even a very small object has lots of kinetic energy if it is moving very fast. Tiny flecks of paint and debris from previous space missions are floating around in space at high speeds. Space shuttles have to be made of very strong materials to protect against damage caused when they are hit by these little pieces of debris.

**B** Fast means lots of kinetic energy.

3 What units is kinetic energy measured in?

4 **a** What is the equation used to calculate kinetic energy?
  **b** Which variable from the equation has the biggest effect on the kinetic energy? Explain your answer.

## Have you ever wondered?

Which parts of the ride make you feel sick?

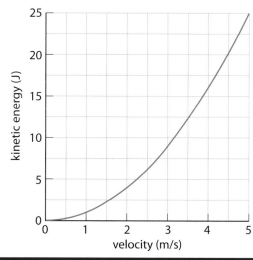

Kinetic energy against velocity for an object with constant mass (2 kg)

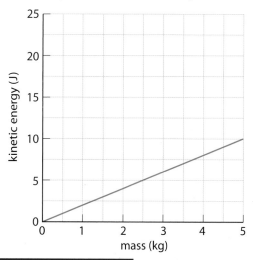

Kinetic energy against mass for an object with constant velocity (2 m/s)

**C** Increasing the velocity increases the kinetic energy much more than increasing the mass.

5 One of the fastest tennis serves ever was at 68 m/s (almost 250 km/h). If the ball had a mass of 0.06 kg, what was its kinetic energy?

6 Explain what kinetic energy is, using examples of objects with large and small amounts of kinetic energy. Include the equation in your answer.

Summary Exercise

Higher Questions

# 4. Potential energy

**By the end of these two pages you should be able to:**

- define potential energy
- recognise what factors affect the gravitational potential energy of an object
- use the equation for calculating gravitational potential energy.

It's obvious that it takes a bit of work carrying a heavy suitcase up a set of stairs, against the force of gravity. There is more energy stored in the suitcase at the top of the stairs than at the bottom. The suitcase has stored energy which is called **potential energy**.

1 What is the name for the type of energy stored in a lifted object?

2 What is the name of the force that you work against when you lift objects up?

When people talk about potential energy they usually are referring to **gravitational potential energy**, the type that is involved in lifting objects. There are also other types of potential energy, including **elastic potential energy**. This describes the energy stored when you change the shape of an object, like when you squash a spring.

The gravitational potential energy stored in an object depends upon three things:
- the mass of the object
- the strength of the force of gravity
- the height it is lifted.

In most cases, the strength of gravity will always be the same. But if you were weightlifting on the moon, the force of gravity would be lower, making it easier to lift the weights.

**A** More potential energy than most of us could provide. If the weights are dropped, they will fall to the ground with a lot of force.

**B** Weaker gravity means less gravitational potential energy and an easier lift.

3 Name one type of potential energy.

4 What three factors affect the amount of gravitational potential energy stored in an object?

5 Why would the gravitational potential energy in a lifted object be less on the Moon than on Earth?

To calculate the change in gravitational potential energy when something is lifted you can use this equation:

gravitational potential energy transferred (J)
= mass (kg) × acceleration of free-fall due to gravity (m/s²) × change in height (m)

This is sometimes written as

GPE = mgh

On Earth the value g will almost always be 10 m/s².

Priya has a mass of 35 kg. She climbs the 1652 steps to the top of the Eiffel Tower in Paris (300 m). How much gravitational potential energy does she gain?

GPE = mgh
$\quad$ = 35 kg × 10 m/s² × 300 m
$\quad$ = 105 000 J (105 kJ)

**C** Even if all these people have the same mass, the highest one has the most gravitational potential energy.

## Have you ever wondered?

How do you make the biggest water splash?

6 What is the equation used to calculate the change in gravitational potential energy?

7 Jumping over 6 m in the pole vault is considered a great achievement. What is the change in gravitational potential energy when an athlete (mass = 60 kg) does this?

8 Write a fact sheet on gravitational potential energy. Include examples of objects with large amounts of this type of energy and the equation to calculate it. Try to include at least one worked example in your answer, using the examples above to guide you.

**Summary Exercise**

**Higher Questions**

# 5. Electrical energy

**By the end of these two pages you should be able to:**
- define electrical energy
- recognise what factors affect the electrical energy in a circuit
- use the equation for calculating electrical energy.

Energy transfer can happen in all kinds of places – even in moving things that are almost impossible to see, like electric currents. As the **current** flows around an electric circuit, energy is being transferred to components like lamps, speakers and motors.

**A** Cars run on petrol but they need electrical energy to start.

The amount of **electrical energy** in a circuit depends on three things:
- the voltage, in volts
- the current, in amps
- the time, in seconds.

If any of these increases, so does the amount of electrical energy. Because current and **voltage** can be controlled easily, electricity is one of the most versatile types of energy available.

The winching motor on a roller coaster is a very good example of something that converts electrical energy into gravitational potential energy as it lifts the roller coaster cars. Because the energy needed to get the roller coaster and passengers up the track is very large, special high power motors are needed. They often run on high currents and higher voltages than normal mains electricity so they can provide enough energy.

1 Give an example, other than a roller coaster, of something that converts electrical energy into gravitational potential energy.

2 What three factors affect the amount of electrical energy available?

**B** Big rides mean big motors and big electricity bills at theme parks.

Electrical power is calculated by multiplying the voltage by the current (P = VI). Electrical energy is simply the amount of electrical power that is generated during a given period of time.

electrical energy (J) = power (W) × time (s)
E = Pt

It we replace P in the above equation with VI then we get the more common equation used to calculate electrical energy:

electrical energy (J) = voltage (V) × current (A) × time (s)

This is sometimes written as:

E = VIt

A motor on the London Eye runs at a voltage of 415 V and a current of 56 A. How many joules of electrical energy does it use in 5 seconds?

electrical energy (J) = voltage (V) × current (A) × time (s)
$$= 415 \text{ V} \times 56 \text{ A} \times 5 \text{ s}$$
$$= 116\,200 \text{ J (116.2 kJ)}$$

**3** What is the equation used to work out the amount of electrical energy available?

**4** How much electrical energy does a toaster have that uses 4 A at 230 V when it is turned on for 10 seconds?

**5** Write down the equation for electrical energy that includes power.

**6** How much energy does a 200 W light bulb use in 60 seconds?

**7** Explain what electrical energy is and how it is related to power. Include both versions of the equation and at least one example calculation.

**C** The motors on the London Eye use over a million joules every minute.

Summary Exercise

Higher Questions

**H** **By the end of these two pages you should be able to:**

- explain what happens when an object moves in a circular path
- describe the forces that give objects a circular motion
- describe and show the direction of the forces causing circular motion.

If you are riding a bike or skating then you will know that if you slip going round a corner then you will fly outwards. A similar thing might happen on a children's roundabout. If you are spinning quickly and you let go, you will fly off. Even though you cannot measure these **forces**, it is easy to get a feel for what is happening.

When anything goes round a corner or is on a circular path, forces act inwards towards the centre of the circle. It is these forces that stop you from flying outwards, unless you lose your grip!

1 If you sit on a merry-go-round, which direction does the force act in?

2 Explain what is happening to the forces when a skier flies off the track when she goes round a corner.

3 When a cyclist goes round a banked corner, where does the force come from to keep him on this path?

4 Name at least three other sports where competitors move in circular paths.

**A** When an object travels on a circular path, the force acts inwards.

In sports such as cycling, skating and skiing, the force that acts inwards is friction. The friction between the wheels, skates or skis and the track keeps the athlete moving in a circular path. If they go too fast round a corner, there will not be enough friction – the force is too small so they will fly outwards.

Exactly the same idea applies to the Earth orbiting the Sun. In this case the gravitational attraction between the Earth and Sun provides the force keeping us orbiting the Sun. If gravity could somehow be turned off then the Earth would fly outwards into space!

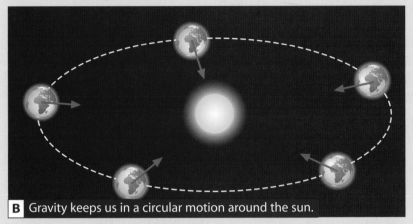

**B** Gravity keeps us in a circular motion around the sun.

As you know, the **velocity** of an object tells you both its **speed** and the direction in which it is travelling. Any object moving in a circular path is constantly changing direction. This means that even if it is travelling at a **constant speed**, its velocity is always changing. The changes in an object's velocity over time tell you its **acceleration**. So when an object travels in a circular motion for any period of time, it is actually accelerating.

To make an object accelerate, a force is needed. If an object is moving in a circular path, then there must be a **resultant force**, this acts toward the centre of the circle.

resultant force

**C** There are many forces on the rider but the resultant force is towards the centre. This makes the girl accelerate and travel in a circular path.

5 When the moon orbits Earth, what forces causes the circular motion?

6 If an object is travelling at a constant speed on a circular path is its velocity constant? Explain your answer.

7 If an object is travelling at a constant speed on a circular path does it have to be accelerating? Explain your answer.

8 Write an information sheet to explain the key ideas about circular motion. Include information about the forces and their direction, as well as labelled diagrams.

**A**

**P**

**Summary Exercise**

**Higher Questions**

**H** *By the end of these two pages you should be able to:*

- recognise that scientists accept theories if they can make accurate predictions
- explain that these predictions need to be testable
- describe how some of the predictions made by Einstein's theory of relativity have been tested and validated.

Scientific theories, like Einstein's **theory of relativity**, need to be tested before they can be accepted. Einstein's theory explains many complex things about space and time that are almost impossible to test experimentally. But scientists can test some of the things that the theory predicts will happen. In this way, they can find evidence to reject or support the theory.

Einstein's predictions could not be tested when the theory was first published in the early 1900s. Since then, science and technology have progressed a great deal. Scientists now have different ways to check whether Einstein's ideas are correct.

**1** What usually has to happen for us to accept new scientific theories?

**2** Give a reason why Einstein's theory was not widely accepted when it was first published.

**3** Explain how a theory can still be considered correct, even if it cannot directly be tested experimentally.

50 m/s                    1 500 000 m/s                    almost the speed of light

**A** If something is going really fast then it will appear squashed to someone watching but everything will look exactly the same to the driver.

One of the things that the theory of relativity predicts is that for anything moving very fast, time slows down. The faster you go, the more time slows down.

This idea was tested in 1971. Two very accurate clocks were set at *exactly* the same time. One was left on the ground and one was put in a jet aeroplane for 45 hours. After the flight they were compared, and the one from the plane was found to be slower. This helped to prove the theory, even though the clock was only slower by about 0.000 000 06 seconds! This test has been carried out many times since, with the same results every time: the faster the clock travels, the slower time gets.

## Have you ever wondered?

Can spaceships fly across galaxies at warp speed (faster than light)?

**B** The faster you go, the more time slows.

Einstein's prediction was also validated in a different way – with a tiny particle called a muon. Muons travel close to the speed of light. They are created when cosmic rays hit the Earth's atmosphere. Muons normally disintegrate in a fraction of a second. This means that we would not expect any to reach the surface of the Earth. However, some of them do reach Earth. Because they travel so fast, time slows down for them and so they arrive before they disintegrate.

**4 a** What was the prediction that was tested with accurate clocks and aeroplanes?
   **b** How was the test carried out?
   **c** What were the results of this experiment?
   **d** Why do you think this test could not have been done in 1915?

**5** What causes muons to be created?

**6** How do these particles show that the predictions made by the theory of relativity are correct?

**7** Write a newspaper article entitled 'What makes relativity a good scientific theory?' Include an explanation of how predictions and tests have led us to believe that the theory is true.

**C** Observing muons helped to prove the theory of relativity.

The results of these tests support the predictions made from Einstein's theory of relativity. The theory is accepted by scientists as giving a good explanation of some of the ways in which space and time behave.

Summary Exercise

Higher Questions

# 8. Einstein and relativity

**By the end of these two pages you should be able to:**

- recognise that developing a scientific theory can be a creative process
- explain why scientists sometimes have difficulty accepting new theories.

Scientific theories are often created by carrying out experiments. Patterns found in the results from these experiments help to develop a theory or law which can be used to make predictions. These are then tested again and again until scientists are satisfied that the theory is supported. Other scientists can then use the data to repeat the experiment and check it themselves.

Other scientific theories are not based on experiments at all. Instead, the scientist uses his or her imagination to bring together different ideas in new ways. This is the creative side of science.

**1** How are experiments used to create new theories?

**2** What is another way that theories can be developed?

**A** Some theories come from thought alone.

**3** What is a thought experiment?

**4** Why is Einstein considered to be a creative scientist?

Einstein's theory of relativity is a good example of creative science. He used his knowledge of existing ideas and experiments and then imagined new possibilities. He called this a *Gedankenexperiment*, which is German for 'thought experiment'. It takes a very special, creative mind to think this way. It was many years before some parts of the theory could be tested and were shown to be correct. There are many other famous thought experiments. They often have odd names such as Schrödinger's cat, Maxwell's demon, quantum suicide and the bucket argument.

How did Einstein come up with the most famous idea in physics – the theory of relativity?

Welcome Home after 30 years

**B** Would you believe that going very fast would slow down time if you did not have any proof? The theory of relativity states that for the person on Earth time will travel much faster than for the astronaut travelling near the speed of light.

experimental analysis

repeatable findings

peer review

new scientific theory

theory accepted

**C** It can take a great deal of work and many years to get a new scientific theory accepted.

Relativity was controversial partly because it disagreed with ideas that scientists already had. It suggested that mass and energy could change into each other – something no-one expected was possible. It also suggested that gravity was much more complicated than previously thought. It was almost impossible to test experimentally and created new areas of scientific study that had not been looked at before. This made it difficult for scientists to accept it.

In the 1500s people could not believe the new idea that the Earth goes round the Sun. People often find it difficult to accept new theories, sometimes even when there is proof. This still happens today with some new scientific theories. Ideas that challenge what we already accept and believe can be threatening and for some scientists it can affect their careers dramatically.

New scientific ideas now go through a long process of checking and testing by other scientists working in similar areas before they are accepted. This is called peer review. Often, it is important that findings can be repeated many times, and any predictions that the theory might make also need to be checked.

5 Why did some scientists find it difficult to accept the theory of relativity?

6 Give an example of another theory that was not accepted at first.

7 Write a fact sheet about scientific theories. Make sure you include:
   **a** the different ways that scientists can come up with new theories
   **b** what a thought experiment is
   **c** why new theories may not be easily accepted.

Summary Exercise

Higher Questions

**By the end of these two pages you should be able to:**

- explain the meaning of conservation of energy
- recognise the different forms of energy involved in a roller coaster ride
- describe the energy transfers that happen during a roller coaster ride
- explain the main principles that make roller coasters work.

Roller coasters can go incredibly fast, sometimes up to speeds of 200 km/h – yet they do not have motors running all the time. This due to the conservation of energy. As you know, this means that you cannot destroy energy. All you can do is move it around. All the energy that the roller coaster needs is given to it by the winches at the beginning of the ride. Once it starts moving it carries on going as the energy transfers from one form to another.

## Have you ever wondered?

Where does the power come from to make a theme park ride accelerate faster than a space shuttle?

At the start of almost all roller coaster rides there is a long slow bit as the cars go up to the highest point of the track. This is not just designed to build up tension for the riders (although it does!) but to give the roller coaster as much gravitational potential energy as possible. Without this, the ride will not work.

**A** Tension builds … and so does the gravitational potential energy!

When a roller coaster is at the top of the track, the force of gravity is acting on the cars. As the brakes are released this force causes it to accelerate to high speeds. As it accelerates,

1 Why do roller coasters go up to the highest point at the start?

2 Why are motors not needed to keep roller coasters going?

3 a What force is acting upon the cars at the top of the ride?
  b What does this make the cars do?

the gravitational potential energy is transferred into kinetic energy. The more kinetic energy it has, the faster it goes.

When the roller coaster reaches the bottom and the track curves upwards, it slows down. The kinetic energy decreases and is transferred back into gravitational potential energy as it goes up the slope. This is the main type of energy transfer that continues throughout the ride.

**4** If a roller coaster has lots of kinetic energy what does that tell you about the ride?

**5** What other types of energy are involved in the ride?

**B** During the ride the car will be at different heights and speeds but the total energy will stay the same throughout.

According to the law of conservation of energy, the total amount of energy that the roller coaster has at the start cannot be destroyed. For most of the ride it stays with the roller coaster, in different forms. Some of the energy during the ride is transferred away from the roller coaster on the corners and loops. Most of it ends up as thermal energy in the brakes when it is brought to a halt at the end. Log flumes are slightly different, as much of the kinetic energy they gain on the big drops is transferred to the water, making a big splash.

**6** When a roller coaster stops, where has all the energy gone?

**7** Explain how the law of conservation of energy applies to roller coaster rides.

**8** What happens to the kinetic energy of a log flume ride when it reaches the bottom of a big drop?

**C** Most of the kinetic energy of this ride goes into the water.

**9** Draw a poster showing a roller coaster you have designed yourself. Add notes to the diagram explaining the energy involved and how it transferred at different points (e.g. top of track, fastest corner). Also include some information about forces, speed and acceleration.

## Have you ever wondered?

If you could design a roller coaster ride, what would it look like?

**Summary Exercise**

**Higher Questions**

# 10. The best rides

**By the end of these two pages you should be able to:**

- predict what type of energy a roller coaster will have at different stages of the ride
- calculate the amount of energy at different points on the ride.

As you know, energy is conserved during a roller coaster ride. Throughout the ride the total energy will stay the same. It is just transferred from one form to another.

| Part of ride | Energy change |
|---|---|
| being lifted up at the start | electrical → gravitational potential |
| going down a slope, speeding up | gravitational potential → kinetic |
| going up a slope, slowing down | kinetic → gravitational potential |

**A** The energy changes happen pretty quickly when the brakes come off.

1  What happens to the total energy of a roller coaster during the ride?

2  What is the energy change involved when the electric motors lift the roller coaster up?

3  Write down the other two main energy changes that happen in a roller coaster ride.

It is possible to follow the energy of the roller coaster at different stages and work out what will happen during the ride. The example below takes an imaginary vertical roller coaster being winched up to the top and then dropping.

The electric motors use a current of 50 A at 415 V. They take 20 seconds to lift the cars and passengers (total mass 1600 kg) to the top of the track. How much gravitational potential energy do they gain? (In all the following examples, you can assume the energy transfer is 100% efficient, even though this would not be the case in reality.)

Use the equation for electrical energy:

E = VIt

Substitute the numbers into the equation:

E = 415 V × 50 A × 20 s = 415 000 J

All of this becomes gravitational potential energy, so the cars will have 415 000 J of gravitational potential energy.

You can also calculate the power of this motor.

power = energy/time
= 415 000 J/20 s = 20 750 W

After the ride starts to drop, just before it reaches the ground, all its gravitational potential energy is transferred to kinetic energy. So it will have 415 000 J of kinetic energy.

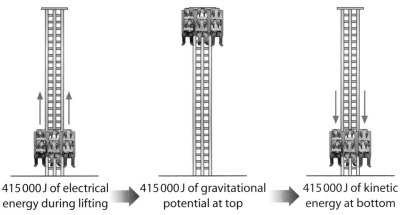

415 000 J of electrical energy during lifting ➡ 415 000 J of gravitational potential at top ➡ 415 000 J of kinetic energy at bottom

**B** During the ride the total energy stays the same, it just transfers from one form to another.

**H** If you know how much kinetic energy the ride has at the bottom of the drop, and you know its mass, you can calculate its velocity. To do this, you need to rearrange the equation for kinetic energy.

KE = $\frac{1}{2}mv^2$

Rearrange this to find the velocity:

$v = \sqrt{\dfrac{KE}{\frac{1}{2}m}}$

Then you can substitute the data:

$v = \sqrt{\dfrac{415\ 000\ J}{\frac{1}{2} \times 1600\ kg}}$

Have you ever wondered?

Can you say why theme park rides are addictive?

**C** This ride can make you feel much heaver than normal as it transfers energy between kinetic and gravitational potential.

**4** A roller coaster has of mass 2300 kg is lifted 34 m up a track How much gravitational potential and kinetic energy does it have
  **a** at the top of the track
  **b** half-way down the track
  **c** when it comes to a stop at the end of the ride?

**5 a** Describe the different forms of energy in a roller coaster ride and how they are transferred.
  **b** Explain how you could prove that energy is conserved throughout the ride. Include equations in your answer.

**Summary Exercise**

**Higher Questions**

# 11. Questions

## Multiple choice questions

1 A hydraulic crane is used to lift a boat into a dockyard. Which of the following lists all the information needed to calculate the work that the crane does?
   A The weight of the boat and the distance it is carried.
   B The weight of the boat and the time it takes to do the lifting.
   C The weight of the boat, the distance it is carried and time it takes to do the lifting.
   D The weight of the boat and the speed it moves at.

2 Which of the following lists all the information needed to calculate the power that the crane in question 1 uses?
   A The weight of the boat and the distance it is carried.
   B The weight of the boat and the time it takes to do the lifting.
   C The weight of the boat, the distance it is carried and time it takes to do the lifting.
   D The weight of the boat and the speed it moves at.

3 What units are work and power measured in?
   A Power and work are both measured in joules.
   B Power and work are both measured in watts.
   C Power is measured in joules and work is measured in watts.
   D Power is measured in watts and work is measured in joules.

4 Choose the response below that places the following objects in order of increasing kinetic energy: a car (1000 kg, 5 m/s), a golf ball (0.05 kg, 70 m/s) and a shark (200 kg, 20 m/s)
   A shark, golf ball, car
   B car, golf ball, shark
   C golf ball, shark, car
   D shark, car, golf ball

5 Which of the following statements about gravitational potential energy is correct?
   A It only depends upon the strength of gravity and how quickly you lift something.
   B It only depends upon the strength of gravity.
   C It only depends upon mass, the strength of gravity and the height something is lifted.
   D It only depends upon how high you lift something.

6 Which is the correct equation used to calculate electrical energy?
   A $E = V/It$
   B $E = VIt$
   C $E = V + It$
   D $E = V + I + t$

7 Which of the following statements about scientific theories is false?
   A It can take many years for some theories to be accepted.
   B Patterns found in experimental results can lead to theories.
   C New theories can sometimes contradict everything that was previously thought about a subject.
   D Theories can only ever be proven by experimental work.

8 Why do roller coasters not need on-board motors?
   A They usually have all the energy they need by the time they reach the top of the first drop.
   B Each time they travel down a slope they gain more energy to keep them going.
   C As they travel faster the total amount of energy they have increases, keeping them going.
   D All the energy they need is stored as kinetic energy before they start.

9 A snake is slithering along at a constant velocity on a horizontal path. Which of the following statements about its energy is correct?
   A The gravitational potential energy increases and the kinetic energy decreases.
   B The gravitational potential energy decreases and the kinetic energy increases.
   C Both the gravitational potential energy and the kinetic energy remain constant.
   D Both the gravitational potential energy and the kinetic energy are decreasing.

10 Which of the following statements about the energy in a vertical drop roller coaster is false?
   A The total amount of energy throughout the ride remains constant.
   B During the ride the kinetic energy increases and the gravitational potential energy decreases.
   C The total amount of energy throughout the ride increases.
   D The ride has its maximum gravitational potential energy at the very top.

**H** **11** Which of the following statement about an object in circular motion is not true?
   **A** There is always force acting towards the centre of the motion.
   **B** The velocity can remain constant.
   **C** The speed can remain constant.
   **D** The object must be accelerating.

**12** Which of the following statements about Einstein's theory of relativity is true?
   **A** As you travel faster, time always speeds up.
   **B** Time does not change, whatever speed you travel at.
   **C** It can be tested experimentally very easily.
   **D** It was not accepted straight away by all scientists.

**13** At what velocity must a school text book (mass 1 kg) be thrown so that it has 32 J of kinetic energy?
   **A** 32 m/s
   **B** 1 m/s
   **C** 8 m/s
   **D** 64 m/s

**14** What happens to the kinetic energy of a moving object if the velocity is tripled and the mass is made three times smaller?
   **A** It gets nine times bigger.
   **B** It gets three times bigger.
   **C** It gets three times smaller.
   **D** It gets six times bigger.

**15** A levitating super-magnet has 72 J of gravitational potential energy. How much gravitational potential energy would a similar sized one have on the Moon if it were hovering three times higher than the one on Earth. (*Note*: the acceleration due to gravity on the Moon is six times smaller than on Earth.)
   **A** 36 J
   **B** 12 J
   **C** 216 J
   **D** 72 J

**Short-answer questions**

**1** A milk float, float fully laden with milk (total mass 800 kg) climbs up a steep hill, 120 m high. The engine provides the energy for this work. The power of the engine is quite low, so it takes 5 minutes to get to the top.
   **a** **i** Define the terms 'work' and 'power'.
   **ii** State the equations used to calculate them, explaining each term used and the units they are measured in.

   **b** What is the work done to raise the m      distance? Show your working.
   **c** What is the power provided by the m      this? Show your working

**2** Read the newspaper article below and answer the questions that follow.

> ## Einstein all wrong! Time goes the other way
> Professor Cameron Bowie, the maverick British scientist has just announced his new theory which suggests that much of what is predicted by Einstein's theory of relativity is completely wrong. Jokingly called 'de-relativity', Bowie's new theory suggests that when you travel close to the speed of light time actually speed up, rather than slowing down, as Einstein famously predicted. When challenged to show evidence for his theory, Professor Bowie said: "We just don't have the technology at the moment, but one day everyone will know I am right. My colleagues around the world don't like what I have to say because it disagrees with everything that they believe to be true, but that's not my fault. I may disagree with Einstein, but I now know how he felt."

   **a** Professor Bowie says that there are currently no experiments that can test his theory. Does this mean that it must be wrong? Explain your answer.
   **b** How might it be possible to check whether or not this theory is correct?
   **c** Assume that this theory is actually correct. Suggest why it might take some time for it to become widely accepted.
   **d** When Professor Bowie says 'I know how Einstein felt', what do you think he means?

**3** Draw a diagram of the Earth in orbit around the Sun. **H**
   **a** On the diagram, draw an arrow to represent the force that causes this circular motion.
   **b** What causes this force?
   **c** As the Earth orbits the Sun, does each of the following quantities for the Earth increase, decrease or stay the same:
   **i** mass
   **ii** speed
   **iii** velocity.

**\*acceleration** A measure of how quickly the velocity of an object is changing. It can be positive (speeding up) or negative (slowing down).

**\*conservation of energy** A law that states that energy can be converted from one form to another but cannot be created or destroyed.

**\*constant speed** The movement of an object that covers the same distance every second, neither accelerating nor decelerating.

**\*current** The flow of electricity around a circuit, measured in amps (A).

**\*distance** A measure of how far apart objects or places are, in metres (m).

**displacement** A measure of the distance in a particular direction, in metres (m).

**elastic potential energy** The energy stored when the shape of an object is changed, like squashing a spring. Measured in joules (J).

**\*electrical energy** The energy made available by a flow of current. Measured in joules (J).

**\*energy transfer** The change in energy from one form to another. For example, in a loudspeaker the energy transfer is from electrical to sound.

**\*force** An action on an object that makes it accelerate, decelerate or change shape.

**\*gravitational potential energy** The energy involved in moving anything against the force of gravity, such as lifting an object. It depends upon the mass of the object, the distance moved and the gravitational field strength. Measured in joules (J).

**\*kinetic energy** The energy of a moving object, measured in joules (J). It depends on the mass of the object and the velocity at which it is travelling at.

**\*mass** The amount of matter in an object, measured in kilograms (kg).

**\*potential energy** The energy stored in an object. Measured in joules (J). Specific examples are gravitational potential energy and elastic potential energy.

**\*power** A measure of how quickly energy is transferred, measured in watts (W).

**\*resultant force** The total force that results from two or more forces acting on a single object. It is found by adding the forces together, taking into account their direction.

**\*speed** A measure of the distance an object travels in a given time. Usually measured in metres per second (m/s).

**\*theory of relativity** A theory put forward by Albert Einstein that connects different areas of physics including mass, energy, gravity, movement, space and time.

**\*velocity** The speed of an object in a particular direction. Usually measured in metres per second (m/s).

**\*voltage** The difference in electrical energy between two points that makes a current flow, measured in volts (V). It is sometimes called the potential difference.

**\*work done** The energy transferred by a force on a moving object, measured in joules (J).

\*glossary words from the specification

# Putting radiation to use

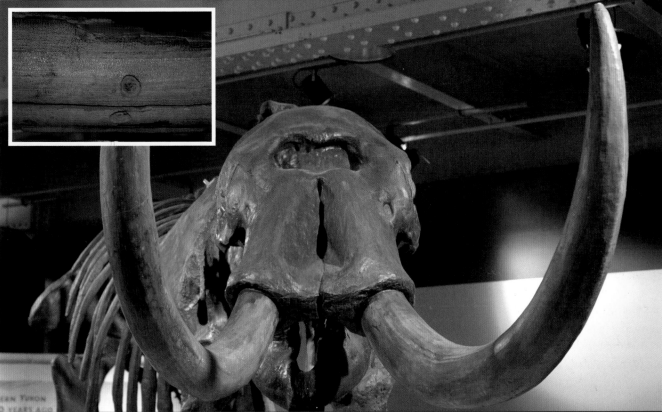

**A** Archaeologists find radioactivity an essential tool. This mammoth's tusk shows where material has been extracted for radioactive dating.

Archaeologists study the past by using scientific methods to analyse ancient remains. They use radioactivity to work out the age of these remains. Radioactivity can also be useful in other ways, for example, to kill cancers and to sterilise food. There are also dangers with radioactive materials. To understand radioactive sources, it is important to know about the particles which make up atoms and how they can break down.

### In this topic you will learn that:

- there are different types of ionising radiations that have different properties
- the activity of a radioactive source can be measured and used in practical situations
- radioactivity has useful applications in everyday life and medicine
- atoms are made from particles that can be combined in different ways to produce isotopes, some of which are unstable.

Look at these statements and sort them into the following categories:

I agree, I disagree, I want to find out more.

- Background radiation all occurs naturally.
- Atoms of one type of element are all identical.
- Things become less radioactive with time.
- Radon gas is poisonous.
- It is impossible to work out how long ago dinosaurs lived.
- During radioactive decay, elements can change into other elements.
- Some parts of the UK are more hazardous to health than others.

**H** **By the end of these two pages you should be able to:**

- explain what background radiation is
- describe how radiation from radon gas varies across the UK
- explain that some unstable atoms emit radiation.

Some substances emit invisible rays. In 1895, a scientist called Wilhelm Röntgen was investigating the light given off by materials when they are exposed to electron beams. He noticed that something was being emitted even when the device was covered. Something invisible was radiating from it. He showed that this new form of radiation was able to pass through materials. Not knowing what they were, he named them X-rays. Doctors soon started to use them to see inside the human body.

Later, another scientist called Antoine Becquerel thought that X-rays might be produced by uranium when it was exposed to sunlight. He tested this with <u>photographic plates</u> that could detect X-rays. His first attempts produced a <u>faint</u> image. Cloudy days stopped his work so he put the plate and uranium rock away in a drawer. Bad weather continued and impatience led him to develop the plate. The result was astonishing – there was a strong image on the plate that was not caused by sunlight. The uranium was emitting something continuously! This chance discovery became known as **radioactivity**.

Radioactivity is all around us. It is called **background radiation**. Becquerel's rock came from the ground – most radiation comes from the ground as well. Detectors called Geiger-Müller tubes can be used to measure the background radiation. They provide a background count, which shows that this radiation varies from place to place.

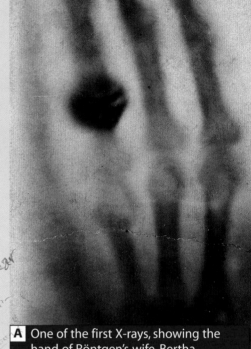

**A** One of the first X-rays, showing the hand of Röntgen's wife, Bertha.

**1** Look at the photograph. Why do you think the ring shows up so clearly?

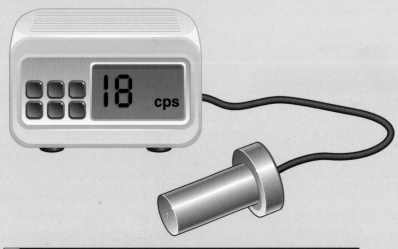

**18 cps**

**B** Using a Geiger-Müller tube to measure background radiation.

Radioactivity comes from the unstable nuclei of **atoms**. Nuclei become more stable by releasing radiation. However, you cannot tell when they will give out radiation – it is a random process. Every time you measure background radiation you may find some variation. Radioactivity is measured by counting the radiation detected over a period of time. This is called the **activity** and is usually in counts per minute (cpm) or counts per second (cps). By repeating your readings, you can calculate an average background count. This gives a clearer indication of background levels.

When you want to measure the radioactivity of different sources, it is important to remember that you should measure the background count at the same time. To make sure you get an accurate reading for the source, you must subtract the background count from your readings.

4 What is meant by background count?

5 Jeremy records background counts of 19, 22 and 16 cpm. Find his average count.

6 Jeremy then tests a rock with apparent activity of 229 cpm. What is its true activity?

Graph C shows where the background radiation comes from in the UK. Radon is a naturally occurring radioactive gas which comes out of the ground. Even some foods, such as shellfish and brazil nuts, can be slightly radioactive. Only a small percentage of background radiation is artificial (from human activity), such as medical applications. Less than 0.3% comes from nuclear activities.

7 What percentage of radiation occurs naturally?

8 How much more radiation comes from space than from what you eat?

## Have you ever wondered?

Why do some people wear radioactive watches that shine in the dark?

**Radon gas** is the main contributor to the background radiation dose. Amounts of radon vary considerably across the UK. A survey in 2001 showed that Blackpool had the lowest concentration of radon, at around 10 counts per second (cps) per cubic metre of air. Some buildings in Cornwall had concentrations 1000 times higher than this. New buildings in some areas must have protection against radon.

2 What part of atoms does radioactivity come from?

3 What is the activity of a radioactive source usually measured in?

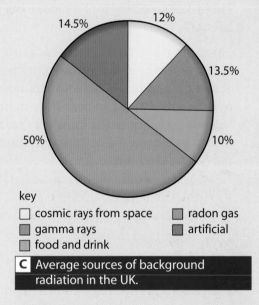

key
☐ cosmic rays from space   ▨ radon gas
▨ gamma rays   ▨ artificial
▨ food and drink

**C** Average sources of background radiation in the UK.

9 Identify two areas of the UK with the highest and lowest levels of radon gas.

10 Write a fact sheet about background radiation. Include the role of atoms and variations due to radon gas.

Summary Exercise

Higher Questions

# 2. What are these rays?

P
V
H

**By the end of these two pages you should be able to:**

- describe how household smoke alarms use radioactivity
- describe the three different types of radiation: alpha, beta and gamma
- explain that different types of radiation have different abilities to penetrate and ionise
- explain how unstable nuclei of atoms can emit radiation.

Every year in the UK, hundreds of people die in household fires. Many deaths could be prevented if all homes had at least one smoke detector. Smoke detectors contain radioactive particles. This is just one way that radioactivity can be important in everyday life.

There are three types of radioactivity: alpha, beta and gamma. Alpha and beta radiation are particles, and gamma is a wave. These three types of radiation differ in size and speed, and also in how easily they can penetrate matter. All three forms of radiation are known as **ionising radiation**. Ionisation is where atoms gain or lose electrons, turning them into charged particles called **ions**.

**1** What is meant by ionisation?

**2** Explain the main similarities and differences between the three types of radiation.

**Alpha particles** are the largest form of radiation, consisting of two neutrons and two protons. The protons give them a large positive charge which also makes them the most ionising type of radiation. Alpha particles travel at the slowest speeds, usually less than 10% of the speed of light.

Alpha particles are large enough to collide with other particles. When they come into contact with matter, they do not penetrate it easily. This makes them useful in smoke detectors. Smoke detectors contain a small amount of americium-241, which gives out alpha particles. The alpha particles ionise the air, which is detected by a sensor. Smoke entering the detector blocks the alpha particles. This makes the sensor trigger a loud alarm to alert people to the fire.

**3** Explain why americium-241 is used in smoke detectors.

**4** Why are alpha particles easily deflected by matter?

Alpha particles ionise the air and these charged particles move across the gap forming a current.

Siren will sound when the detector current falls.

Am-241 alpha source

Smoke enters smoke detector.

Americium-241 source gives off a constant stream of alpha particles.

detector

battery

Smoke in the machine will absorb ions so current falls.

A detector senses the amount of current of ionised particles.

**A** Smoke detectors use radioactivity to save lives.

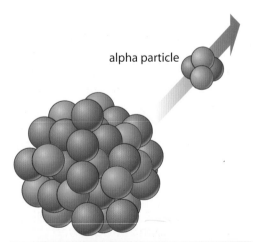

alpha particle

**B** Alpha particle being emitted from an americium-241 nucleus.

**Beta particles** are much smaller than alpha particles. This allows them to penetrate matter more easily. They are made up of electrons, so they have a single negative charge. They are much less ionising than alpha particles – as much as ten times less. They also travel faster than alpha particles, at up to half the speed of light.

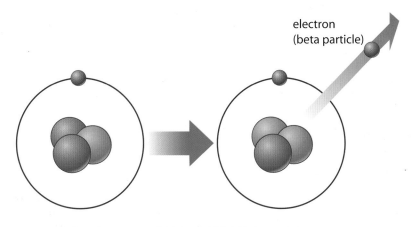
electron
(beta particle)

**C** Beta particle being emitted from an atomic nucleus.

**Gamma rays** are high frequency electromagnetic waves. It is the fastest type of radiation, travelling at the speed of light. They have no electric charge, so they are the least ionising of the three types of radiation – about ten times less ionising than beta particles. Gamma rays can penetrate matter very easily.

5  What charge do beta particles have? Explain your answer.

6  Explain why gamma radiation is the least ionising of the three types of radiation.

gamma ray

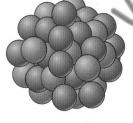

**D** Gamma ray being emitted from an atomic nucleus.

**H** All three types of radiation come from the nuclei of unstable atoms. Nuclei are unstable if they have too many or too few neutrons, as the forces holding the nucleus together are too weak. Nuclei can become more stable by emitting radiation. Alpha emission means nuclei lose two protons and two neutrons; beta emission changes a neutron into a proton, whereas gamma emission does not change the nucleus.

7  Where do all three forms of radiation come from?

8  Why are some atoms unstable?

9 **a** Copy and complete this table:

| Radiation | Form | Speed | Charge | Penetration | Ionisation |
|-----------|------|-------|--------|-------------|------------|
| alpha | | | +2 | | |
| beta | electrons | | | | medium |
| gamma | | speed of light | | high | |

**b** Write a short paragraph summarising the data in the table.

Summary Exercise

Higher Questions

# 3. Finding underground leaks

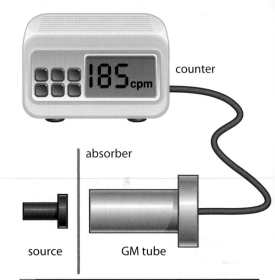

counter

absorber

source          GM tube

**A** This experiment shows how much each type of radiation is absorbed by different materials.

**By the end of these two pages you should be able to:**

- compare the ability of alpha, beta and gamma radiations to penetrate and ionise.

All forms of radiation can penetrate materials. But alpha, beta and gamma radiation are very different from each other. This has a big effect on how easily they penetrate things. You can test how penetrating each radiation is by using radioactive sources and materials with different densities. Place different thicknesses of paper, aluminium foil and lead between a radiation source and a detector. After you subtract the count due to background radiation, you can measure the effect of each material on radioactivity.

| Material | Thickness (mm) | Corrected count rate (cpm) | | |
|---|---|---|---|---|
| | | **Alpha** | **Beta** | **Gamma** |
| air | 20 | 370 | 24 376 | 770 |
| paper | 0.10 | 180 | 23 202 | 722 |
| | 1.00 | 0 | 16 750 | 702 |
| aluminium | 0.25 | | 14 950 | 664 |
| | 0.80 | | 8350 | 650 |
| | 1.50 | | 2560 | 638 |
| | 2.30 | | 694 | 632 |
| | 2.55 | | 358 | 600 |
| lead | 3 | | | 564 |
| | 6 | | | 454 |
| | 9 | | | 423 |
| | 12 | | | 386 |
| | 20 | | | 262 |

**B** Typical results for absorption experiment.

**1** Which material is the densest? How can you tell this from the results shown?

**2** What does the corrected count rate take into account?

Alpha particles are absorbed by a few centimetres of air or a few sheets of paper. Beta particles are smaller and less ionising than alpha, making them harder to stop. Paper hardly affects them, but a few millimetres of aluminium normally stops them. Paper and aluminium have little effect on gamma rays. Thick lead will absorb some of them, but not completely. Many metres of concrete will also absorb a large amount of gamma radiation.

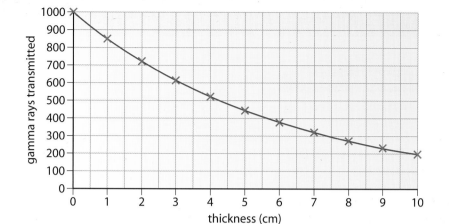

**C** Graph showing how the absorption of gamma rays changes with thickness.

The different penetrating abilities of radiation can be useful. Beta particles are used in industry to monitor the thickness of aluminium foil during manufacture. Beta radiation is directed through the foil and detected on the other side. If the foil is too thin, more radiation gets through. If it is too thick, less radiation will get through. Adjustments are made to maintain the same thickness.

Gamma radiation can be used to detect leaks in underground pipes. For this, you need a small amount of material that emits gamma radiation for a short time. The gamma source is placed into the pipe. Where the fluid is leaking into the ground, gamma radiation becomes concentrated. The gamma rays penetrate through the ground to the surface, where it can be detected. The leak can then be pinpointed and repaired more quickly.

Ionisation from alpha sources can be detected using a cloud chamber. The air inside is saturated with alcohol and cooled by dry ice underneath. Alpha particles ionise air molecules as they pass through. These ions cause droplets of alcohol to form, leaving a trail. Beta particles are around 100 times less ionising then alpha. This means their trails are much harder to see. Gamma rays are around 100 times less ionising than beta – too weak to cause trails.

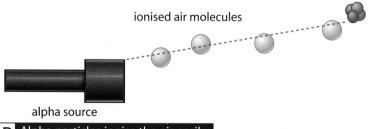

**D** Alpha particles ionise the air easily.

**3** Which materials absorb:
**a** alpha particles
**b** beta particles?

**4** Explain why gamma rays are more easily stopped by lead than aluminium.

**5** Nuclear power stations produce high levels of gamma rays. Explain why large amounts of concrete are used to build them.

**6** Why do you think leaks in pipes underground can't be found using sources of alpha particles?

**7** Describe what happens when an alpha particle ionises the air.

**8** Explain why alpha particles are more ionising than beta particles.

**9** Explain the ability of each type of radiation to penetrate and ionise. Give examples of how these abilities can be used in industry.

**Summary Exercise**

**Higher Questions**

**By the end of these two pages you should be able to:**

- explain the sources and properties of X-rays and gamma rays
- describe how radioactivity is used in hospitals to find and treat illnesses
- explain how equipment can be sterilised with radioactivity
- explain how radioactivity is used to treat food so it keeps longer.

**X-rays** and gamma rays are electromagnetic waves. In a vacuum, they both travel at 300 000 km/s. Both are very penetrating and can be damaging. They ionise materials when they pass through them. Remember that ionised atoms are electrically charged. Living cells can be seriously damaged by ionisation, but radioactive sources still have many important uses.

## Have you ever wondered?

Could a low dose of radiation actually be good for you?

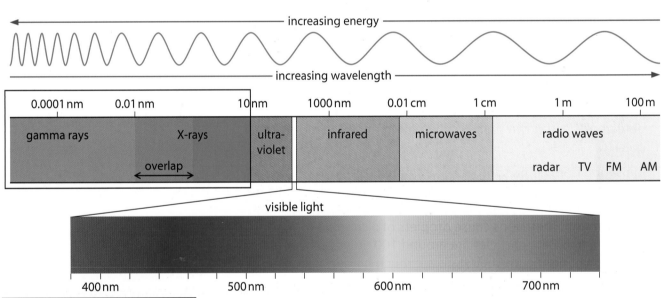

**A** The electromagnetic spectrum.

X-rays and gamma rays come from different sources. Gamma rays are produced naturally from the nuclei of atoms when they undergo radioactive decay. On earth, X-rays are artificially produced in special X-ray machines. X-rays and gamma rays have similar frequencies. So you can only tell them apart if you know where they come from.

X-rays help doctors see bones inside patients. Gamma rays also have a wide range of uses in medicine. Cancer cells are more easily damaged than normal cells by gamma rays. Radiotherapy uses gamma rays to kill cancer cells. Other cells suffer relatively

1 What is the speed, in km/s and m/s, of X-rays and gamma rays?

2 How are X-rays and gamma rays produced?

minor damage, depending on where in the body the radiation is used. Specific areas, such as brain tumours, can also be targetted. Multiple beams are directed at the cancer from different angles, so they overlap when they reach the cancer.

## Have you ever wondered?

Radioactivity destroys cancers, but does it leave a patient radioactive afterwards?

Sources of low-level gamma rays can also be useful when injected into the body. They can be detected with a special gamma camera, revealing problems with thyroid glands and blocked kidneys. Alpha and beta sources are not used because they are easily absorbed by the body and would cause damage. Gamma rays are less easily absorbed, so cause less damage. It is important to use sources that do not remain radioactive for long, such as technetium or iodine. This reduces the chances of patients becoming ill from the exposure.

3 Explain why gamma rays can be used to help cure cancer.

4 Explain why only gamma sources that do not remain radioactive for a long time should be used when injected into the body.

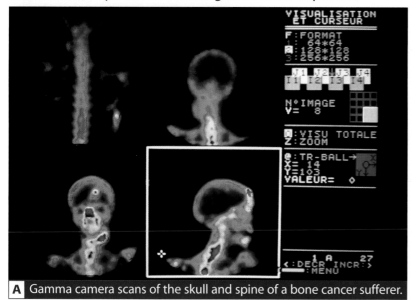

**A** Gamma camera scans of the skull and spine of a bone cancer sufferer.

Another important use of gamma rays is for **sterilisation**. Surgical equipment needs to be completely clean. Powerful gamma rays are used to kill any viruses and bacteria on it. This is especially helpful for sensitive instruments that cannot be sterilised using heat. Food can be sterilised with gamma rays in a process called **irradiation**. The gamma rays kill microbes and bacteria, which cause food to spoil. This keeps the food fresh for much longer without leaving any harmful residue.

## Have you ever wondered?

Irradiating food makes it last longer, so why won't the supermarkets sell it?

5 Explain how medical equipment and food can be sterilised using radiation.

6 Write a paragraph comparing X-rays and gamma-rays. Include their sources, properties and uses.

**Summary Exercise**

**Higher Questions**

# 5. Are all hydrogen nuclei the same?

**By the end of these two pages you should be able to:**

- describe the structure of atoms in terms of protons, neutrons and electrons
- describe the nuclei of different atoms in the form $^{m}_{p}X$
- explain the existence of isotopes using atomic number and mass number.

The Sun is made mostly of the elements hydrogen and helium. The difference between these elements is the number and types of particles they are made from. In 1897, J J Thomson (1856–1940) discovered that atoms contain tiny, negatively charged particles called **electrons**. Atoms have a neutral charge overall, so he realised that they must also contain positively charged matter.

Years later, students Geiger and Marsden performed an investigation with gold foil. They discovered that there is a tiny positively charged **nucleus** in the centre of all atoms. The negative electrons orbit the nucleus – much like planets orbit the Sun. Their teacher, Rutherford, discovered that the positive charge came from particles with opposite charges to electrons, but with much more mass. These are known as **protons**.

In 1932 neutrally charged particles, called **neutrons**, were discovered in the nucleus. They had a very similar mass to protons. This meant that atoms consisted of the following particles:

| Particle | Electric charge | Relative mass |
| --- | --- | --- |
| electron | −1 | 0.0005 |
| neutron | 0 | 1 |
| proton | +1 | 1 |

**A** The Sun – a hydrogen fireball.

1 What charge do electrons have?

2 What charge do the nuclei of atoms have?

3 What particles give nuclei their charge?

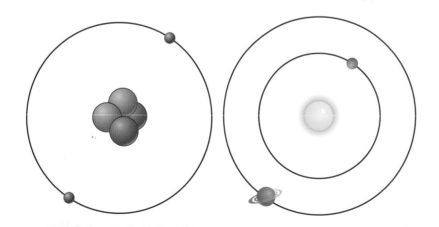

**B** Electrons orbit nuclei in a similar way to how planets orbit the Sun.

You can show in detail what all atoms look like by drawing diagrams with neutrons and protons in a central nucleus with electrons outside, such as that in diagram C.

You can use shorthand to represent different atoms. You already know about the symbols that stand for the chemical name, such as H for hydrogen. You can use the chemical symbol together with two numbers to describe the nucleus. The **atomic number** tells you the number of protons in the nucleus. This is represented by the letter $p$, and can also be called the **proton number**. The **mass number** is the total number of protons and neutrons. This is represented by the letter $m$. The particles found in the nucleus are sometimes called nucleons, so the mass number is sometimes called the **nucleon number**. You can write these symbols together like this: $^m_p X$, for example $^1_1 H$.

The X stands for the element (e.g. hydrogen, H). You can find the number of neutrons by subtracting the atomic number from the mass number. It is also easy to find the number of electrons. Atoms normally have neutral charge, so the number of electrons is the same as the number of protons.

**H** All atoms of the same element have the same number of protons and electrons, but some have different numbers of neutrons. This means they have different masses. Atoms of the same element with different masses are called **isotopes**. Heavier isotopes have more neutrons and lighter isotopes have fewer neutrons.

There are three naturally occurring isotopes of hydrogen: $^1_1 H$, $^2_1 H$, and $^3_1 H$. As they all have just one proton, they have the same atomic number (1). But they have a different atomic mass because they have extra neutrons. All atoms have different isotopes.

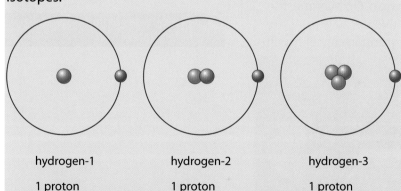

| hydrogen-1 | hydrogen-2 | hydrogen-3 |
| --- | --- | --- |
| 1 proton | 1 proton | 1 proton |
| 0 neutron | 1 neutron | 2 neutrons |
| 1 electron | 1 electron | 1 electron |

**D** The three isotopes of hydrogen.

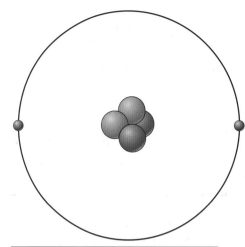

**C** Simple diagram of a helium atom.

**4** What is meant by atomic number?

**5** What is a nucleon?

**6** Helium can be written $^4_2 He$. How many of the following particles does it contain:
   **a** protons
   **b** neutrons
   **c** electrons?

**7** Use a Periodic Table to complete the following atoms: $^{14}_{7}\,—$, $^{18}_{\_\_}O$, $^{\_\_}_{79}Au$.

**8 a** Draw a diagram of a lithium atom, showing the particles in the nucleus and their charges. Make sure you label your diagram.
   **b** Write a description of the lithium atom, including the masses and charges of the particles in the nucleus.
   **c** Write the symbol for this atom showing the mass number and the proton number.

**9** What is an isotope?

**10** The atomic number of carbon is 6. Its most common isotope has six neutrons. Show how this isotope is written.

**Summary Exercise**          **Higher Questions**

# 6. How long will it be radioactive?

**By the end of these two pages you should be able to:**

- describe how radioactivity decreases over time
- explain the term half-life
- use radioactive decay graphs to calculate half-lives
- compare half-life graphs created on paper to graphs from a computer.

If you pull the plug out of a bath, the water flows away. At first it flows quickly because there is a lot of water creating more pressure over the plug hole. When there is less water in the bath the flow is slower.

A similar thing happens with radioactive decay from unstable atoms. All unstable atoms will eventually decay. At the start there are more atoms available to decay – it's like having more water above the plug hole. As the unstable atoms decay, there are fewer atoms left to decay. So the amount of radioactivity reduces over time.

You can find out how quickly different types of atoms decay using a measure called the **half-life**. This is the average time taken for half the atoms to decay. This is more reliable than measuring the time it takes for all the atoms in a sample to decay because that would depend on how many atoms you started with. Even if you have more or fewer atoms, the half-life is always the same for the same type of atom.

Look at graph A. The blue curve is source A, which has 120 atoms at the start. It takes 5 seconds for half the nuclei to decay, leaving 60 nuclei. So the half-life of source A is 5 seconds. After another 5 seconds, another half have decayed. On average, the half-life will always be 5 seconds. Radioactive decay graphs are always curves, starting more steeply and gradually levelling off.

**Radioactive decay**

*no. of undecayed nuclei* (y-axis: 0, 20, 40, 60, 80, 100, 120)

*time (s)* (x-axis: 0, 5, 10, 15, 20, 25, 30, 35, 40)

key
- ◆ source A
- ■ source B

**A** Different types of atoms decay at different rates.

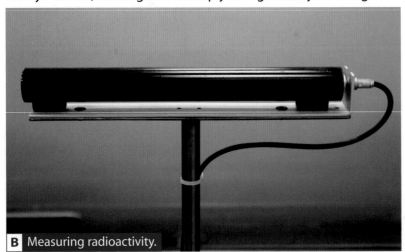

**B** Measuring radioactivity.

**1** In your own words, explain what is meant by the term half-life.

The half-life of a sample can also be found by looking at how its radioactivity decreases over time. To do this, you need to measure the number of decays over a period of time. The average time taken for the activity to fall to half the original count rate is the half-life.

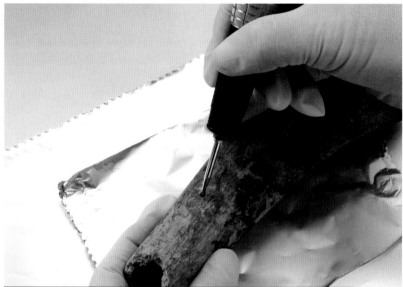

**C** A scientist extracting some material for radioactive analysis.

It is common to use computers to analyse the radioactive decay of nuclei. They can produce accurate graphs very quickly. Plotting graphs by hand is less accurate and can take a long time if you have lots of data to plot. Radiation detectors can be connected to a computer using data-loggers. Software can then record the activity at different times and can produce graphs as the readings are taken. Some types of atom decay so fast that computers must be used to record their decay.

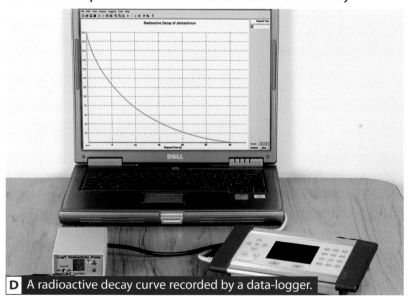

**D** A radioactive decay curve recorded by a data-logger.

**Summary Exercise**

**2 a** Copy and complete the table of data below for a radioactive source:

| Time (minutes) | Activity (counts per minute) |
|:---:|:---:|
| 0 | 12 000 |
| 1 | 6000 |
| 2 | |
| 3 | |
| 4 | |

**b** How many complete minutes would be needed until the activity falls to less than 50 counts per minute?

**3** Write a paragraph explaining how radioactivity decreases over time. Include an explanation of half-life and how this can be found from decay graphs.

**4** John records the activity of a sample over a 30 minute period. His results are shown below.
**a** Plot a graph on paper of activity (y-axis) against time (x-axis).
**b** Find the half-life of this decay.
**c** Explain why this might be easier to do with a computer program.

| Time (minutes) | Activity (counts per minute) |
|:---:|:---:|
| 0 | 600 |
| 5 | 335 |
| 10 | 190 |
| 15 | 105 |
| 20 | 60 |
| 25 | 35 |
| 30 | 20 |

**Higher Questions**

# 7. How old is the Earth?

**By the end of these two pages you should be able to:**

- explain how scientists draw conclusions from techniques like radioactive dating
- recognise that there are often some uncertainties in these conclusions.

## Have you ever wondered?

How do we know things like 'Woolly mammoths died out 10 000 years ago', which is before humans learned to write?

All living things have carbon in their bodies. Plants get their carbon by absorbing carbon dioxide during photosynthesis. Animals eat plants, so they take in some of the carbon. A tiny proportion of the carbon atoms are radioactive. These are known as carbon-14. While the plant is alive, the amount of carbon-14 in the plant remains constant. When the plant dies, the proportion of carbon-14 decreases (its half-life is 5730 years). By measuring how much carbon-14 remains, you can estimate when the plant or animal died. This is called **radioactive dating** (or radiocarbon dating).

**A** Computers are always used in radioactive dating.

1 Where do living things get carbon-14 from?

2 Why does the amount of carbon-14 in dead animals decrease over time?

One problem with radioactive dating is that it assumes the amount of carbon-14 in the air is the same today as it was in the past. Fossil fuels do not contain any carbon-14 because almost all carbon-14 decays after about 50 000 years. So the amount of carbon-14 in the air decreased after the industrial revolution. Nuclear weapons tests then nearly doubled the amount of carbon-14 in the air. As a result, it is not possible to give entirely accurate answers using radioactive dating.

Another problem for scientists using radioactive dating is that different plants can absorb slightly different amounts of carbon-14. This means scientists cannot be completely certain about the ages they give to organic remains.

Results from radioactive dating are still very useful. For example, one Dead Sea scroll was dated to between 159 BCE and 16 CE. Part of the Turin Shroud was dated by scientists in Oxford, Tucson and Zurich to between 1260 and 1390 CE. By taking an average of different measurements, the conclusion is considered more reliable.

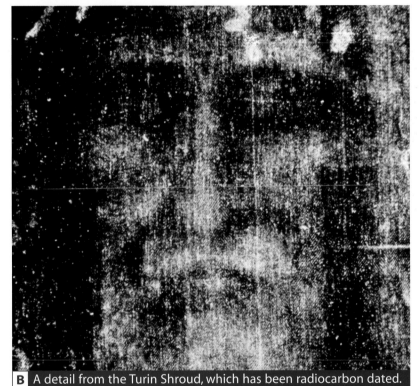

**B** A detail from the Turin Shroud, which has been radiocarbon dated.

Scientists have to be careful about the assumptions they make. This is another reason why their conclusions might be uncertain. In 1862, Lord Kelvin assumed the Sun produced its heat from burning (combustion). He concluded that the Sun was 100 million years old. Once radioactivity was discovered, it became clear that his assumption was wrong. Even though his measurements and calculations were accurate, his results were meaningless.

One type of uranium has a half-life of 4500 million years. Uranium can be found in some rocks. Through radioactive decay, uranium turns into lead. By measuring the amounts of lead and uranium, the age of the rock can be found. This radioactive dating suggests that the Earth is 4600 million years old. Scientists believe this is accurate to within 2 million years – a very good level of accuracy.

**Summary Exercise**

3 Why is it particularly important to repeat radioactive measurements and find an average?

4 A plant absorbed more than the normal amount of carbon-14. Explain what difference this would make to its radioactive age.

5 Where did Kelvin think the Sun got its energy from?

6 In what two ways has the amount of carbon-14 in the air been changed by human activities?

7 When scientists use radioactive dating they cannot be completely certain about the date they give the sample. Explain the reasons for this.

**Higher Questions**

# 8. How did Marie Curie die?

**By the end of these two pages you should be able to:**

- explain that scientific ideas develop over time
- discuss some of the risks associated with radioactive sources
- describe the dangers of ionising radiation and the possible damage it can cause
- discuss the precautions that must be taken when handling radioactive sources.

Marie Sklodowska was born in Poland in 1867. She moved to Paris to study chemistry, where she met and married Pierre Curie. Marie and her husband discovered that thorium gave off rays similar to those Becquerel had found from uranium. Marie used the term radioactivity to describe them. The Curies discovered two previously unknown elements. They named the first polonium (after Poland) and the second radium (after ray).

In 1903, Marie and Pierre shared the Nobel Prize for physics for their work on radioactivity, with Becquerel, who originally discovered it. Marie also won the Nobel Prize for chemistry in 1911 for discovering the new elements.

The dangers of radioactivity were not understood for decades. In the 1920s, miracle cures involving radium were sold. Jars of 'Vitalizer' containing radium water supposedly cured just about anything! Radium-based paint was also used to make watch hands glow in the dark. The women who did the painting used their mouths to make fine points on brushes. Many of the women became ill and even died. But it was not until later that people discovered that radiation was the cause.

**A** The Curie family.

1 Who first used the word radioactivity?

2 What new elements did the Curies discover?

**B**
Radium sprayers working around 1950 could not get insurance because of the dangers.

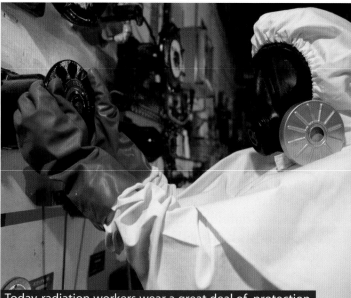

Today, radiation workers wear a great deal of protection.

**3** What was used to make watch hands glow in the dark?

**4** Explain why the women painting the hands became ill.

The Curies didn't know about the dangers of radioactivity. Marie eventually developed leukaemia, a cancer of the blood. She died in 1934, almost certainly as a result of overexposure to radiation. It took a long time before enough evidence built up to show that radioactivity caused health problems.

**5** How did Marie Curie die?

Today we understand the dangers of radioactivity. If radiation enters your body, cells can be killed. Some may simply stop working properly. If DNA in the cells is damaged, **mutations** can occur. A mutation is when a cell develops differently from the way it is supposed to. This is normally dangerous; cells may become cancerous.

**6** Why are radioactive sources dangerous?

It is important to be very careful when you handle radioactive sources. You need to use tongs to keep the source away from your hands. Also you should not point them at people. All sources should be kept in a lead-lined container. This stops the alpha and beta particles from escaping and reduces the strength of any gamma rays. Radiation is used in hospitals every day. Staff who work with these sources have to wear special badges that monitor their exposure.

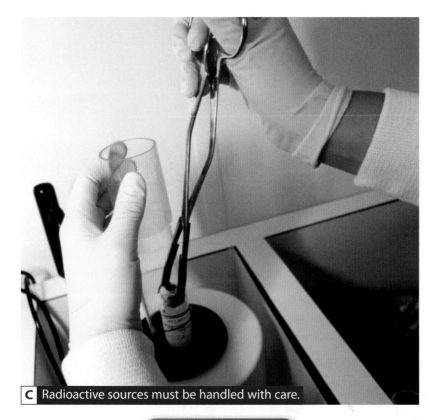

**C** Radioactive sources must be handled with care.

**7** What containers are necessary to store radioactive sources safely?

**8** Why is it important to monitor radiation exposure for some hospital workers?

**9** Our understanding about the dangers of radioactive sources have changed over time. Explain some of these changes and describe what precautions we use today.

**Summary Exercise**

**Higher Questions**

# 9. Radioactivity in depth

**By the end of these two pages you should be able to:**

- describe where natural background radiation comes from
- describe how background radiation from radon gas varies across the UK.

Radioactivity is natural. On earth it comes from rocks, but it also comes from space as cosmic rays. One of the sources of background radiation is radon gas from uranium in the ground. The two most common isotopes of radon are radon-222 and radon-220. Concentrations vary dramatically around the world. Diagram A shows how levels of radon gas inside buildings vary considerably across the UK.

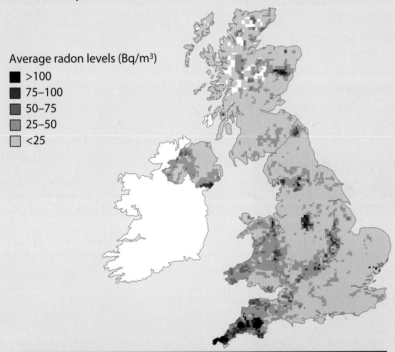

Average radon levels (Bq/m³)
- ■ >100
- ■ 75–100
- ■ 50–75
- ■ 25–50
- □ <25

**A** Some areas of the UK receive much higher exposure to radon gas.

The map shows the average indoor levels of radon gas. The darker areas have higher levels and the lighter areas have lower levels. Concentrations are measured in becquerels per cubic metre. A becquerel (Bq) is a unit of radioactivity, named after Becquerel who discovered radioactivity. 1 Bq is defined as 1 decay per second. The average level of radon gas is 20 Bq/m³.

In 1990 the UK Government declared concentrations of 200 Bq/m³ as an action level. It advised that above this level action should be taken to remove the gas as it was considered a health hazard. A small proportion of people living at the action level run the risk of developing lung cancer. But this gas occurs naturally, so what can be done?

1 Where does radon gas come from?

2 What parts of the UK have the highest levels of radon gas?

3 Find out radon's atomic number from a Periodic Table. Use this to write its two most common isotopes in the form $^{m}_{p}X$.

New buildings in high-radon areas are built with vented floors. Where particularly high concentrations exist, extractor fans are also fitted to draw the gas out before it can pass into the home. Another way of reducing radon levels is to use more impenetrable damp-proof membranes on the ground floor. This costs around £100 per house.

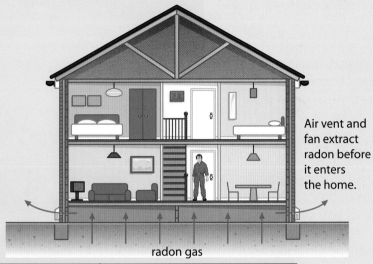

Air vent and fan extract radon before it enters the home.

radon gas

**B** It is easy to prevent radon gas from entering a house.

Radon-220 has a half-life of 55.6 seconds. This means it is unlikely to be a risk as it decays before it has the chance to enter buildings. But radon-222 has a half-life of just under four days. This means it has time to enter buildings. There are a total of eight decays from radon-222 until a stable isotope is reached. Half are alpha emissions and half are beta emissions. The emission of alpha or beta particles inside the lungs can lead to lung cancer. Around 5% of the 34 000 UK deaths each year from lung cancer are attributed to radon.

**4** Why do some houses have vented floors?

**5** What else can be done to reduce radon levels in homes?

**6** Calculate the number of people who die, on average, from lung cancer as a result of radon in the UK.

**7** The table below shows results of a survey carried out in 2001 for three counties in England. Calculate the percentage of homes at or above the action level in each county.

| County | Average radon concentration (Bq/m³) | Number of homes at or above action level | Number of homes measured |
|---|---|---|---|
| Cambridgeshire | 37 | 12 | 1200 |
| Cornwall | 162 | 15 800 | 67 800 |
| Cumbria | 90 | 440 | 4500 |

**8** Explain how home owners can reduce radon concentrations.

**9** Explain why background radiation levels vary across the UK.

Summary Exercise

Higher Questions

# 10. What are the northern lights?

P

**H** | **_By the end of these two pages you should be able to:_**

- describe the origin of the background radiation in space
- explain how the Earth's atmosphere and magnetic field protect us from radiation from space.

The Earth is constantly under attack from space! Ultra-violet radiation comes from the Sun, and the Earth's ozone layer absorbs the most dangerous rays. But there's much more than just light coming to Earth.

Streams of charged particles travelling at nearly 300 000 km/s hurtle towards our planet. These come from all directions and are called cosmic rays. We know they come from outer space and not the Sun as they are just as strong at night as they are during the day. Their strength also increases if you get higher above the ground. Fortunately the upper atmosphere absorbs large amounts of them, reducing their danger at ground level.

Astronomers believe that cosmic rays come from some of the most violent objects in the universe – supernovae, neutron stars and black holes. These rays were first discovered by Victor Hess (1883–1964) in 1912. By flying hot air balloons to altitudes of 5 km, he found that the air was much more ionised higher in the atmosphere.

**A** The Crab Nebula – a supernova remnant over 1000 years old.

**P**

**1** Name two forms of radiation that are reduced by the atmosphere.

**2** What are cosmic rays and where do they come from?

**?**

### Have you ever wondered?

Do you get a dangerous dose of cosmic rays if you fly often?

The Earth's **magnetic field** can also protect us from radiation from space. Streams of charged particles evaporate from the surface of the Sun in all directions. This is called the solar wind. The solar wind heads towards the Earth at around 400 km/s. It would erode the atmosphere but the magnetic field deflects most of the solar wind away from the planet. Some is channelled towards the north and south poles, where they ionise the air and create the northern and southern lights.

## Have you ever wondered?

What makes the northern lights the most colourful sight on Earth?

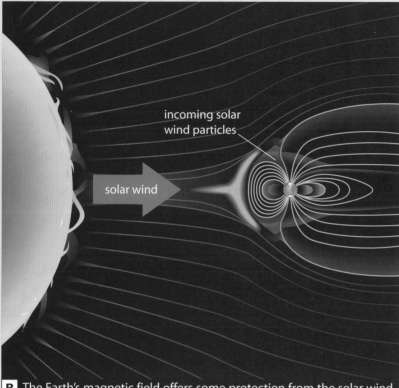

**B** The Earth's magnetic field offers some protection from the solar wind.

You can show how beams of charged particles are deflected by magnetic fields using a horseshoe magnet. Beams of alpha and beta particles can be deflected. They have opposite charges, so they are deflected in opposite directions. Alpha particles have twice the charge of beta particles, but as they have so much more mass they are harder to deflect. Beta particles are strongly deflected because they have a low mass.

6 Why do magnetic fields deflect alpha and beta particles in different directions?

7 Gamma rays have no charge. Will a magnetic field deflect them?

The European Space Agency has plans to send people to Mars by 2030. Mars has no magnetic field and its atmosphere is very thin. This means that many precautions will need to be taken while they are there, and also during the journey.

8 a Explain why living on Mars will be much more dangerous than on Earth.
   b What would Mars need to be better protected from radiation?

3 What is the solar wind?

4 What part of the Earth protects us from the solar wind?

5 What are the Northern Lights?

**C** The northern lights are produced by the solar wind.

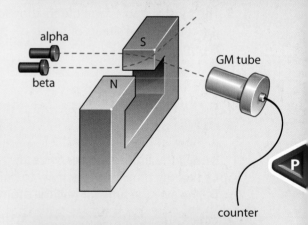

**D** Alpha and beta particles are electrically charged and can be deflected by magnetic fields. Detection of alpha deflection is normally only possible in a vacuum.

**Summary Exercise**

**Higher Questions**

# 11. Questions

## Multiple choice questions

**1** The most penetrating form of radiation is
**A** alpha particles.
**B** beta particles.
**C** gamma rays.
**D** X-rays.

**2** The most ionising form of radiation is
**A** alpha particles.
**B** beta particles.
**C** gamma rays.
**D** X-rays.

**3** The largest form of radiation is
**A** alpha particles.
**B** beta particles.
**C** gamma rays.
**D** neutrons.

**4** The most suitable form of radiation for monitoring the thickness of aluminium foil is
**A** alpha.
**B** beta.
**C** gamma.
**D** X-rays.

**5** The most suitable form of radiation for monitoring the thickness of sheets of paper is
**A** alpha.
**B** beta.
**C** gamma.
**D** X-rays.

**6** Half-life is
**A** how long it takes for half an atom to decay.
**B** half the time for atoms to decay.
**C** half the time for the activity to halve.
**D** the average time for half the atoms to decay.

**7** Radiocarbon dating can be used to find out how long ago something died up to about
**A** 5730 years ago.
**B** 6000 years ago.
**C** 14000 years ago.
**D** 50000 years ago.

**8** Smoke detectors commonly use a source of
**A** alpha particles.
**B** beta particles.
**C** gamma rays.
**D** neutrons.

**9** Food can be treated so it keeps longer by exposing it to
**A** alpha particles.
**B** beta particles.
**C** gamma rays.
**D** X-rays.

**10** In what way are gamma rays and X-rays similar?
**A** They have the same wavelength.
**B** They have the same speed in a vacuum.
**C** The have the same ability to penetrate.
**D** They have the same frequency.

**H** **11** Background radiation comes mostly from
**A** space, as cosmic rays.
**B** the ground, as gamma rays.
**C** the ground, as radon gas.
**D** the air, from nuclear bomb tests and leaks from power stations.

**12** An isotope is an atom of the same element with different numbers of
**A** electrons.
**B** protons.
**C** ions.
**D** neutrons.

**13** The northern lights are caused by
**A** radioactivity in the atmosphere.
**B** the solar wind.
**C** light reflecting off Venus.
**D** cosmic rays from outer space.

**14** For an atomic nucleus, the nucleon number is the number of
**A** neutrons.
**B** electrons.
**C** protons and neutrons.
**D** protons.

**15** Regional variations in levels of radon gas in the UK are considerable. The area with the highest concentrations is
**A** Northern Ireland.
**B** East Anglia.
**C** the South West.
**D** North Wales.

## Short-answer questions

1 Juman is going in to hospital to have a gamma-ray scan of her kidneys. She is worried about remaining radioactive for a long time after the procedure and also about possible damage from the radiation. Explain why:

 a she won't remain radioactive for very long

 b why the gamma rays will cause very little damage to her.

2 Brian uses a data-logger to record how the activity of a sample of thoron reduces over time. He wants to use the results to find its half-life. Here are his results:

| Time (s) | Activity (counts per second) |
|---|---|
| 0 | 240 |
| 10 | 212 |
| 20 | 187 |
| 30 | 165 |
| 40 | 146 |
| 50 | 129 |
| 60 | 114 |
| 70 | 100 |
| 80 | 89 |
| 90 | 78 |
| 100 | 69 |
| 110 | 61 |
| 120 | 54 |

 a Using graph paper, or a graph-plotting program, plot a graph to show Brian's results. Plot time on the horizontal axis and activity on the vertical axis.

 b Use your graph to find three values of the half-life of Brian's source.

 c Write down an average value for the half-life. Explain why this average is more reliable than just one measurement.

**H** 3 Rowland's teacher carried out some experiments with radioactive sources. He used a Geiger-Müller tube to record the strength of the radiation received when different absorbers were present in front of the tube. He did not have time to repeat his readings. Here are his results:

| Source | Count rate (counts per minute) | | | |
| | No absorber | 5 sheets of paper | 3 mm of aluminium | 20 mm of lead |
|---|---|---|---|---|
| No source | 18 | 17 | 18 | 16 |
| $^{60}_{27}$Co | 956 | 962 | 948 | 342 |
| $^{90}_{38}$Sr | 2302 | 2296 | 25 | 17 |
| $^{226}_{88}$Ra | 1243 | 18 | 17 | 17 |

 a Explain why radiation was received, even with no source present.

 b Look carefully at the results for different absorbers. Write down which type of radiation is being emitted for each of the three sources.

 c Can you explain why more radiation was received for $^{60}_{27}$Co when a paper absorber was present than without?

 d For each of the sources used, calculate how many of the following particles a neutral atom would contain:

 i protons

 ii neutrons

 iii electrons.

 e $^{60}_{27}$Co is cobalt, which is a magnetic material. Can you think of a reason why it should be disposed of with extreme care?

 f $^{90}_{38}$Sr was produced in the fallout from the Chernobyl nuclear accident in the Ukraine. It is very similar to calcium, so cows eating contaminated grass ingested it. Predict what problems this could cause for humans.

 g $^{226}_{88}$Ra decays into $^{222}_{86}$Rn, which is radon. Explain why Rowland's teacher must store the $^{226}_{88}$Ra in a ventilated cupboard.

# 12. Glossary

**activity** The number of emissions of radiation from a sample in a given time. Normally this is given as counts per minute (cpm) or counts per second (cps).

**\*alpha particle** The largest form of particle that can be emitted as radiation from unstable nuclei. They consist of two protons and two neutrons held together as a single particle. This is the same as the helium-4 nucleus.

**\*atom** Smallest possible particle of any given element. Atoms are themselves made up of electrons, neutrons and protons (so-called sub-atomic particles).

**\*atomic mass** The mass of an atom. Normally measured in kilograms. Do not confuse with relative atomic mass.

**\*atomic (proton) number** The number of protons present in the nucleus of all atoms of one particular element.

**\*background radiation** Radiation that is all around us all the time from a number of sources. Some background radiation is naturally occurring, while some has its origins in human activities.

**\*beta particle** Particle form of radiation that can be emitted from the nucleus of radioactive atoms when they decay. Typically the beta particle is an electron.

**\*electron** Negatively charged particle that forms part of every atom. Electrons orbit the positively charged nucleus.

**\*gamma ray** An electromagnetic (EM) wave emitted from the nucleus of some radioactive atoms. Gamma rays are the highest frequency EM waves and like all EM waves they travel at the speed of light.

**\*half-life** A measure of how quickly some radioactive substances decay. It is the average time for half of the atoms originally present to have decayed.

**ion** An atom or group of atoms with an electrical charge. Ions can either be positively or negatively charged due to losing or gaining electrons.

**\*ionising radiation** Form of radiation that causes ionisation in atoms through which it passes – the atoms lose or gain electrons from their outer shells and so become charged overall – they become ions.

**irradiation** A process whereby powerful doses of gamma rays are used to sterilise food so that it stays fresh for a longer period of time prior to consumption.

**\*isotope** Name given to atoms of the same element with different mass (nucleon) numbers. Isotopes occur because fewer or greater neutrons can be present in the nucleus without it changing the type of atom.

**\*magnetic field** Region where moving charged particles experience a force.

**\*mass (nucleon) number** The combined total number of neutrons and protons in the nucleus of one particular isotope of an element. Also called nucleon number.

**\*mutation** Change that takes place in a living organism, often as a result of interaction with radiation.

**\*neutron** Neutral-charge particle that is found in the nucleus of all atoms, except hydrogen.

**\*nucleus (plural: nuclei)** The central, positively charged, part of all atoms.

**\*proton** Positively charged particle that is found in the nucleus of all atoms.

**\*radioactive dating** Method of determining the approximate age of a material or substance.

**\*radioactivity** The random emission of radiation from the nuclei of unstable atoms. The process of emission changes the type of atom.

**\*radon gas** Naturally occurring, radioactive gas that is emitted from rocks under ground. In some parts of the world, including the UK, it is emitted at dangerous levels. As a result, buildings have to be designed to protect their occupants from the gas.

**\*sterilisation** Process where bacteria and viruses on an object are destroyed. Sterilisation can be carried out using radioactive sources.

**\*X-rays** Electromagnetic (EM) waves emitted by metals when they are bombarded with electrons. X-rays are nearly as high in frequency as gamma rays and, like all EM waves, they travel at the speed of light.

\*glossary words from the specification

# Power of the atom

**A** The UK government is planning to build new nuclear power stations like this one at Hinkley in Somerset, to help solve our energy needs.

Modern life relies on electricity. But there is an environmental cost to generating the amount of electricity that we need. Burning fossil fuels is causing a steady change to global climates – a change that we may not be able to reverse.

Some scientists and politicians suggest that nuclear power may be the answer. But people are afraid of the devastating results of accidents and concerned about the radioactive waste. Understanding the physics of nuclear power and learning about some of the issues can help you form opinions and make decisions about using energy.

## In this topic you will learn that:

- nuclear power stations use chain reactions to produce electricity
- the Sun produces its energy using nuclear fusion
- the movement of charged particles forms an electric current
- static charges have useful applications but they can also create hazards.

Look at these statements and sort them into the following categories:

I agree, I disagree, I want to find out more.

- Gas power stations are a better option than nuclear.
- When Arctic sea ice melts it will make sea levels rise in the UK.
- The Chernobyl disaster was like a small atomic bomb exploding.
- Nuclear waste is safe after about 50 years.
- The UK has no permanent solution for disposing of its nuclear waste.
- Nuclear waste is hazardous because it is very hot.

# 1. Chain reactions

**By the end of these two pages you should be able to:**

- explain how a chain reaction works
- describe what happens in the fission of uranium-235
- **H** describe a simple decay series starting from the daughter products of uranium-235.

Uranium-235 is an energy source that is used in nuclear power stations. If a **nucleus** of uranium-235 absorbs a **neutron** it becomes highly unstable. It will split into two smaller nuclei, called **daughter nuclei**. This process is called nuclear **fission**.

A nuclear fission reaction releases a large amount of energy. It also releases three more neutrons. If each of the neutrons is absorbed by another nucleus of uranium-235, these three nuclei will also break apart. Each of them will release three more neutrons. Those nine neutrons will trigger fission reactions in nine more nuclei, and so on. The neutrons keep the reaction going by creating a **chain reaction**.

1 **a** What particle triggers a uranium-235 nucleus to break apart?
  **b** What is the name for this process?

2 Which of the following are produced by the splitting nucleus?
  **i** two daughter nuclei
  **ii** carbon dioxide
  **iii** energy
  **iv** three neutrons
  **v** water

3 Use a calculator to do the following. Enter 3; multiply it by 3; multiply it by 3 again; and so on. Each multiplication is a link in the chain. How many links does it take to get to more than:
  **a** 500   **b** 5000   **c** 5000000?

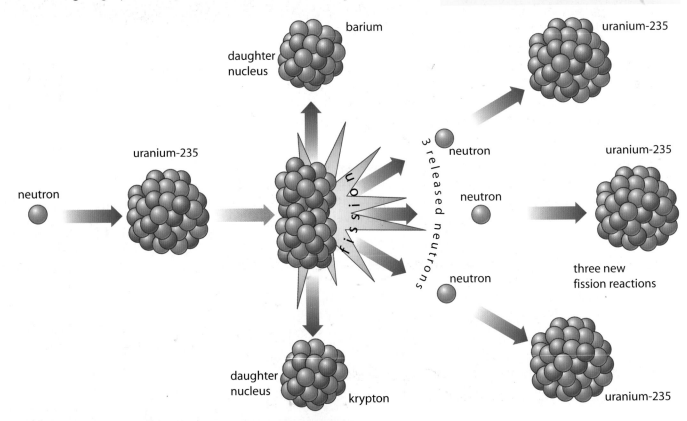

**A** How the decay of Uranium-235 can lead to a chain reaction.

This chain reaction is out of control. It will grow very quickly and be explosive – like an atomic bomb. But it is not like this inside a **nuclear reactor**.

The chain reaction in a nuclear reactor is steady. For each link in the chain, only one of the three neutrons causes a new fission. This means that each fission reaction leads to one more fission reaction instead of three. The links in the chain do not increase the number of fissions – they keep them constant. The reaction is sustained but not explosive.

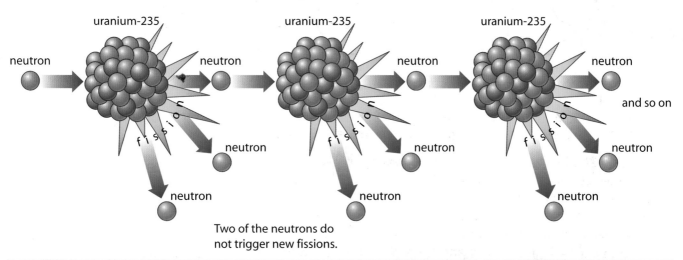

Two of the neutrons do not trigger new fissions.

**B** In a nuclear reactor, the chain reaction is steady. Only one of the three neutrons released is reabsorbed by a nucleus of uranium-235.

In nature, the links in the chain are even weaker. Natural uranium contains about 0.7% uranium-235. Most of the spare neutrons do not trigger a new fission. So the chain reaction does not get started. To make nuclear fuel from natural uranium, it has to be enriched. Uranium-235 is added to natural uranium to raise the concentration to 3%. **Enriched uranium** can then be used in a nuclear reactor.

**H** The daughter nuclei of uranium-235 will be the nuclei of lighter elements like barium and krypton. They will always be radioactive and form the beginning of a **decay series**. This involves a number of steps before it reaches a stable nucleus.

krypton-89 ⟶ rubidium-89 ⟶ strontium-89 ⟶ yttrium-89 (stable)

beta      beta      beta

**C** Krypton-89 starts a decay series which ends with the stable yttrium-89. Each step in the series gives out beta radiation.

4 Describe what happens in a nuclear fission reaction.

5 Look at the decay series in diagram C. Which atom is:
   **a** stable
   **b** a daughter of a fission reaction
   **c** a daughter of the beta decay of rubidium?

6 How many of the materials in the decay series are radioactive?

7 **a** Are all three neutrons absorbed by another uranium-235 nucleus in:
   **i** a bomb
   **ii** a nuclear reactor
   **iii** nature?
   **b** In each case, is the reaction explosive, sustaining or will it stop?

Summary Exercise

Higher Questions

# 2. Controlling the chain reaction

**By the end of these two pages you should be able to:**

- explain how a chain reaction can be used for both peaceful and destructive purposes
- explain how a chain reaction can be controlled in a nuclear reactor.

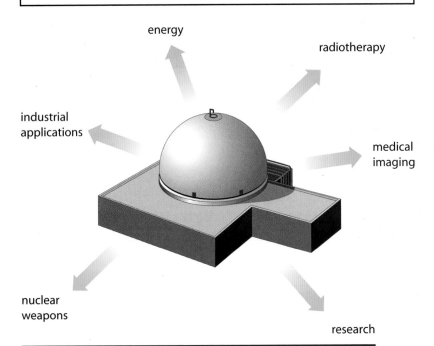

energy

radiotherapy

industrial applications

medical imaging

nuclear weapons

research

**A** Nuclear fission is used for peaceful and destructive purposes.

At dawn on 6 August 1945, 60 kg of uranium was forced into a chain reaction over the Japanese city of Hiroshima. It unleashed an explosion equivalent to 18 000 tonnes of **TNT**, and killed 700 000 people. The radioactive daughter products caused sickness, death and birth defects for years afterwards.

Scientists have found ways of harnessing the same energy for peaceful purposes: in nuclear power stations. These rely on the same chain reaction but in a controlled way.

The first nuclear bomb was made from 60 kg of pure uranium-235. This is called the **critical mass**. It is big enough to produce a chain reaction that grows in an instant. The chain reaction in a nuclear power station cannot grow in such an explosive way because:

- the uranium is put in fuel rods with a mass of 5 kg – much less than the critical mass
- it is only about 3% uranium-235.

## Have you ever wondered?

How easy is it to build an atom bomb?

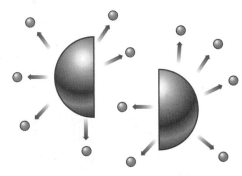

More neutrons are escaping from the edges of the smaller pieces.

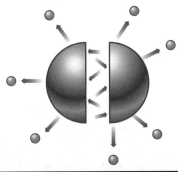

**B** Two small pieces of uranium-235 lose more neutrons than one big piece. When they are put together in one big piece, above, more of the neutrons are reabsorbed. This speeds up the chain reaction. Once the piece reaches the critical mass, it will explode.

1 What mass of TNT would be required to produce the same explosion as the first atom bomb?

2 Suggest why governments have continued to develop nuclear weapons.

The fission reactions in a nuclear power station take place inside fuel rods. These are made from pellets of enriched uranium held in a casing that is about the size of a fat billiard cue. The fission reactions make the fuel rod hot. However, a single fuel rod loses neutrons from its edges. So the fuel rods are put close together in the reactor core, which means that more of the neutrons are absorbed. This sets off more fission reactions. The temperature of the rods is over 500°C.

If the fuel gets too hot, the engineers slow the chain reaction down by lowering **control rods** between the fuel rods. When demand is high, the engineers raise the control rods, the reaction rate goes up and the fuel rods get hotter.

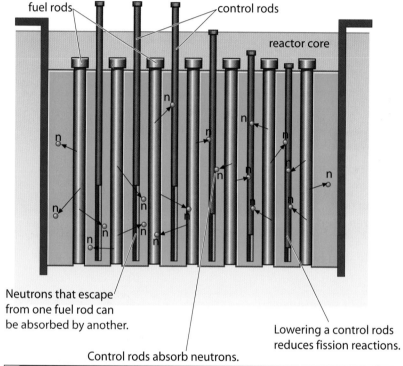

fuel rods
control rods
reactor core

Neutrons that escape from one fuel rod can be absorbed by another.

Control rods absorb neutrons.

Lowering a control rods reduces fission reactions.

**C** Control rods are positioned between the fuel rods. These are made of boron, which absorb some of the neutrons and slow down the chain reaction.

Nuclear reactors produce many new **radioactive** materials which do not exist in nature. Some of these are useful in industry, medicine and research. More than 100 different types are used for diagnosis or treatment in hospitals.

Carbon-13 allows doctors to 'see' brain activity using a special scanner. The carbon-13 is taken into the brain cells and gives out low levels of radiation, which is built into an image.

Iodine-131 is used to treat thyroid cancer. The iodine concentrates in the patient's thyroid gland. It gives out beta radiation, which kills the cancer cells.

**Summary Exercise**

3 Give three examples of peaceful applications of nuclear fission.

4 Why do nuclear fuel rods get hotter when they are put next to each other?

5 Control rods are put between the nuclear fuel rods. What effect does this have on the rate of the chain reaction?

6 A reactor core is getting too hot. Should the engineers raise the control rods or push them in further?

7 Describe how a chain reaction is controlled in a nuclear reactor.

**Higher Questions**

# 3. Electricity from nuclear power

**By the end of these two pages you should be able to:**

- describe how a nuclear reaction is used to generate electricity
- discuss the benefits and drawbacks of nuclear power.

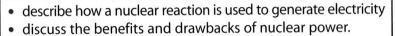

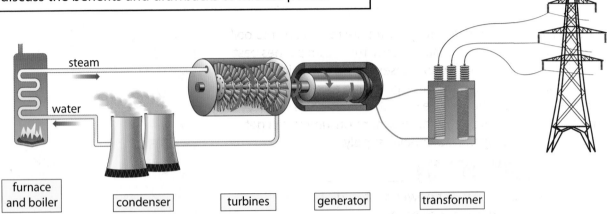

**A** The stages in using a fossil fuel to generate electricity.

A nuclear power station is similar to one that burns fossil fuels. It uses steam to turn a turbine which then drives a generator. The main difference is the way steam is produced:

- a fossil fuel power station uses the energy released by combustion when a fuel burns
- a nuclear power station uses the energy released by nuclear fission.

The central part of a nuclear reactor is the core. It is the equivalent of a furnace in a fossil fuel power station. But there are no flames and there is no noise. The fission of uranium-235 silently heats the fuel rods to over 500°C.

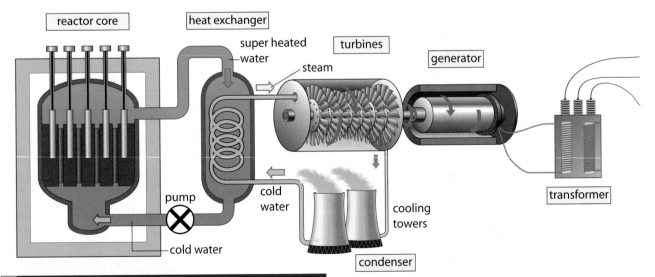

**B** The stages in using a nuclear fuel to generate electricity.

**1** Copy and complete the following table:

| Type of power station | Fossil fuelled power station | Nuclear power station |
|---|---|---|
| An example of a fuel | | |
| The type of reaction that heats the water | | |
| Where the reaction takes place | | |
| Where steam is produced | | |

In a nuclear reactor, **thermal energy** from the rods is used to boil water and produces high pressure steam. The steam pushes past the blades of a turbine, and a condenser on the other side turns it back into water. The steam pushes the turbine round which drives the generator. The voltage from the generator is connected to the National Grid through a transformer. Consumers can get their **electrical energy** from the mains supply.

## Have you ever wondered?

Should we switch to nuclear power to stop global warming, as it doesn't produce greenhouse gases?

The world's first commercial nuclear reactor was opened in Cumbria in 1956. It was seen as a clean, smoke-free alternative to fossil fuels, like coal. But some people were opposed to nuclear power because of the radioactive waste it produces. Public fears and opposition grew after the devastating explosion at Chernobyl in 1986. Governments became nervous and stopped building new nuclear power stations.

But governments are now considering building them again, this time because of a new environmental problem – climate change. Burning fossil fuels produces carbon dioxide, which is a greenhouse gas. Most governments are committed to reducing the production of carbon dioxide. As the French have found out, using nuclear power to generate more electricity is one way to achieve this.

**C** The core of a nuclear reactor. The fuel rods are under the floor, where they heat water to 200 °C.

**2 a** Why did governments build nuclear power stations in the 1950s?
   **b** Why did they stop in the 1990s?

**3** Nuclear power is now being reconsidered. Explain why.

**4** France has much lower carbon dioxide emissions per kW h than the UK. Explain how they achieve this.

**5** What is the difference between the electricity generated by fossil fuels and nuclear power?

**6** Imagine you are a researcher for the Government's energy minister. Prepare a brief outline of how electricity is generated in a nuclear power station. Include a summary of the main benefits and drawbacks of nuclear power.

| | Total annual consumption (billion kW h) | Number of nuclear power stations | Percentage of electricity from nuclear power | Mass of carbon dioxide released per kW h of electricity produced (g/kW h) |
|---|---|---|---|---|
| France | 550 | 59 | 78% | 20 |
| UK | 320 | 14 | 28% | 160 |

**D** France produces less carbon dioxide but generates more electricity than the UK. This is because France relies on nuclear power more than the UK does.

**Summary Exercise**

**Higher Questions**

# 4. Are nuclear power stations safe?

**By the end of these two pages you should be able to:**

- explain that the products of nuclear fission are radioactive
- describe some of the options for storing or disposing of nuclear waste
- describe how a nuclear power station might affect a local environment and the people who live there.

The fission reactions in nuclear power stations produce radioactive material. Some of this is useful, but most becomes radioactive waste, which is hazardous. There are three categories of waste. Each of these is treated differently.

**High-level waste** (HLW) is made up of spent nuclear fuel. It is very radioactive and has to be stored in steel and concrete to contain the radiation. However, it does not remain highly radioactive for very long. Within a few years, its activity has decreased and it is reclassified as intermediate-level waste.

**A** High-level waste is made of spent nuclear fuel. This picture shows a steel container of waste being lowered into the store. It has to be shielded to prevent radiation escaping.

**Intermediate-level waste** (ILW) is made up of pieces of equipment like fuel cladding, which are radioactive because they have been in the reactor core. Unlike high-level waste, ILW is radioactive for tens of thousands of years. It is currently contained in concrete and steel drums in a temporary store at Sellafield. Scientists and politicians are still considering what to do with it in the long term. It must be put somewhere where there is no chance of it leaking out. It must be secure for tens of thousands of years.

1 Why is nuclear waste hazardous?

2 a Where does HLW come from?
  b Why does it have to be shielded?

put it into deep boreholes in solid rock

dispose of it at sea in special containers

bury it under the sea bed

continue to store it above ground

launch it into space

dispose of it at the edges of tectonic plates in the Earth so it is dragged into the Earth's mantle

**B** Disposing of ILW is a big problem. There is no perfect solution. It has to be kept secure over tens of thousands of years. The storage has to prevent it from leaking out and contaminating the environment.

**Low-level waste** (LLW) is made up of clothing, paper towels and medical equipment from nuclear power stations and hospitals. It is slightly radioactive and cannot be buried with domestic waste, so it is compacted and buried in special landfill sites.

## Have you ever wondered?

Is it safe to bury nuclear waste underground in the UK?

In 2006, there were 14 nuclear power stations in the UK. Although they are usually built in remote areas, they are not completely isolated. They affect the price of houses and the structure of the local community. The two main concerns people have are:

- the small risk of a major disaster
- the possibility of radioactive material escaping into the water or air.

A leak of radioactive material at Windscale in 1957 meant that farmers had to throw away their milk. A study of the area suggests that there is still an increased risk of childhood leukaemia. But other studies have shown that there is no effect on the number of adults contracting cancer.

3 Why is ILW such a concern?

4 Look at the list of possible solutions for permanently disposing of ILW.
  a Draw up a list of advantages and disadvantages of each method.
  b Which method do you prefer? Explain your answer.

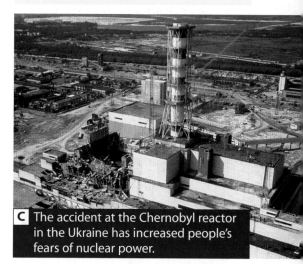

**C** The accident at the Chernobyl reactor in the Ukraine has increased people's fears of nuclear power.

5 Copy and complete the following table.

| Category of waste | HLW | ILW | LLW |
|---|---|---|---|
| Source | | | hospitals; clothing |
| Activity | very high | | |
| Lifetime | | | variable but radiation is very low |
| Volume in 2001 | 2000 m³ – about the volume of an Olympic swimming pool | 75 000 m³ – an area the size of a football pitch covered to 15 m high | 1 500 000 m³ |
| Issues | theft; radiation | | |
| Disposal/storage | | not decided; temporarily packed in stainless steel drums and held in a surface store at Sellafield | |

6 Nuclear power stations affect the area around a local community. Give one example of:
  a an environmental effect
  b a social effect.

7 Imagine you live near a nuclear power station and the local community is worried about the hazards. Write a fact sheet describing how the power station deals with the different types of waste, explaining the dangers of each type.

**Summary Exercise**          **Higher Questions**

# 5. Making predictions from theories

**By the end of these two pages you should be able to:**

- explain how Einstein predicted the possibility of releasing enormous amounts of energy
- explain how scientists use theories to make predictions.

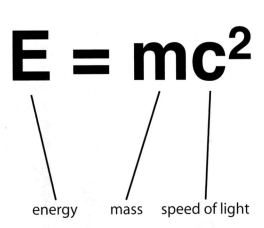

$$E = mc^2$$

energy     mass     speed of light

**A** Einstein proposed his famous equation to solve a problem about light. It was later used to predict the energy released by nuclear fission.

## Have you ever wondered?

What does $E = mc^2$ really mean?

Theories are a vital part of the scientific process. Einstein's Special Theory of Relativity, published in 1905, contains what is probably the most famous equation in physics: $E = mc^2$. All scientific theories need to be able to make predictions. Einstein developed his theory to solve a puzzle about the speed of light. But no one realised that another incredible prediction would be made from this equation 40 years later: the massive explosive power of the atomic bomb.

In 1905, Einstein was not thinking about atomic bombs. At this time, physicists did not even know that atoms have a nucleus.

1 In 1905, was Einstein a nuclear physicist? Explain your answer.

2 **a** What is the famous equation he published in his special theory of relativity?
   **b** What does each symbol in the equation stand for?

One of the predictions Einstein made from his theory was that the mass of an object will decrease if it loses energy. At the time, this prediction could not be tested. Even the most explosive chemical reactions did not release enough energy. For example, burning 1 g of hydrogen in air makes a big bang. But it loses only a millionth of a millionth of a gram. This is too small to measure – and certainly was in 1905.

In 1938 two German chemists, Otto Hahn and Lise Meitner, found that if they bombarded uranium with neutrons, barium was produced, which is much lighter. This seemed impossible. But Meitner realised that the uranium nucleus must have split in two. She called this process fission.

Meitner confirmed that the products had a much smaller mass than the uranium. About a million times more mass was lost in this reaction than for burning hydrogen. Using Einstein's equation, she calculated that the fission reaction would release a million times more energy than a chemical reaction.

**B** Lise Meitner's insight led to new experiments, and showed it was possible to create a fission reaction with uranium-235.

**C** The first atom bomb test site. Einstein realised that Hitler would try to use fission to produce a weapon. Although he was a pacifist, Einstein wrote to President Roosevelt to urge him to develop a weapon before the Germans.

Einstein's theory ended up being used in a way that he never imagined. The power of his equation was that it could make astonishing predictions which were later tested – to devastating effect. Like other well-established scientific theories, Einstein's has continued to make predictions that, when tested, turn out to be true. This makes it a successful and strong theory. Another example is Newton's laws of motion, which continue to predict the paths of satellites and space rockets successfully.

3 The fission of a nucleus of uranium-235 produces nuclei of barium and krypton (and some spare neutrons).
   **a** How will the mass of the products compare with the mass of the uranium nucleus?
   **b** What prediction did Lise Meitner make about the amount of energy that would be released?

4 Give an example, other than the special theory of relativity, of theories that can make predictions.

5 Describe how Einstein's theory eventually led to the exploding of the atom bomb. Make sure you include the predictions that were made from the theory and how they were tested.

**Summary Exercise**

**Higher Questions**

# 6. How are new theories accepted?

**By the end of these two pages you should be able to:**

- explain that new scientific theories have to be validated by other scientists before they are accepted.

The Power of the Sun in a Test-Tube

**Cold Fusion Dream becomes Reality!**

**A** In 1989, Martin Fleishmann and Stanley Pons stunned the world with their announcement that they had achieved 'cold fusion'. Their claim received massive publicity before it had been reviewed or tested by other scientists.

## Have you ever wondered?

Two scientists claimed they could make a nuclear power station in a test tube. Are they crazy?

On 23 March 1989, Martin Fleischmann and Stanley Pons held a press conference to announce an amazing scientific breakthrough. They claimed that they had achieved nuclear **fusion** – getting hydrogen nuclei to fuse – in a simple electrolytic cell.

It promised to revolutionise the way that electricity is generated and help solve the world's energy problems. Scientists had been trying for 30 years to produce energy from nuclear fusion. Like fission, nuclear fusion can produce an enormous amount of energy without releasing any carbon dioxide. But unlike fission, the fuel needed for this is hydrogen. This is readily available, safe to use, and produces practically no radioactive waste.

To produce nuclear fusion, scientists have been using huge pressurised containers which heat the hydrogen to 50 million °C – over three times the temperature of the Sun. Fleischmann and Pons claimed to have made it work at 50 °C. This is why their claim became known as 'cold fusion'.

1 Give some advantages of cold fusion over:
   **a** hot fusion
   **b** fission
   **c** fossil fuels.

2 Why was the reaction known as cold fusion?

3 Why was their announcement so exciting?

**B** This 'nuclear reactor' fits on a laboratory bench. Fleishmann and Pons claimed the temperature of the apparatus went up due to fusion.

Soon, scientists began to doubt the claims made by Fleischmann and Pons. They had not taken the usual steps for publishing a new breakthrough. Normally, scientists make sure that their results are:

- **peer** reviewed: this means that the article is checked by other scientists before being published in a scientific journal
- explained by theory: the results carry more weight if there is a way to understand what is happening using scientific ideas
- reproducible: this means that other researchers can do the same experiment and get the same results. This **validates** the claim and makes sure the results are not fake or just luck.

Following these conventions gives scientists faith in each other's work.

Fleischmann and Pons did not follow any of these conventions because:

- the announcement was made at a press conference
- there was no explanation of how it worked
- scientists were soon reporting that they could not reproduce the results.

Most scientists became sceptical of their claims. All attempts to reproduce it have failed. But there is still a fierce debate about cold fusion. Fleischmann and Pons stand by their claims and there is plenty of ongoing research. However, the scientific community is still waiting for reliable, reproducible experiments that will validate the claims.

**Summary Exercise**

**4 a** How did Fleischmann and Pons announce their results?
 **b** What is the more respected way of publishing results?

**5** Explain what is meant by the term peer-review.

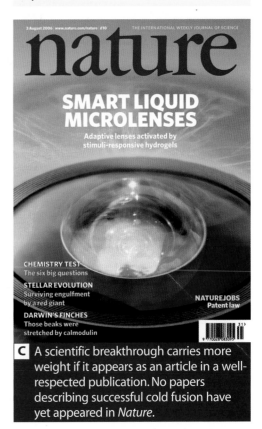

**C** A scientific breakthrough carries more weight if it appears as an article in a well-respected publication. No papers describing successful cold fusion have yet appeared in *Nature*.

**6 a** What does reproducible mean?
 **b** Why is it important that scientific experiments are reproducible?

**7** Is a press conference a good way to announce the results of a scientific discovery? Explain your answer.

**Higher Questions**

# 7. Nuclear reactions in stars

**H** **By the end of these two pages you should be able to:**

- describe how fusion differs from fission
- recognise fusion as the energy source for the Sun and stars
- recall that nuclear fusion requires extremely high temperatures and densities
- explain the difficulty of generating electricity from fusion.

Nuclear power stations rely on nuclear fission. But there is an even more energetic nuclear reaction: nuclear fusion. This is the reverse of fission. If two small nuclei get close enough to each other they join together – or fuse. Hydrogen nuclei can be fused to form helium. This releases lots of energy. It is the reaction that keeps the Sun and all the other stars alight.

Scientists are trying to find ways of harnessing this energy because hydrogen is plentiful and there is no radioactive waste. But it is not straightforward. The hydrogen nuclei have to get within a million millionth of a millimetre of each other to fuse. But both nuclei are positive and repel each other – they are held apart by an **electrostatic** force of **repulsion**. The nuclei will only fuse if they are forced together at extremely high temperatures and pressures.

High temperatures make the particles move extremely fast. The faster they are moving, the closer they get to each other before the repulsive force pushes them apart. At normal pressures, the gas has to be heated to about 50 million °C to give the particles enough speed. The Sun has a core temperature of about 15 million °C. But the reaction can take place here despite the lower temperature because of the huge pressures in the core of the Sun. This forces the particles closer together.

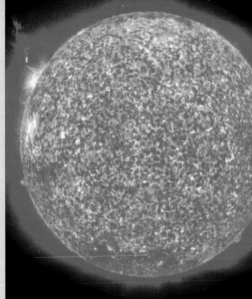

**A** The Sun relies on nuclear fusion to keep shining. You can see huge plumes of hot gas that have risen from its core where fusion takes place.

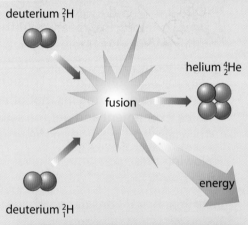

deuterium $^2_1$H

helium $^4_2$He

fusion

energy

deuterium $^2_1$H

**B** The two hydrogen nuclei fuse to form helium.

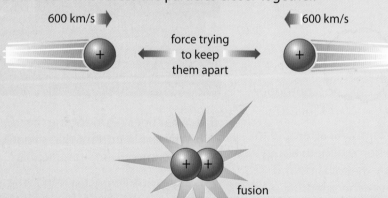

600 km/s

600 km/s

force trying to keep them apart

fusion

**C** Hydrogen nuclei are both positive. The two positive charges repel each other. The hydrogen nuclei have to move at about 600 km/s to overcome the electrostatic force and fuse.

1 Where can you see nuclear fusion reactions most nights of the year?

2 Describe what happens when two hydrogen nuclei get close to each other.

3 What conditions are needed to achieve fusion?

4 What is the product of hydrogen fusion?

Scientists have had some success with fusion reactors called tokomaks. The tokomak of the Joint European Torus (JET) project in Oxfordshire has produced up to 16 MW of power – enough to run 20 000 homes. However, it needed more power than this to keep it going. So it is not yet a viable source of energy. But scientists are still working on fusion.

**D** A tokamak is a like a hollow doughnut. It has a doughnut-shaped ring of magnets to hold the intensely hot hydrogen under pressure without touching the sides.

5 Fusion is more likely to happen if the gas is held together under pressure. What holds the hydrogen gas together in:
**a** the Sun    **b** a tokomak?

6 In a tokomak, the hot gases must not touch the edges of their container. Explain why.

7 Look at the table of energies.

| Reaction | Energy released by 1 kg ($\times 10^6$ J) |
|---|---|
| Combustion of hydrogen | 197 |
| Fission of uranium | 81 000 000 |
| Fusion of hydrogen | 630 000 000 |

Burning hydrogen releases lots of energy. How many times more energy is released by:
**a** the fission of uranium    **b** the fusion of hydrogen?

8 People think that fusion would be a more desirable means of producing energy than nuclear fission. Write an article explaining what fusion is, why it is difficult to make it work and why people are still trying to solve the problems.

Summary Exercise

Higher Questions

**By the end of these two pages you should be able to:**

- explain that electrostatic effects are due to the movement of electrons
- explain how you get shocks from car doors, synthetic fibres and lightning
- explain why objects discharge to earth.

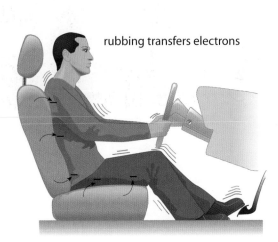
rubbing transfers electrons

charged up

charge jumps off

**A** As your clothes rub against the car seat, they pick up electrons. This gives you a negative charge which causes a spark.

You may have found that you sometimes get a shock when you touch a car door. This is usually because your clothes have been rubbing against the seat cover. Some materials, like nylon, will pick up extra electrons when they are rubbed. Electrons carry a negative charge. So if you wear clothes containing nylon in a car, your clothes (and you!) can become negatively charged. This is **static electricity**.

When you leave the car, you are still negatively charged. The charge will eventually leak away and spread out in the Earth. But if you touch the car door, all the **electrostatic charge** jumps to the car, in one go. This is a spark – like a small bolt of lightning. And it gives you a little jolt.

When charge builds up, it will try to even out, or discharge. A charge will always flow from a place where it is concentrated to a place where it can spread out. A boy getting out of a car will be charged up – the charge is concentrated. When he touches the metal door handle, the charge can spread out through the car.

1 If an object picks up extra electrons, what type of charge will it have?

2 What can cause your clothes to get an electrostatic charge in a car?

3 Give two examples of electrostatic charging that can cause a spark.

The charge can become even more spread out if it is transferred to the ground. This is called **earthing**. Whenever there is an opportunity for charge to flow to Earth, it will do so.

concentrated

spread out

**B** Charge goes from where it is concentrated to where it can spread out.

Lightning is also caused by the discharge of static electricity. Storm clouds get charged up as water particles and ice crystals move through them. When the charge becomes very high, it looks for a way to discharge. Sometimes it discharges in the air between clouds. At other times the charge is discharged to the Earth in a dramatic arc of electric current or lightning.

**C** Lightning takes the shortest path to the Earth, often through tall buildings. A lightning conductor can channel the electrostatic charge safely into the ground.

Lightning has very large electrostatic charges. It can cause serious damage to buildings and people when it strikes. Lightning **conductors** can help. The point at the top of a lightning conductor can discharge a thunder cloud and prevent the lightning strike. If it does strike, it will hit the highest point and the conductor will carry the charge safely to earth.

4 You walk on a nylon carpet in shoes with rubber soles and you get charged up.
   a What will happen if you touch, for example, a metal rail? Explain your answer.
   b The rail is connected to earth. Why does the charge tend to flow to earth?

5 How does a lightning conductor help prevent damage from a lightning strike?

6 Explain how you become charged in a car and then get a small shock when you touch the car door.

**Summary Exercise**

**Higher Questions**

289

# 9. How does static electricity work?

**By the end of these two pages you should be able to:**

- describe the force of repulsion between like charges
- describe the force of attraction between unlike charges
- explain how insulating materials can be charged.

## Have you ever wondered?

Your teacher can create lightning bolts and make objects levitate – is this magic or physics?

Static electricity causes shocks and sparks when the charge jumps across a gap. This is because of the forces between the charges. You can see these forces directly. If you run a nylon comb through your hair you can use it to pick up tiny pieces of paper. This effect was discovered by the ancient Greeks, who did it with amber and feathers. The Greek word for amber is electron. This is the origin of our modern word for the tiny particle that causes these electrostatic effects.

Nylon and Perspex are **insulating** materials. This means that a charge cannot flow through them. Instead the charge stays on the surface. So, when you rub an insulator with a cloth, you charge it up. A piece of nylon will get a negative charge. This is because it *gains* negative electrons from the cloth. A piece of Perspex will get a positive charge. This is because it *loses* electrons to the cloth.

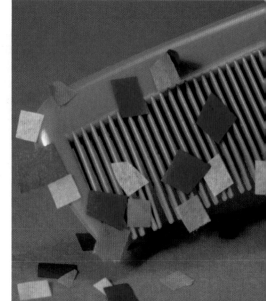

**A** Charging an insulator makes it attract neutral material. So if you charge up a nylon comb, you can pick up little bits of paper.

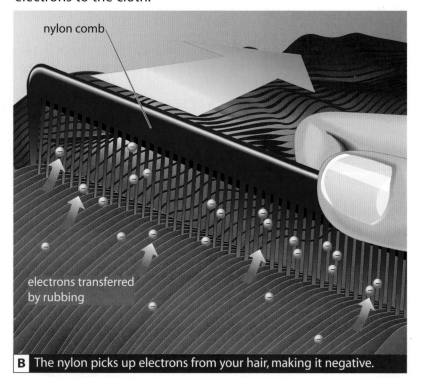

nylon comb

electrons transferred by rubbing

**B** The nylon picks up electrons from your hair, making it negative.

1 **a** What is the name of the tiny charged particle that causes electrostatics?
   **b** Where does the name come from?

2 **a** What is meant by the term insulator?
   **b** Give two examples of an insulator.

Two pieces of charged insulator will exert a force on each other. A piece of nylon will **attract** a piece of Perspex. The nylon and Perspex have opposite charges. This shows that opposite charges attract each other.

However, a piece of charged nylon will repel another piece of charged nylon. And a piece of charged Perspex will repel another piece of charged Perspex. In each case, the charges are alike – both negative or both positive. This shows that like charges repel each other – they are held apart by repulsion.

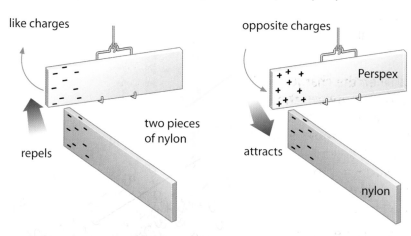

**C** Nylon repels another piece of nylon because their charges are alike. But nylon and Perspex attract each other because they have opposite charges.

If you hold the dome of a Van de Graaff generator, your hair stands on end. This happens because the dome has an electrostatic charge. This comes from a belt below the dome, which picks up electrons from a wire at the bottom. When you hold the dome, you get charged up. All of your hairs have the same charge so they repel each other. They also repel your scalp, which has the same charge. So the hairs are pushing away from each other and from your scalp. This makes them stand up.

**3** What is the rule for the force between two:
  **a** like charges
  **b** opposite charges?

**4** A piece of rubbed polythene is repelled by a piece of rubbed nylon.
  **a** What is the charge on the nylon?
  **b** What must the charge on the polythene be?
  **c** What will the force be between the polythene and a piece of Perspex?

**D** A Van de Graaff generator charges up your hair and it stands on end.

**5** Photo D shows a girl's hair standing on end. Write a short paragraph explaining how this happens.

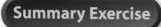

**Summary Exercise**

**Higher Questions**

# 10. Dangers and uses of electrostatics

## By the end of these two pages you should be able to:

- describe some of the dangers and uses of electrostatic charges.

## Have you ever wondered?

What should you do if you're in the countryside when lightning strikes?

Lightning can be very destructive. On average, five people die every year in the UK when the charge from a lightning bolt hits the ground. Static electricity can also be dangerous in other situations. For example, refuelling an aeroplane could be hazardous were it not for our understanding of electrostatics.

The fuel pipe used for refilling aeroplanes is an insulator. The moving fuel rubs along the inside of the pipe. The friction causes the pipe to get charged up as it picks up electrons from the fuel. The pipe gets a negative charge that could lead to a spark. A spark here would be explosive because there is jet fuel vapour in the air. So the pipe, the truck and the aeroplane are all **bonded** to earth using a good conductor. This is called a bonding line. Earthing the pipe in this way helps to spread out the charge through the earth, so it does not build up and cause a spark.

**A** Without a bonding line, opposite charges can build up on the pipe and the plane. If they are bonded to earth, there is no build up of charge.

Electrostatic charges are not always dangerous – they have many uses. Laser printers use charges to create an image, made from tiny dots of ink, or toner. A laser pulses over the drum inside the printer, covering it with a pattern of negatively charged dots. The toner is picked up by the drum wherever there is a charged dot. The dots of toner are then transferred from the drum onto paper to make up text and images.

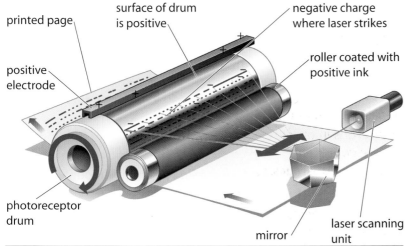

- printed page
- surface of drum is positive
- negative charge where laser strikes
- positive electrode
- roller coated with positive ink
- photoreceptor drum
- mirror
- laser scanning unit

**B** How a laser printer works. A similar electrostatic process is used in photocopiers.

When you use a comb to pick up some paper, the paper is neutral. Neutral insulators are often attracted to charged objects. The police use this effect to collect fingerprints from dusty surfaces. It only works if the dust is dry. They need to lift the dusty print without damaging it. To do this, they use an electrostatic machine. It has a thin plastic film that is charged up by a battery. The officer holds the machine over the surface and the charged film lifts up the dusty print. This sticks to the film and can be taken away.

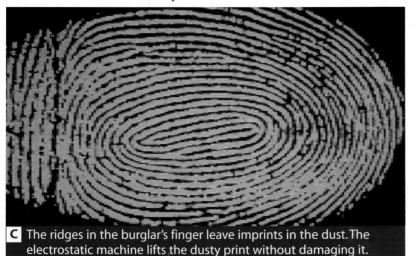

**C** The ridges in the burglar's finger leave imprints in the dust. The electrostatic machine lifts the dusty print without damaging it.

1 **a** Explain how a fuel pipe can get charged up when an aeroplane is refuelling.
  **b** Why is this a hazard?
  **c** Describe how you can prevent a charge from building up.

2 In a laser printer, what is the job of:
  **a** the charged drum
  **b** the laser?

3 What would the page look like if the laser stopped working?

4 **a** What type of fingerprint can be lifted by electrostatics? Explain your answer.
  **b** Use a sequence of bullet points to describe the steps in lifting this type of fingerprint.

5 Write a short information leaflet about the dangers and uses of electrostatic charge.

**Summary Exercise**

**Higher Questions**

# 11. Questions

## Multiple choice questions

**1** Nylon and polythene both get a negative charge when they are rubbed. What will happen when a rubbed piece of nylon is brought close to a rubbed piece of Perspex?
- **A** They will attract each other.
- **B** They will repel each other.
- **C** They will stick together.
- **D** They will get hot.

**2** Which of the following machines does *not* rely on static electricity to work?
- **A** a laser printer
- **B** a fingerprint machine
- **C** a Van de Graaff generator
- **D** a cold fusion reactor

**3** Which part of a nuclear power station is driven by high-pressure steam?
- **A** the reactor core
- **B** the heat exchanger
- **C** the turbine
- **D** the generator

**4** A nucleus of uranium-235 will break up when it absorbs a neutron. What is the name of this process?
- **A** nuclear fission
- **B** nuclear fusion
- **C** chain reaction
- **D** nuclear combustion

**5** When a nucleus of uranium-235 breaks up, the following things happen. Which of these is essential to start the process in question 4?
- **A** It releases energy.
- **B** It breaks into two smaller nuclei.
- **C** It releases three neutrons.
- **D** The products are radioactive.

**6** During normal operation, which one of these would not be found in the core of a nuclear reactor?
- **A** fuel rods
- **B** control rods
- **C** flames
- **D** superheated water

**7** Look at these categories of waste. Which one is currently stored in cooling tanks of water?
- **A** high-level waste
- **B** intermediate-level waste
- **C** low-level waste
- **D** domestic waste

**8** Einstein published his equation $E = mc^2$ in 1905. Look at the statements below. Which one of these is the main reason it is so well accepted?
- **A** It has been used to make accurate predictions.
- **B** It is mathematical.
- **C** It was about the speed of light.
- **D** Einstein was a patent officer.

**9** Nuclear fusion releases a huge amount of energy. In which of these has nuclear fusion not taken place?
- **A** the Sun
- **B** the Moon
- **C** a tokomak
- **D** a hydrogen bomb

**10** Before a new scientific discovery is published in a scientific journal, it is checked by other scientists. What is the name of this process?
- **A** peer review
- **B** marking
- **C** publication
- **D** sub-editing

**H** **11** Perspex gets a positive charge when it is rubbed with a cloth. Which of these statements best explains why?
- **A** The cloth loses positive charge to the Perspex.
- **B** The cloth loses negative charge to the Perspex.
- **C** The Perspex loses positive charge to the cloth.
- **D** The Perspex loses negative charge to the cloth.

**12** In 1987, there was an explosion at the nuclear power station in Chernobyl. Which one of these is *not* a true statement about this explosion.
- **A** The explosion was like a large atomic bomb.
- **B** The land around the power station is still uninhabitable.
- **C** Welsh farms were contaminated with radioactive fallout.
- **D** Many countries stopped building new nuclear power stations.

13 Radioactive waste can last for a very long time. Which of these does *not* help explain its long life?
 A Fission products are often the start of a long decay series.
 B Some of the isotopes have long half-lives.
 C There is no way of speeding up radioactive decay.
 D The fission of uranium releases lots of energy.

14 Control rods reduce the rate of a chain reaction. Which of these is the best explanation of how they do this?
 A They absorb neutrons.
 B They absorb uranium-235.
 C They absorb energy from gamma rays.
 D They cool the uranium-235 and reduce fission.

15 Which one of these is *not* true about nuclear fusion and fission?
 A Fusion requires extremely high temperatures; fission does not.
 B Fission is currently used to generate electricity; fusion is not.
 C Fusion is when two nuclei join to make one; fission is when one nucleus splits to make two.
 D A fission reaction releases more energy per kilogram than combustion; fusion does not.

## Short-answer questions

1 a In a thunder storm, it is a bad idea to shelter under a tree. Explain why.
 b Suggest a safe place to shelter. Explain your answer.

2 Look at these parts of a nuclear power station:

 reactor core   generator   transformer   turbine heat exchanger

 a Starting from the reactor core, put them in the order in which they are connected together.
 b Briefly describe what happens in each part.

3 a Give an example of a scientific theory that is well established.
 b Describe one reason why it was accepted.
 c Give an example of a scientific claim that has not been accepted by the scientific community.
 d Describe one reason why it failed to be accepted.

4 a Look at the statements below about a chain reaction. Draw a flow diagram like the one shown and put the statements into the empty boxes so that they are in the correct sequence.

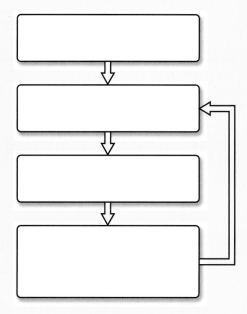

 One or more of these is absorbed by another nucleus of uranium-235

 The nucleus splits into two smaller nuclei.

 A nucleus of uranium-235 absorbs a stray neutron.

 It releases lots of energy and two spare neutrons.

 b Explain how the upward pointing arrow leads to a chain reaction.

**H** 5 A nucleus of uranium-235 will break up into two smaller nuclei when it absorbs a neutron.
 a How does the mass of the products compare with the original mass?
 b Can the difference in mass be measured?
 c Explain why the mass is different.
 d Hydrogen burns in oxygen to form water. Repeat parts **a** and **b** for this reaction.
 e Explain why your answers to **b** and **d** are different.

D

P

# Glossary

pulls two objects together.
...e earth using a good electrical
...a thick cable) with good connections.

**...action** The sequence of reactions produced
when a nuclear fission reaction triggers one or more
new fissions.

**critical mass** The amount of uranium-235 that is needed
to start an uncontrolled, explosive chain raction.

**conductor** A material that will let an electric current flow
through it. Metals are good conductors.

**control rod** A rod made from carbon or boron that can
be lowered into the core of a nuclear reactor, absorb
neutrons and slow down the chain reaction.

**\*daughter nucleus** The nucleus produced when the
nucleus of a radioactive atom decays by giving out an
alpha or beta particle.

**\*decay series** A sequence of radioactive isotopes and
their radiation. When a radioactive isotope decays, it
may form a new radioactive isotope. This in turn decays
into another isotope. The series goes on until it reaches
a stable isotope.

**earthed** Connected to the earth by a good electrical
conductor so that there is no build up of charge.

**\*electrical energy** The energy made available by a flow
of current. Measured in joules (J).

**electrostatic** A force created by electrical charges that
do not move.

**\*electrostatic charge** Charge that builds up on an
insulator and does not move (it is static). It causes
forces between objects and can cause sparks when it
moves.

**enriched uranium** Uranium that has had uranium-235
added to it to increase the concentration to 3%. At this
level, it will sustain a chain reaction.

**\*fission** The reaction caused when the nucleus of a
heavy atom splits into two smaller nuclei.

**\*fusion** The reaction caused when the nuclei of light
atoms, like hydrogen, join together to make the
nucleus of a heavier atom.

**high-level waste (HLW)** Highly radioactive waste which
is hazardous. The radioactivity decreases over a few
years and it becomes intermediate-level waste.

**\*insulation** A piece of material that does not conduct
electricity. It stops charge from flowing.

**intermediate-level waste (ILW)** Materials which have
become radioactive because they have been in a
nuclear reactor. Radioactive for tens of thousands of
years.

**low-level waste (LLW)** Slightly radioactive waste, usually
clothing, paper towels and medical equipment.

**\*nuclear reactor** The part of a nuclear power station that
holds the fuel rods and control rods. It is where
controlled fission takes place to produce heat for
generating electricity.

**\*nucleus** The tiny structure at the centre of an atom. It
holds all the positive charge of the atom and most of
its mass.

**\*neutron** A particle found in the nucleus of an atom. It
has no charge.

**peer** Someone who is on the same level. In this case, they
will be another scientist with similar background and
experience.

**\*radioactive** Describes a substance that gives out
ionising radiations like alpha, beta and gamma.

**\*repulsion** Describes a force that pushes two objects
apart.

**static electricity** See electrostatic charge.

**\*thermal energy** The energy associated with a hot body.

**TNT** Trinitrotoluene – an explosive used in weapons. It is
taken as the standard measure of explosive power.

**validate** To confirm that something, in this case a
scientific theory, is true or that it works.

*glossary words from the specification

# Periodic Table

Key:

| relative atomic mass → | 1 |
|---|---|
| | H |
| | hydrogen |
| atomic number → | 1 |

**Group**

| Period | 1 | 2 | 3 | 4 | 5 | 6 | 7 | 8 | 9 | 10 | 11 | 12 | 3 | 4 | 5 | 6 | 7 | 0 |
|---|---|---|---|---|---|---|---|---|---|---|---|---|---|---|---|---|---|---|
| 1 | 1 H hydrogen 1 | | | | | | | | | | | | | | | | | 4 He helium 2 |
| 2 | 7 Li lithium 3 | 9 Be beryllium 4 | | | | | | | | | | | 11 B boron 5 | 12 C carbon 6 | 14 N nitrogen 7 | 16 O oxygen 8 | 19 F fluorine 9 | 20 Ne neon 10 |
| 3 | 23 Na sodium 11 | 24 Mg magnesium 12 | | | | | | | | | | | 27 Al aluminium 13 | 28 Si silicon 14 | 31 P phosphorus 15 | 32 S sulphur 16 | 35.5 Cl chlorine 17 | 40 Ar argon 18 |
| 4 | 39 K potassium 19 | 40 Ca calcium 20 | 45 Sc scandium 21 | 48 Ti titanium 22 | 51 V vanadium 23 | 52 Cr chromium 24 | 55 Mn manganese 25 | 56 Fe iron 26 | 59 Co cobalt 27 | 59 Ni nickel 28 | 63.5 Cu copper 29 | 65 Zn zinc 30 | 70 Ga gallium 31 | 73 Ge germanium 32 | 75 As arsenic 33 | 79 Se selenium 34 | 80 Br bromine 35 | 84 Kr krypton 36 |
| 5 | 85 Rb rubidium 37 | 88 Sr strontium 38 | 89 Y yttrium 39 | 91 Zr zirconium 40 | 93 Nb niobium 41 | 96 Mo molybdenum 42 | (98) Tc technetium 43 | 101 Ru ruthenium 44 | 103 Rh rhodium 45 | 106 Pd palladium 46 | 108 Ag silver 47 | 112 Cd cadmium 48 | 115 In indium 49 | 119 Sn tin 50 | 122 Sb antimony 51 | 128 Te tellurium 52 | 127 I iodine 53 | 131 Xe xenon 54 |
| 6 | 133 Cs caesium 55 | 137 Ba barium 56 | 139 La lanthanum 57 | 178 Hf hafnium 72 | 181 Ta tantalum 73 | 184 W tungsten 74 | 186 Re rhenium 75 | 190 Os osmium 76 | 192 Ir iridium 77 | 195 Pt platinum 78 | 197 Au gold 79 | 201 Hg mercury 80 | 204 Tl thallium 81 | 207 Pb lead 82 | 209 Bi bismuth 83 | (209) Po polonium 84 | (210) At astatine 85 | (222) Rn radon 86 |
| 7 | (223) Fr francium 87 | (226) Ra radium 88 | (227) Ac actinium 89 | (261) Rf rutherfordium 104 | (262) Db dubnium 105 | (266) Sg seaborgium 106 | (264) Bh bohrium 107 | (277) Hs hassium 108 | (268) Mt meitnerium 109 | (271) Ds darmstadtium 110 | (272) Rg roentgenium 111 | | | | | | | |

# Index

**Edexcel**
190 High Holborn
London WC1V 7BH
UK

© **Edexcel Limited 2006**
Fifth impression 2010

**ISBN: 978-1-903133-61-3**

| | |
|---|---|
| Designed by | Roarrdesign |
| Illustrated by | Oxford Designers and Illustrators Ltd |
| Picture research | Kay Altwegg |
| Indexer | Indexing Specialists (UK) Ltd |
| Printed in China | GCC/05 |

The publisher's policy is to use paper manufactured from sustainable forests.

**Acknowledgments**

We are grateful to the following for permission to reproduce photographs:

**Action Plus:** pg22 (Philippe Millereau), pg68(t), pg209 (Glyn Kirk), pg190, pg206(b), pg218(l), pg232 (Neil Tingle); **AgCenter:** pg48 (b) (Stephen A Harrison); **Agripicture.com:** pg57 (Peter Dean); **Alamy:** pg37, pg60 (imagebroker), pg51 (Phototake Inc.), pg61(r) (Allan Ivy), pg66 (r) (Richard Sheppard), pg76(r) (BananaStock), pg87(t) (Visual&Written SL), pg94 (l) (A Room With Views) (r) (Imageshop), pg105 (G P Bowater), pg111 (John James), pg114 (Wally Bauman), pg115 (foodfolio), pg129 (Topix), pg148 (Mark Scheuern), pg158(t) (D. Hurst), pg160 (Image Source), pg162 (Sciencephotos), pg164 (Nahum Budin), pag 166(l) (Jack Sullivan), pg178(1) (Popperfoto), pg180(t) (Stockbyte Platinum), pg186(r) (Keith Dannemiller), pg196(r) (Glyn Thomas), pg204(tl) (picturebyrob), (tr) (Motoring Picture Library), pg206(t) (Shotfile), pg208 (Glyn Kirk), pg216(t) (Cut and Deal Ltd), pg219(r) (Associated Press) (l) (SuperStock), pg228(l) (Anthony Collins), pg229(t) (Richard Robinson), pg233 (1Apix), pg235(b) (Arco Images), pg237 (Tim Gainey), pg243(t) (David Pledger), pg290 (Leslie Garland Picture Library); **Ardea London Ltd:** pg36(r) (Jean Michel Labat), pg83(t) (Auscape International); **Car & Bike Photo Library:** pg 234; **BAA Aviation Photo Library:** pg212 (David Hares), pg292; **Broads Authority:** pg92(r) (Simon Finlay), pg98, pg100, pg101(all); **British Energy:** pg273; **BNFL:** pg280; **Corbis:** pg188 (Rober Ressmeyer), pg196(l) Eleanor Bentall), pg279 (Bernard Annebicque/Sygma), pg283(l), pg284 (Bettmann), pg289 (Scott Stulberg); **DCP Microdevelopments Ltd:** pg261(b); **Department for Transport:** pg218(r); **Dorling Kindersley Media Library:** pg61(l), pg197; **Empics:** pg24 (Associated Press), pg50 (Sports Photo Library); **FLPA:** pg202 (Malcolm Schuyl); **Food Features:** pg14 (all), pg20, pg28(t); **Forest Stewardship Council:** pg73(t); **Galaxy Picture Library:** pg210(l), pg258; **Getty Images:** pg28(b), pg167(r) (Rice University/AFP), pg182(t), pg207, pg210(r), pg264(l) (Evans/Three Lions); **Andrew Harmsworth:** pg249 (all); **honda-engines-eu.com:** pg228(r); **Kimbleton Fireworks:** pg192; **Kobal Collection:** pg226 (Warner Bros/DC Comics); **Nature Publishing Group:** pg285(b) (Reprinted by permission from Macmillan Publishers Ltd: [Nature] (Vol. 442, No. 7102), copyright (2006); **naturepl.com:** pg88(r) (Tom Mangelsen), pg87(l) (Tom Vezo), pg99(r) (William Osborn), pg171 (Reinhard/ARCO); **NHPA:** pg45 (John Shaw), pg49, pg63 (Ernie Janes), pg62 (George Bernard), pg64 (Geoff Bryant), pg83(b) (Andy Rouse), pg89 (Roger Tidman), pg99(l) (Kevin Schafer); **Redferns:** pg229(b) (Ian Dickson); **Rex Features:** pg26(r), pg29, pg281; **Science Photo Library:** pg9, pg13, pg116, pg287 (Maximilian Stock Ltd), pg12 (E Gray), pg25(all) (Adrienne Hart-Davis), pg33 (Pasquale Sorrentino), pg34, pg53, pg58 (Dr Gopal Murti), pg36(l), pg68(tr) (Gusto), pg40 (John Paul Kay, Peter Arnold Inc), pg41 (Edelmann), pg42 (James Stevenson), pg43 (Victor Habbuck Visions), pg44 (A C Seinet), pg46 (Adam Hart-Davis), pg47 (Tony McConnell), pg48 (t) (Leonard Rue Enterprises), pg59 (J C Revy),

pg68(bl) (Lawrence Lawry) (br) (Daniel Sambraus, Thomas Luddington), pg71, pg113 (Robert Brook), pg72 (Dr Morley Read), pg77(tl) (Michael Marten) (b) (Alex bartel), pg82 (Dr Ken MacDonald), pg90(t) (Ian Boddy), pg90(b), pg168(l) (Simon Fraser), pg95 (Jerry Mason), pg96, pg204(b) (NASA), pg109, pg124 (Andrew Lambert Photography), pg110, pg130 (Martyn F Chillmaid), pg117, pg166(r) (Tek Images), pg122 (Paul Rapson), pg123 (Russ Munn/AgStock), pg131 (Pascal Goetgheluck), pg138, pg140, pg156(l) (Charles D Winters), pg141 (James Holmes, Hays Chemicals), pg143 (Los Alamos National Laboratory), pg146, pg159 (Laguna Design), pg163 (Claude Nuridsany & Marie Perennou), pg165 (St. Bartholomew's Hospital, London), pg167(l) (Geoff Tompkinson), pg170(l) (Martin Clarke), pg177(r) (David Hay Jones), pg194(l) (Keith Kent), pg195, pg283(r) (Emilio Segre Visual Archives/American Institute of Physics), pg215 (Lea Paterson), pg257, pg285(t) (Philippe Plailly), pg 261(t) (James King-Holmes), pg263 (Gianni Tortoli), pg264(t) (Humanities & Social Sciences Library/New York Public Library) (br) (Steve Allen), pg265 (Josh Sher), pg268 (NASA/ESA/STScI), pg269 (Chris Madeley), pg282, pg286 (European Space Agency), pg291 (Peter Menzel), pg293 (Alfred Pasieka); **Soil Association:** pg73(b); **Sportsbeat Images:** pg26(l) (Richard Eaton); **Still Pictures:** pg66(l) (ullstein – Goettlicher), pg76(l) (George Mulala), pg77(tr) (Mike Kolloffel); **Martin Stirrup:** pg156(r), pg158(b); **Thorpe Park, Surrey:** pg243(b), 244, 245; **volvocars.co.uk:** pg201, pg209(t), pg213, pg216(b), pg217, pg221; **Wellcome Trust:** pg19 (T Blundell & N Campillo), pg250.

The following photographs were taken on commission © **Pearson Education Ltd by:**
**Trevor Clifford:** pg157, pg161, pg182; **Mari Tudor-Jones:** pg81, pg84, pg86, pg88(l), pg92(r), pg153, pg168(r), pg169, pg170(r), pg172(all), pg177(l), pg178(r), pg180(b), pg186(l), pg190(r), pg191, pg194(r), pg225, pg227, pg231, pg235(t), pg236, pg242, pg260, pg262.

Front cover photo and back cover shot: David Parker/Science Photo Library

# Licence Agreement: *Edexcel 360Science Additional Science ActiveBook*

**Warning:**

This is a legally binding agreement between You (the user) and Edexcel Limited, 190 High Holborn, London WC1V 7BH, United Kingdom ('Edexcel Ltd').

By retaining this Licence, any software media or accompanying written materials or carrying out any of the permitted activities, You are agreeing to be bound by the terms and conditions of this Licence. If You do not agree to the terms and conditions of this Licence, do not continue to use the Disk and promptly return the entire publication (this Licence and all software, written materials, packaging and any other component received with it with Your sales receipt to Your supplier for a full refund.

*Edexcel 360Science Additional Science ActiveBook* consists of copyright software and data. The copyright is owned by Edexcel Ltd. You only own the disk on which the software is supplied. If You do not continue to do only what You are allowed to do as contained in this Licence you will be in breach of the Licence and Edexcel Ltd shall have the right to terminate this Licence by written notice and take action to recover from you any damages suffered by Edexcel Ltd as a result of your breach.

**Yes, You can:**

1. use *Edexcel 360Science Additional Science ActiveBook* on your own personal computer as a single individual user;

**No, You cannot:**

1. copy *Edexcel 360Science Additional Science ActiveBook* (other than making one copy for back-up purposes);

2. alter *Edexcel 360Science Additional Science ActiveBook*, or in any way reverse engineer, decompile or create a derivative product from the contents of the database or any software included in it;

3. include any software data from *Edexcel 360Science Additional Science ActiveBook* in any other product or software materials;

4. rent, hire, lend or sell *Edexcel 360Science Additional Science ActiveBook*;

5. copy any part of the documentation except where specifically indicated otherwise;

6. use the software in any way not specified above without the prior written consent of Edexcel Ltd.

**Grant of Licence:**

Edexcel Ltd grants You, provided You only do what is allowed under the Yes, 'You can' table above, and do nothing under the 'No, You cannot' table above, a non-exclusive, non-transferable Licence to use *Edexcel 360Science Additional Science ActiveBook*.

The above terms and conditions of this Licence become operative when using *Edexcel 360Science Additional Science ActiveBook*.

**Limited Warranty:**

Edexcel Ltd warrants that the disk or CD-ROM on which the software is supplied is free from defects in material and workmanship in normal use for ninety (90) days from the date You receive it. This warranty is limited to You and is not transferable.

This limited warranty is void if any damage has resulted from accident, abuse, misapplication, service or modification by someone other than Edexcel Ltd. In no event shall Edexcel Ltd be liable for any damages whatsoever arising out of installation of the software, even if advised of the possibility of such damages. Edexcel Ltd will not be liable for any loss or damage of any nature suffered by any party as a result of reliance upon or reproduction of any errors in the content of the publication.

Edexcel Ltd does not warrant that the functions of the software meet Your requirements or that the media is compatible with any computer system on which it is used or that the operation of the software will be unlimited or error free. You assume responsibility for selecting the software to achieve Your intended results and for the installation of, the use of and the results obtained from the software.

Edexcel Ltd shall not be liable for any loss or damage of any kind (except for personal injury or death) arising from the use of *Edexcel 360Science Additional Science ActiveBook* or from errors, deficiencies or faults therein, whether such loss or damage is caused by negligence or otherwise.

The entire liability of Edexcel Ltd and your only remedy shall be replacement free of charge of the components that do not meet this warranty.

No information or advice (oral, written or otherwise) given by Edexcel Ltd or Edexcel Ltd's agents shall create a warranty or in any way increase the scope of this warranty.

To the extent the law permits, Edexcel Ltd disclaims all other warranties, either express or implied, including by way of example and not limitation, warranties of merchantability and fitness for a particular purpose in respect of *Edexcel 360Science Additional Science ActiveBook*.

**Governing Law:**

This Licence will be governed and construed in accordance with English law.